"In this volume, scholars and practition[...] innovations in Christian mission. The resulting kaleidoscope of approaches demonstrates a global transition from an outdated model of mission to a centered appreciation of diversity. As these writers show, that shift has massive implications. It opens the way for collaboration and further innovation in mission contexts around the world."

Frances S. Adeney, William A. Benfield Professor Emerita of Evangelism and Global Mission, Louisville Presbyterian Theological Seminary

"This collection of essays captures numerous insightful perspectives on contemporary approaches to the study and practice of Christian mission, and is a worthy testimony to Fuller's powerful ongoing contributions to missiology."

Paul Kollman, University of Notre Dame

"Beginning with several assessments of the pioneering work and contribution of Donald McGavran and his successors at Fuller's SWM/SIS, the contributors to this volume touch critically on historical developments, contemporary issues and future possibilities for Christian communities who hear the Spirit's enduring invitation to intercultural missional engagement. Practitioners, students and scholars will find much to ponder, discuss and act on by attending to these thoughtful voices from around the world."

Thomas John Hastings, executive director, Overseas Ministries Study Center, New Haven, Connecticut

"*The State of Missiology Today* captures the presentations given on the fiftieth anniversary of Fuller Seminary's School of Intercultural Studies. Both well-known and emerging missiologists from around the world and across ecclesiastical communities met to honor and critique the past and anticipate the future of innovations in global mission. Beginning with Charles Van Engen's introduction, noting ten missiological innovations that have been connected to Fuller, and ending with Scott Sunquist's eight trends in mission to guide us into the future, the chapters in between are loaded with deep insights, relevant perspectives and practical applications. Bravo! for a great book that will surely become a lasting landmark in missiology."

Darrell Whiteman, missiological anthropologist, former professor, Asbury Theological Seminary

THE STATE OF MISSIOLOGY TODAY

Global Innovations in Christian Witness

Edited by
CHARLES E. VAN ENGEN

IVP Academic

An imprint of InterVarsity Press
Downers Grove, Illinois

InterVarsity Press
P.O. Box 1400, Downers Grove, IL 60515-1426
ivpress.com
email@ivpress.com

InterVarsity Press® is the book-publishing division of InterVarsity Christian Fellowship/USA®, a movement of students and faculty active on campus at hundreds of universities, colleges and schools of nursing in the United States of America, and a member movement of the International Fellowship of Evangelical Students. For information about local and regional activities, visit intervarsity.org.

Cover design: David Fassett
Interior design: Beth McGill
Images: We the Peoples . . . by Ron Waddams / Private Collection / Bridgeman Images

ISBN 978-0-8308-5096-9 (print)
ISBN 978-0-8308-9349-2 (digital)

Printed in the United States of America ♾

Library of Congress Cataloging-in-Publication Data
A catalog record for this book is available from the Library of Congress.

P 23 22 21 20 19 18 17 16 15 14 13 12 11 10 9 8 7 6 5 4 3 2 1

Y 36 35 34 33 32 31 30 29 28 27 26 25 24 23 22 21 20 19 18 17 16

This book is dedicated to the Advisory Council of the School of Intercultural Studies for their guidance, prayers and financial contributions to the 2015 Missiology Lectures, celebrating the fiftieth anniversary of the School of Intercultural Studies (formerly the School of World Mission).

Contents

Preface

Charles E. Van Engen

Most of the chapters in this book were presented initially at the fiftieth-anniversary conference of Fuller Theological Seminary's School of Intercultural Studies (formerly School of World Mission)—"Telling Our Unfinished Story: 50 Years of Innovation in Christian Mission . . . and Looking to the Next 50 Years"—held on the Pasadena, California, campus on October 21–24, 2015. Innumerable hands made the conference and this volume possible:

- President Mark Labberton and Provost C. Douglas McConnell supported this venture at every turn.

- Dean Scott Sunquist and his wife, Nancy Sunquist, and the School of Intercultural Studies staff, including Wendy Walker and Silvia Gutierrez, each spent many hours planning for and making the conference happen.

- Irene Neller, vice president for Communications, Marketing and Admissions, and her "events" staff, especially Sarah Bucek and Tamisha Tyler, among many others, oversaw the details of the event.

- Our Fuller Seminary colleagues Bob Freeman, Jude Tiersma Watson, Enoch Kim, Dan Shaw, Roberta King, Veli-Matti Kärkkäinen, Wilmer Villacorta, Ryan Bolger, Peter Im, Evelyne Reisacher, Juan Martinez and Diane Obenchain were respondents to the presentations.

- Bob Freeman, Matthew Lee, Charles Van Engen, Lee Jongill, Delonte Gholston, Clare Wiggins, Diane Obenchain, David Muthukumar, Dwight Radcliffe, Roberta King, Leah Fortson, Eric Sarwar, Wilmer Villacorta, Matthew Kraybill and Toni Kraybill assisted with worship at each of the sessions.

- Kirsteen Kim, Darrell Whiteman and Jehu Hanciles were "listeners" to the conference and pulled together many of the threads and themes from the conference.

- Amos Yong, the director of the School of Intercultural Studies Center for Missiological Research, and his graduate assistant, Hoon Jung, helped with the editing and indexing of the book.

- Scott W. Sunquist, Amos Yong and John Franke, as coeditors of the Missiological Engagements series, and David Congdon and the InterVarsity Press staff have been professional at every step.

It was a joy to have the opportunity to work with these colleagues to bring the conference papers together in the present volume.

Introduction
∙∙

Innovating Mission

Retrospect and Prospect in the
Field of Missiology

Charles E. Van Engen

We gathered from the four corners of the globe to remember, celebrate
and rethink together the significance of the past, present and future of
mission theory and practice of the first fifty years of the Institute of Church
Growth (ICG) / School of World Mission (SWM), now the School of Intercultural Studies (SIS), founded by Donald A. McGavran.[1] With several
hundred mission leaders and practitioners gathered for the event, recognized leaders in the field from around the globe offered short lectures reflecting on the innovations in missiology associated with Donald McGavran
and his associates. The chapters of this book bring together their thoughts.

Having known Donald McGavran personally, I found the celebration to be
inspiring, fun, stimulating and thought provoking. For me, it turned out to be
a kind of back-to-the-future event. The reader will remember the film trilogy
called *Back to the Future*. In the first episode (1985) of that sci-fi classic, Marty
McFly (Michael J. Fox) must go back to 1955 in a plutonium-powered De-
Lorean car invented by eccentric scientist Emmett "Doc" Brown (Christopher
Lloyd). Traveling back in time, Marty must make sure his then teenage
parents-to-be (Crispin Glover, Lea Thompson) meet and fall in love so he can
get back to the future—or he will not exist. In addition, Marty must return to

---

[1]In chapter one, Gary McIntosh offers us a brief biographical history of Donald McGavran and
his missiological perspectives.

his own time and save the life of Doc Brown, who is a very important scientist for the future.[2] As the reader will see in the chapters of this book, our gathering in Pasadena this past October was a similar kind of back-to-the-future experience during which we reconsidered some of the innovations stimulated by McGavran and his colleagues and we reflected on the significance of the past for missiological thought and practice in the future.

BACK TO 1965

Come with me back fifty years to the early 1960s in missiology. Huge changes had occurred in the world with significant impact on the prevailing concepts and action of Christian mission. Here are a few examples of the phenomenal global changes that had taken place prior to the 1960s.

- Two world wars had devastated the globe.
- The Korean War had divided that subcontinent.
- China had closed its doors to outside influence.
- The United Nations was born.
- The World Council of Churches was born.
- Over fifty new nations, for example, Indonesia, Japan, India and South Korea, were born or reconstituted in Africa, Asia and the Middle East.
- Dictatorships were being re-evaluated and replaced in Latin America.
- Airplane travel was expanding around the globe.
- Radio, telephone and television were transforming communication all over the world.

Parallel to these changes, the way the Christian churches and their mission agencies thought about mission was undergoing significant scrutiny. Here are a few examples.

- National churches began to mature and assert themselves as active agents of their own destiny and directors of their own mission endeavors.
- Many folks expressed a strong anticolonial critique of the mission perspectives and actions of older European and North American churches.

---

[2]This summary is adapted from "*Back to the Future* (franchise)," *Wikipedia*, https://en.wikipedia.org/wiki/Back_to_the_Future_(franchise), accessed January 22, 2016.

- The anticolonial critique rose to the point of some mission leaders in Asia and Africa calling for a "moratorium" on sending missions from Europe and North America.

- At the same time, major "faith" mission sodalities were born, especially in North America.

- Simultaneously, the *aggiornamento* of the Second Vatican Council meeting from 1962 to 1965 transformed the Roman Catholic Church's view of Christian mission, among a host of other changes.

- Meanwhile, a strong ecumenical movement took shape in the birth and expansion of the World Council of Churches (WCC).

- Somewhat in response to what was happening in the WCC, evangelical Protestants expressed their view of mission, which eventually split evangelism and social action, a divide that Latin American Protestant missiologists decried.

- Pentecostal cross-cultural and international mission continued to grow, planting thousands of churches and forming hundreds of new denominations around the world.

- African-initiated churches with no historic ties to any Western missions continued to grow exponentially throughout Africa.

Such radical changes in contexts and concepts forced many mission thinkers to choose between the glass half empty and the glass half full. For many, the missiological glass was half empty. By the early 1960s much of the discussion surrounded the already declining churches in the West, the rise of so many competing creeds, the reality of so much disunity in the church, and the existence of so many churches and mission endeavors vying for position and status. All this produced a deep uncertainty and increasing concern over the authenticity of the church and the viability of Christian mission.

In the 1960s, there was deep pessimism and perplexity concerning the church's mission. Some called it more a venture than ever. Others felt that its foundations had been shaken. Some called the discussion surrounding it a "great debate" while others felt that it belonged to an era long past and should suffer "euthanasia," or at least be placed under a "moratorium." Some felt the church should administer mission, but others believed the church itself was the problem. Some were convinced that mission should lead to a personal spiritual conversion, but others stressed that its motivations and goals should involve a life-and-death struggle against hunger, disease, poverty, racism and unjust sociopolitical and economic structures. Still others wanted to replace the whole idea of mission with such notions as interchurch aid or dialogue. Such feelings of uncertainty, coupled with strong appeals for support in mission, were nowhere more apparent and critical in the 1960s than in the discussion, critique and caricaturing of Donald McGavran and what became known as the church-growth movement, the central creating and forming initiative of the School of World Mission at Fuller Theological Seminary.[3]

McGavran and his associates were among those who saw the glass of missiological reflection as half full and affirmed that classic mission had been at the center of the church's life throughout the centuries and especially in 1965, when they established the SWM. They recognized that mission endeavors had absorbed tremendous energy, people power and money. They admitted that in some cases mission was that part of the church's life that had made it (wittingly or not) a partner in the worldwide expansion of Western influence. They admitted that mission was an enigmatic aspect of the church's nature that exhibited sometimes the church's vitality but sometimes its decadence. But they also reminded folks that in the eighteenth and nineteenth centuries mission was seen clearly as the church's primary task, one of its major contributions to world civilization. Yet these same more optimist folks felt the need in the early 1960s for tangible, concrete and clear criteria by which to judge the authenticity and effectiveness of mission. Amid the uncertainties of the day, they wanted to be able to recognize authentic Christian missionary expression. Into this controversy stepped Donald McGavran.

McGavran and his associates affirmed that it was God's will that the church grow in all aspects, including in the numbers of believers, their spirituality and their impact on their surrounding cultures and contexts. McGavran emphasized that money, manpower and planning should be aimed at converting to Christ what at that time were estimated to be "the

---

[3]The preceding paragraph is adapted from Charles Van Engen, *The Growth of the True Church* (Amsterdam: Rodopi, 1981), 1-2.

three billion." Somewhat in reaction to his own experience and background in mission in India, McGavran stated that, where that was not happening, some "good things" were possibly being done but the true aim of mission was not being fulfilled. In speaking, teaching, writing and publishing, he told the world that the command of Jesus Christ to his disciples was to make more disciples and, as a result, to see the church grow. Thus McGavran and his associates believed, in opposition to those who believed the church to be at the sunset of mission, that the worldwide Christian church was at the sunrise of mission in the second half of the twentieth century.

What transformed these discussions into red-hot debate was the simultaneous rise of three major paradigms of mission that took shape in parallel, with few bridges and little overlap between them. In the late 1950s and early 1960s three major perspectives of missiology arose. Each spawned its own movement in mission. At the risk of oversimplification, let me offer a summary description of these views of mission.

(1) Due to the disastrous silence of the churches in Western Europe during the Third Reich and its genocide, especially regarding Jewish people, a missiology of relevance arose that some would call a missiology of the guilty conscience. With Dietrich Bonhoeffer as its main inspiration, this view of mission stressed the importance of socioeconomic and political action on the part of the church. Most strongly involving the older Protestant churches and mission agencies of Western Europe and North America associated with the World Council of Churches (WCC), this perspective called for the church to recognize what God was doing in the world and to join God's efforts by carrying out actions of compassion and justice.

(2) With Gustavo Gutiérrez among its main proponents, a second view of mission offered a strongly economic Marxist-Leninist rereading of history and reality and called for a renewed awareness of structural evil. Born in Latin America and drawing from a predominantly Roman Catholic paradigm that had emerged as one of the fruits of the Second Vatican Council, liberation theology encouraged a number of additional very important theological and missiological perspectives. Theology of struggle in the Philippines, Dalit theology in India, Minjung theology in Korea, and black and feminist theology in North America would be pertinent examples.

Some of the WCC mission thinking, including God's preferential option for the poor, borrowed much from liberation theology.

(3) The third major missiological movement of the 1960s was church growth. Begun by McGavran, this movement involved mostly conservative evangelical churches and missions in North America. This perspective called for a reaffirmation of classic mission theology and a renewed commitment to world evangelization.[4] Drawing from his life experience in India, McGavran focused his attention on the local congregations around the world. Being at heart an evangelist interested in persons becoming followers of Jesus every-where in the world, McGavran asked the question, why do some local churches thrive and grow, and others decline? Such growth and decline related to all aspects of congregational life but could be primarily recognized by examining the congregation's numerical growth like a kind of thermometer used to test the health of a patient. McGavran wanted to research the factors of growth and decline of local congregations in order to change the prevailing mission practice. Of the three paradigms, McGavran and the church-growth movement focused primarily on the life and health of local congregations.

It is interesting to note here that all three of these missiological move-ments were multidenominational, global and activist. All three wanted to bring about change—but they disagreed about what change should be sought. None of the three paradigms of mission was monolithic and unified within itself. They all exhibited a rather wide spectrum of perspectives. There were some mission thinkers who did manage to bridge all three view-points.[5] But differences within each paradigm were small compared to the difference of each from the other two paradigms. The reader will hear echoes of some of these discussions in the chapters of this book.

The uncertainty and questioning of the 1960s appear once again today. Echoes of the misgivings of fifty years ago may be heard today as we look forward into the future of mission theory and practice in this new century: we are "back to the future." In fact, the reader may recognize that a number of the authors of this book seem to suspect that a full-orbed biblical missi-ology for the twenty-first century will need to draw water from the wells of

---

[4]In several places in this book the reader will observe authors quoting Donald McGavran's defini-tion of mission.

[5]It is beyond the scope of this brief overview to begin to name these persons.

all three paradigms and combine elements of all three with discernment, creativity and wisdom.

THE GROWTH OF A DISCIPLINE

In response to uncertainty about Christian mission in the late 1950s and early 1960s, McGavran and his associates set out to create a movement that would stimulate new efforts in classic global mission and world evangelization on the part of missionary practitioners, churches, denominations, mission agencies and missiologists. They became quite intentional about what they called the "diffusion of innovation." As a result, although missiology as a discipline had been known in Europe, the faculty members of the School of World Mission were the principal agents who fostered the recognition of missiology as an academic discipline in North America. Offering master's degrees in church-growth-oriented missiology in the 1960s and early 1970s, by the mid-1970s they were offering accredited doctoral degrees at Fuller Seminary in the discipline: first a doctor of missiology (DMiss) and later a PhD.

In library science there has long been an effort to track the development of an academic discipline or field of inquiry. Of course, library science wanted and needed that ability in order to best archive, arrange, catalog and organize all the materials related to a particular discipline. Some years ago Edgar Elliston shared with me a table derived and adapted from library science (see table I.1). I have found it to be very helpful in understanding the growth and development of church-growth missiology as an academic discipline in its own right. The reader will notice that the creators of the original table, Cerise Oberman and Katina Strauch, mark four stages in the growth of a discipline: pioneering, elaboration, proliferation and establishment. The reader will also note that the authors mark four aspects of that development, stages and activities that utilize appropriate methods of communication and produce source material, which can then be tracked by means of certain control tools of library science. The church-growth movement mirrored most of the aspects described in this table. Amid severe criticism, particularly from those associated with the World Council of Churches, the faculty of the Institute of Church Growth/School of World Mission devoted much of their energy to research, teaching, writing, speaking and spreading concepts associated with their view of mission. As an example, McGavran began *The Church Growth Bulletin*, which was sent all over the world.[6]

In 1955, Donald McGavran published his groundbreaking book, *The Bridges of God: A Study in the Strategy of Mission*, which became the cornerstone of church-growth theory and the foundation of ICG/SWM/SIS at Fuller.[7] Missiological thinking and missionary practice were transformed by the energy, vitality, insight and stubborn tenacity of Donald McGavran. McGavran's style of writing was quite polemical and made a lot of people angry—but they did not seem to be able to ignore him.[8] Whether they agreed with McGavran or not, after the publication of *The Bridges of God*, mission professors, executives and practitioners could no longer do business as usual, nor their usual business.

In my opinion, after John R. Mott, Donald Anderson McGavran was the second most influential missiologist of the twentieth century. He forced the world of mission to reexamine what had been accepted missionary practice for the previous hundred years. He challenged mission agencies and churches to return to a biblical and classical view of mission that gave center stage to the primary purpose of mission: to fulfill God's will that women and men become disciples of Jesus Christ and responsible members of Christ's church. Affirmation of this purpose became the foundation of the church-growth movement.

---

[6]Readers interested in getting a flavor of this history may enjoy reading Donald A. McGavran, ed., *Church Growth and Christian Mission* (New York: Harper & Row, 1965); idem, *Understanding Church Growth*, 3rd ed. (Grand Rapids: Eerdmans, 1990); idem, "My Pilgrimage in Mission," *International Bulletin of Missionary Research* 10, no. 2 (1986): 53-68; C. Peter Wagner, "A Vision for Evangelizing the Real America," *International Bulletin of Missionary Research* 10, no. 2 (1986): 59-64; George Hunter III, "The Legacy of Donald A. McGavran," *International Bulletin of Missionary Research* 16, no. 4 (1992): 128-62; Darrell L. Whiteman, "The Legacy of Alan R. Tippett," *International Bulletin of Missionary Research* 16, no. 4 (1992): 163-66; Ken Mulholland, "McGavran, Donald A.," in *Evangelical Dictionary of World Missions*, ed. A. Scott Moreau, Harold Netland and Charles Van Engen (Grand Rapids: Baker Academic, 2000), 607; Douglas McConnell, "Tippett, Alan R.," in Moreau, *Evangelical Dictionary of World Missions*, 961; and Charles Kraft, *SWM/SIS at Forty: A Participant/Observer's View of Our History* (Pasadena, CA: William Carey Library, 2005). A complete bibliography of the works published by the prolific faculty of SWM during this formative time is beyond the scope of this volume.
[7]Donald McGavran, *The Bridges of God: A Study in the Strategy of Missions* (1955; repr., Eugene, OR: Wipf & Stock, 2005).
[8]For example, one does not usually win many friends by publishing an important article titled, "Will (the WCC Gathering in) Uppsala Betray the Two Billion?," *Church Growth Bulletin* 4, no. 5 (1968), and follow it up with, "Yes, Uppsala Betrayed the Two Billion: Now What?," *Christianity Today* 16, no. 17 (1972): 16-18.

Table I.1. The growth of a discipline

STAGES AND ACTIVITIES	METHODS OF COMMUNICATION	SOURCE MATERIAL	CONTROL TOOLS
Pioneering Stage			
single great thinker, "prophet" emerges	informal meetings	minutes of meetings	assuming primary materials have been preserved, they can be identified via the following:
group with similar "maverick" interest	correspondence and pamphlets	letters, pamphlets, notes, clippings, tapes	directories to archives and special collections
initial data/idea generation	lectures, news stories, interviews	articles with data	standard (existing) indexes
propaganda	first articles	articles with interpretation	bibliographies
financing through own efforts, possibly through philanthropy	newsletters and sections of annual reports	newsletter back files and report collection	subject headings
Elaboration Stage			
more followers	first organization	member roster	reviewing medium in journal
more contributions/ funding	first courses developed	collections of essays	bibliographic essays
new terminology	first journals	collection of data	glossaries or thesauruses
founder(s) recognized	articles in textbooks	memoirs/biography/ autobiography of early proponents	first published books
Proliferation Stage			
worldwide spread of interest	international organization	international directory	guide handbooks
undergraduate major	more journals	proceedings of meetings/ gatherings	histories
methodology established	whole textbooks	annual report of funded projects	who's who in the new discipline
professional training organized	monographs		encyclopedia articles
conferences			special bibliographies, indexes, classifications
branching/twigging begins			subject headings
new sources of funding established			annual review of outside research

STAGES AND ACTIVITIES	METHODS OF COMMUNICATION	SOURCE MATERIAL	CONTROL TOOLS
Establishment Stage			
academic departments established	course catalogs	dissertations	dissertation bibliographies
doctorates awarded/ standards	publisher series	government reports and documents	separate professional encyclopedia
research proliferates			directory of consultants
institutionalized specialized publishers			list of special journals and collections
endowed chair			
federal research grants			

Source: Eddie Elliston, who adapted it from Cerise Oberman and Katina Strauch, Theories of Bibliographic Education: Designs for Teaching *(New York: Bowker, 1982), 13-21. Used by permission.*

McGavran revitalized global missiological thinking by introducing entirely new disciplines into missiology—and it all began with the publication of *The Bridges of God*. McGavran founded what would become the largest school of missiology in the world. Those in the church-growth movement who studied with him quickly spawned branch movements in North America, England, India, Australia, Canada, Korea and numerous other countries in Asia and Africa. He founded a journal, *Global Church Growth*. One of his associates, Ralph Winter, founded a publishing house, William Carey Library; the US Center for World Missions; William Carey University; and the Perspectives Study Program, a college-level course in which thousands have studied missions. McGavran's teaching and writing stimulated research and writing that resulted in hundreds of published works in numerous denominations. C. Peter Wagner, McGavran's disciple and colleague, popularized McGavran's writings and, with McGavran, founded the North American church-growth movement. A professional society called the North American Society for Church Growth was born to continue the development of McGavran's ideas. From the late 1970s through the beginning of the 1990s, hundreds of pastors in the United States studied church growth in Fuller's doctor of ministry (DMin) program. In Korea, one of McGavran's disciples, David Yonggi Cho, founded what would become the largest church in the world. Nearly all the theories about church planting taught today flow from the fountainhead of Donald McGavran's missiology.

McGavran called for the careful examination of social and cultural cohesion that could provide relational bridges along which the gospel could spread naturally. He suggested that there might be significant cultural and worldview factors affecting a group's receptivity or resistance to the gospel. He challenged everyone in mission to think about people groups rather than isolated individuals as the appropriate audience for gospel presentation. He called for new converts to immerse themselves—and remain immersed—in their cultures and among their kin rather than being extracted from their culture into mission stations, as had been the practice during the previous century. He challenged everyone who would listen to find culturally appropriate ways to present the gospel (a missionary approach later known as indigenization and contextualization).

McGavran forced churches and mission agencies the world over to reconsider the importance of calling persons and people groups to faith in Jesus Christ rather than establishing large institutions and building huge buildings, as had previously been the practice of most mission agencies. Donald McGavran and his associates also exerted a definitive, shaping influence on the Lausanne Movement, born in 1974. A host of other movements such as Discipling a Whole Nation (DAWN), Adopt-a-People and NCD (Natural Church Development) cut their missiological teeth on McGavran's theories. In fact, many of McGavran's ideas are now standard practice for many evangelical Protestant church planters, pastors, crosscultural missionaries and mission agencies, so much so that McGavran's concepts are often taken for granted as the assumed way that evangelical mission is to be done, with little or no awareness of the one who first proposed them, or of how revolutionary—and controversial—they were in the 1950s and 1960s.[9]

Readers will find sprinkled throughout the chapters of this work many brief references to the issues discussed above. There were glaring omissions in the missiology of the ICG/SWM, and many highly respected missiologists did not hesitate to point them out. Yet, when one goes "back to the

---

[9]The previous five paragraphs are adapted from Charles Van Engen, "Bridges of God: The Mission Legacy of Donald Anderson McGavran," *Great Commission Research Journal* 1, no. 1 (2009): 27-32.

future" and compares the missiology of the mid-1960s with missiology as we know it today, the number of innovations is remarkable—and the ICG/SWM/SIS faculty have been at the forefront of, or have encouraged others in, the rise of a significant number of these innovations in missiology. In preparation for this fiftieth anniversary celebration, several of us created a list of innovations in mission theory and practice that involved the SWM/SIS faculty. The list includes a rather large number of items. An analysis of all these in a history of the school and the movement it spawned remains to be done sometime in the future. However, one can categorize these innovations according to ten major missiological issues, as seen below. There is not enough space in this introduction to explain the items in the following list, nor to list the specific SWM/SIS faculty members who researched, taught and wrote about them. When the organizers of the fiftieth anniversary celebration invited the world-class scholars whose presentations appear in this book, they asked the contributors to consider one or two innovations of ICG/SWM/SIS that they might deem noteworthy (both positively and negatively) and to craft their presentations and write their chapters in relation to these. I will leave it to the reader to connect the emphases found in the chapters of this book with one or more of the following ten innovations.

1. Indigeneity, people groups, multi-individual conversion, contextualization

2. Strategies of mission, diffusion of innovations, mobilization of mission efforts to evangelize those who are not yet followers of Jesus, formation of societies of church growth, publications

3. Social sciences employed in missiological analysis: for example, cultural anthropology, linguistics, communication theory, language learning, sociology

4. Mission history reexamined and reread from the point of view of the expansion of the church

5. Biblical theology of mission, Bible and mission, theological perspectives in missiology

6. Revivals and awakenings that have impacted the health and growth of the church

7. Studies of the growth or decline of local congregations, cell-based churches, megachurches

8. Leadership, theological education, theological education by extension

9. Spiritual issues in mission, issues of spiritual power

10. Ecclesiological issues of the nature of the church and its mission, Church Next, the mission of the local congregation

OVERVIEW OF THE BOOK

The chapters in the rest of this book elaborate on this list of innovations (focus of part one) even as they chart trajectories of innovation looking forward (emphasis of part two). We begin with Gary L. McIntosh, who originally presented on Donald A. McGavran during the preconference proceedings. McIntosh has spent a lifetime studying the SWM founder and argues that McGavran's missiological church-growth principles continue to reverberate throughout the missionary world of the early twenty-first century. Shawn B. Redford, an SWM PhD graduate who studied under Charles Van Engen, was invited to write a chapter on the Bible and mission since this has been such an important theme in SWM/SIS history and ought not to be neglected in the publication celebrating, honoring and remembering the event. His chapter makes the case that missiological, thematic, ethno-, spiritual and scientific hermeneutics all offer unique interpretational capabilities for a holistic understanding of God's mission as found in Scripture for the purpose of questioning, shaping, defining, directing, guiding and evaluating today's ongoing missional activity.

The rest of the chapters were plenary presentations originally invited for the book. Sarita D. Gallagher focuses on how the church-growth movement established by Donald A. McGavran and Alan R. Tippett marked a monumental paradigm shift, specifically in twentieth-century indigenous mission theory, that has continued to influence indigenous people movements toward active participation in the global mission of God. Wonsuk Ma writes as the quintessential missionary, expressing his conviction that this generation lives with an unprecedented possibility of world evangelization but that this requires every believer and every congregation to become active mission players, which in turn compels all of us to seriously reexamine our understanding of and approach to mission and theological education. Pascal D. Bazzell then turns more specifically to intercultural and interreligious encounter and outlines how the Cornelius encounter (Acts 10) contributes to a missiological paradigm shift from *missio ecclesiae* to *missio Dei*, which is explicated in terms of what Bazzell refers to as Christian mission "with the people." This is a radical embrace of the divine in the other, together seeking and proclaiming who God is. Consequently, mission is not only about giving but also about receiving, not only about evangelizing but also about being evangelized; mission is about sharing with and hearing from the mysterious work of the triune God in the other in order to participate with God's mission.

Moonjang Lee writes from a South Korean missiological perspective to point out that, as global Christianity is in the midst of great and rapid changes, we need to rethink the nature of the current crisis in Christian mission and find ways to reinvent Christianity, beginning with a renovation of the churches and then also of theological education. Stephen Bevans asks, in the final chapter of part one, what does Rome have to do with Pasadena? And he answers, a lot! SWM/SIS has inspired Catholic scholars and has explored issues that Catholic missiology has also explored. Roman Catholics, of course, have also broken ground that Fuller's evangelical missiologists have not. In the end, however, it is clear that Fuller's evangelical understanding of missions and Roman Catholic missiology have worked together for the establishment of God's reign.

The chapters in part two of the book highlight past innovations of SWM/SIS, but the accent is on future challenges and possibilities. Jayakumar Christian urges that, since the poor and the oppressed are no longer merely objects of mission but have become its agents and bearers, there is a need for the community of missiologists to develop an alternate missiology that provides credible forms of engagement with this reality. Terry C. Muck then applies his extensive experience in the interfaith encounter and maps strategies of contestation, confession and consilience, suggesting the strength and weaknesses of each. Referring to these principles, he recommends how evangelicals can move forward on the world religious ground in the next century. John A. Azumah then dives deeper into the interreligious arena but focuses on Islam, unpacking how recent events reveal how the question of Muhammad's prophetic status is not merely a theological or philosophical one but a political and existential one that calls for a carefully considered response from Christians.

Sister Mary Motte's chapter returns to engagement with Roman Catholic missiology but focuses on its future trajectories. She shows how in the context of recent history, when our planet is situated between chaos and transformation, emerging paths from Vatican II are gradually leading to a new way of seeing, doing and missionizing among Roman Catholics. Anne-Marie Kool then identifies images of Europe and European Christianity in the *Atlas of Global Christianity 1910–2010* and delineates the conceptual and methodological problems of their formation. Kool also examines the assumptions of missiometrics and the underlying mission theory of the atlas, including clarifying some of the criticisms that have emerged over time vis-à-vis McGavran's church-growth theory and principles.

In the thirteenth chapter, J. Kwabena Asamoah-Gyadu writes about how in the twenty-first century Africa has developed as a major heartland of Christianity and how the single most important factor in this development is the power and presence of the Holy Spirit working through ordinary people. He unpacks thereby the claim that Pentecostalism has never been alien to the African experience. In the final chapter derived from the plenary presentations, Pablo A. Deiros, reflecting from a Latin American missiological perspective, urges that as we move deeper into the new millennium, we need to consider the future as our hermeneutical key and develop an eschatological missiology that follows a tri-dimensional model of the Christian mission. The conclusion by current SIS dean Scott W. Sunquist was written specifically for this volume, and he attempts to anticipate the implications for the future of mission thinking and practice suggested by the chapters in this volume.

As Marty McFly learned, sometimes we need to go back to the future in order to receive new lenses and gain new understanding of our present and future. Has the movement founded by Donald A. McGavran run its course, or is it poised to embark on a new journey into the future of global innovation in world evangelization? Time will tell. We invite the reader of these chapters to accompany us back to the future.

PART 1

··

The Diffusion of Innovation

Looking Backward to Look Ahead

1

....

Donald A. McGavran

Life, Influence and Legacy in Mission

Gary L. McIntosh

INTRODUCTION

It was Sunday, September 16, 1923. Donald and Mary McGavran rose early to make final preparations for their trip to India. Beyond the sounds of packing, a crying baby and emotional goodbyes lay a future that was unimaginable at the time—the tragedy of a child's death, the pain of rejected leadership resulting in a demotion, the struggle to evangelize a low-caste tribe and the loss of a dream to train leaders in how to achieve greater growth in the church. Yet, as God would script it, the ministry of Donald McGavran was destined to be one of the twentieth century's glittering triumphs. The pains and losses of his life were mixed with the joys of discovering new insights for reaching lost people with the ageless gospel, of winning over one thousand precious souls to Christ, of planting fifteen churches, of writing groundbreaking books, of starting a worldwide movement, of establishing a profoundly influential school of missiology and of changing the entire face of mission. No one could have foretold that Donald McGavran would eventually become the premier missiologist of the twentieth century, but that is just what happened.[1]

EARLY LIFE

Donald Anderson McGavran was born in Damoh, India, on December 15, 1897. His parents, John and Helen McGavran, were living in Damoh because

---

[1]For a complete biography chronicling the life and ministry of Donald McGavran, see Gary L. McIntosh, *Donald A. McGavran: A Biography of the Twentieth Century's Premier Missiologist* (Boca Raton, FL: Church Leader Insights, 2015).

of a famine that had hit central India. Their primary job was to care for ap-
proximately four hundred orphaned boys, as well as to alleviate the suffering
of those in need as far as resources allowed. The famine slowly ended in the
year following Donald's birth, and John was assigned to the work of evangelism. He focused on the task of winning men and women to Christ until
1910, when the McGavran family returned to the United States.

Except for a few short months of formal education, Donald was home-
schooled, learning primarily through unsupervised reading. He described
his early education as follows: "There was nothing else to do, so we picked
up all kinds of books and at first laboriously and later effortlessly read
through them. We thus accumulated a lot of information and an excellent
ability to read."[2] After entering the United States, Donald enrolled in the
seventh grade and made a good adjustment to American life in general and
to school life in particular. His previous homeschooling having proved sufficient, he was able to adjust quickly to normal classrooms.

When their furlough came to an end, John and Helen faced a serious
decision about the future. Their hearts were in India, but their children
would soon be in need of better schools than were available in the Central
Provinces of India. In the end, after several months of prayer and anguished
discussions, they determined to take a leave from missionary service and
stay in the United States. John became the pastor of the First Christian
Church of Tulsa, Oklahoma, but his reputation and experience, particularly
with the Hindi language and culture, made him the choice for professor of
Indian subjects at the newly formed College of Missions in Indianapolis,
Indiana. The family moved to Indianapolis in 1913, and Donald started attending Shortridge High School, where he graduated in 1915. That fall he
entered Butler College, where he became active on the debating team, in the
Philokurian Literary Society and in the YMCA.

In April 1917 the United States declared war against Germany, and he
enlisted on April 28 in Troop B of the First Indiana Cavalry, a National
Guard unit. However, his unit did not arrive in France until November 10,
1918. After marching for nearly a day, he could hear the guns of battle, but

---

[2]Donald A. McGavran, quoted by Vernon James Middleton, "The Development of a Missiologist:
The Life and Thought of Donald Anderson McGavran, 1897–1965" (PhD diss., Fuller Theological Seminary School of World Mission, 1990), 8.

on November 11 armistice was declared. Donald never saw action and soon returned to the United States for his discharge.

Profoundly glad to be back at Butler College, Donald promptly enrolled in spring classes for 1919. He rejoined the Butler College YMCA, where he chaired the religious committee and, later, the membership committee. During June 13-22, 1919, he attended a YMCA camp at Lake Geneva, Wisconsin, which changed the entire direction of his life. Until that time, Donald had seen himself as a reasonably good Christian but was determined that his career would be in some field other than missions or ministry. "My family has done enough for the Lord," was his attitude. "I will make money." He was attracted to law, geology and forestry as possible fields of study. Day by day, those at the camp were challenged to completely surrender their lives to Christ. They were told to let God decide everything in their lives, including making money and choosing one's life work. For several days, Donald resisted. Finally he yielded and said, "Very well, Lord. It is clear to me; either I give up all claim[s] to being a Christian, or I go all the way. Since that is the situation, I choose to go all the way."[3] Donald did not tell anyone about his decision, but from then on he was sure that if God called him to the mission field, he would go.

In October 1919, the senior class elected Donald as their president. During his senior year two key events occurred that were major turning points for his life. That year Donald met and got acquainted with a sophomore from the Christian church in Muncie, Indiana, Mary Elizabeth Howard. Soon after Christmas, Donald and Mary attended the Eighth International Convention of the Student Volunteer Movement for Foreign Missions in Des Moines, Iowa, from December 31, 1919, to January 4, 1920.[4] The spiritual dynamic at the meetings touched many lives, and Donald and Mary made commitments to give their lives to missionary service. Looking back on that conference, McGavran remembered:

---

[3]Donald Anderson McGavran, "The McGavrans in America: A History of Two Hundred Years, 1775–1966" (unpublished family history, 1983), 40. Private collection of Patricia (McGavran) Sheafor. Copy in author's files.

[4]Addresses delivered at the Eighth International Convention of the Student Volunteer Movement can be found in *North American Students and World Advance*, ed. Burton St. John (New York: Student Volunteer Movement for Foreign Missions, 1920).

There it became clear to me that God was calling me to be a missionary, that
he was commanding me to carry out the Great Commission. Doing just that
has ever since been the ruling purpose of my life. True, I have from time to
time swerved from that purpose but never for long. That decision lies at the
root of the church-growth movement.[5]

Shortly after arriving back at Butler, they were engaged in the spring of 1920,
and Donald graduated on June 17.

That summer he decided to attend Yale Divinity School for two years of
theological training, leading to a BD (bachelor of divinity) degree. Special-
izing in Christian education, he did well at Yale, winning the annual senior
sermon contest, and he graduated in June 1922. Mary Howard graduated
from Butler College on June 12, 1922, and that summer they were married
on August 29.

A year later he graduated with an MA degree in June 1923 from the
College of Missions and was asked to be a faculty member during the
summer for twelve youth conferences being held throughout the United
States. Donald accepted; the opportunity allowed him to do for others what
the Lake Geneva YMCA conference had done for him in the summer of 1919.
A report on his summer activities prophetically evaluated his abilities: "With
his clear-cut thinking and ability of expression, he is always able to make a
strong and convincing address."[6]

A MISSIONARY IN INDIA

When Donald arrived in India in 1923 as a missionary with the United
Christian Missionary Society (UCMS), he brought training that no colleague before him had—he was a specialist in religious education. The main
tasks before him were to improve the training of teachers, revamp the curriculum and reemphasize the purpose of Christian schools, which he understood to mean "to give their pupils a thoroughly good education; to bring
the non-Christian students to a knowledge of Jesus Christ and into discipleship to him; and with the Christian pupils, to look ahead twenty years,
see the church of that day, and mold for it a fit, useful and consecrated

---

[5]Donald A. McGavran, "My Pilgrimage in Mission," *International Bulletin of Missionary Research*
10, no. 2 (1986): 53.
[6]"Loaned to the Department of Religious Education," *World Call*, July 1923, 50.

membership."[7] After inspecting the schools and the teaching staff, he turned his attention to improving the quality of instruction. To meet this challenge, he organized a teachers' institute to inspire new teaching ideals and methods. The training greatly improved the teaching, curriculum and overall rating of the schools, which led to his election as director of religious education for the Indian Mission of the Disciples of Christ in 1927. This role effectively placed him in a position to bring about a uniformity of instruction and courses across all the mission schools.

Early in 1930, as Donald and Mary prepared to leave in June for their first furlough, tragedy struck when Mary Theodora, their oldest daughter, died of appendicitis on March 1. Mary Theodora's death caused Donald and Mary great suffering. Yet, the pain served to turn Donald's life in two new directions. His spiritual life deepened, and he became more concerned for evangelism. Mary Theodora's death made him aware of the shortness of life and thus the importance of reaching as many people as possible with the gospel of Jesus Christ.

After visiting family in Indianapolis during the summer of 1930, the McGavrans relocated to New York, where Donald began studies for a PhD in religious education. His course work was completed during the 1930–1931 school year, and in the fall of 1931 he finished his preliminary research and experimentation project for his final dissertation and passed his examination for the doctor of philosophy degree. Final copies of his dissertation, "Education and the Beliefs of Popular Hinduism," were deposited with Columbia University in 1935, and the degree was awarded officially on August 7.

Upon his arrival for a second term in India, Donald was elected secretary-treasurer of the India Mission during the annual convention held in Jubbulpore November 17-23, 1932. Many challenges lay ahead for the young mission secretary, and holding the mission together during financial depression was a primary one. Funding from home was reduced by 50 percent, and sometimes only 25 percent was received. It took calm nerves, strong management and lots of faith to lead the mission during the early 1930s. It was during this time that Donald began seriously thinking about the church's growth.

---

[7]Donald A. McGavran, "Sending the Church to School," *World Call*, February 1925, 22.

While there were several forerunners who contributed to developing his insights, such as William Carey, Roland Allen, Kenneth Scott Latourette and his own father, the most direct influence that started Donald thinking about church growth was Methodist missionary J. Waskom Pickett, about whom McGavran would later say, "I lit my candle at Pickett's fire."[8]

In 1928, Pickett was asked by the National Christian Council of India, Burma and Ceylon to make an extensive study of Christian mass movements in India. For nearly one hundred and fifty years, missionaries in India had struggled to win Christian converts one by one in the face of Hindu and Islamic resistance. Then, suddenly, religious revivals began, and people started coming to Christ in masses. Such movements caught most missionaries by surprise, and they struggled to ascertain the meaning of it. Pickett's study sought to determine how effective mass movements really were at winning and nurturing new Christian believers. The results of Pickett's study were published in *Christian Mass Movements in India* (1933).[9] McGavran read Pickett's book and was thrilled with the results Pickett found. McGavran wrote, "There came a book sent by God and its name was *Christian Mass Movements in India*."[10] Pickett's intense study concluded that mass movements, or group movements as some preferred to call them, were valid and legitimate in God's plan for India's redemption.

During this same time period, McGavran was quietly changing his view of mission and theology. In his formative childhood years, mission was understood to be carrying out the Great Commission, winning the world for Christ and saving lost humanity. At Yale Divinity School, however, he was introduced to the teachings of theologian H. Richard Niebuhr. According to McGavran, Niebuhr "used to say that mission was everything the church does outside its four walls. It was philanthropy, education, medicine, famine relief, evangelism, and world friendship."[11] McGavran espoused this view of mission when he went to India in 1923. As he became involved in education, social work and evangelism in the real-world context of India, he gradually

---

[8]Donald A. McGavran and George G. Hunter III, *Church Growth: Strategies That Work* (Nashville: Abingdon, 1980), 14.

[9]For the complete story of J. Waskom Pickett's life and ministry, as well as the details on his study of mass movements, see Arthur G. McPhee, *The Road to Delhi* (Lexington, KY: Emeth, 2012).

[10]Donald A. McGavran, "Book Chat," *World Call*, June 1935, 29.

[11]McGavran, "My Pilgrimage in Mission," 54.

reverted to the classical view that mission was making disciples of Jesus
Christ. Regarding this change of view he commented,

> As my convictions about mission and church growth were being molded
> in the 1930s and '40s they ran headlong into the thrust that mission is
> doing many good things in addition to evangelism. I could not accept this
> way of thinking about missions. These good deeds must, of course, be
> done, and Christians will do them. I myself was doing many of them. But
> they must never replace the essential task of mission, discipling the
> peoples of earth.[12]

As a result of his return to a more traditional theology of mission and after
reading Pickett's book, McGavran became deeply concerned that after
several decades of work his mission had only about thirty small churches,
all of which were experiencing no growth. At the same time, he saw mass
movements (people movements) in scattered areas of India where thousands of people in groups, rather than as individuals, were coming to Christ.
He wondered why his denomination's churches were not seeing the same
type of growth. Soon he determined to study the growth of the church in
the Central Provinces area of India.

After preliminary investigations, he found that only 11 of the 145
mission stations were growing; the overall growth rate was about 1 percent
a year. Surprisingly, some of the 11 growing stations were seeing rates of
100 to 200 percent a decade, or about 10 to 20 percent a year. He eventually persuaded the Mid-India Christian Council—an interdenominational group of British, Swedish, American and German missions—to
obtain the services of Pickett for a fact-finding survey. McGavran traveled
with Pickett as his assistant during January and February 1936 conducting
interviews. During the survey tour, Pickett was elected a bishop and had
to leave before the surveys were completed. They agreed that McGavran
would finish the surveys of two important fields and write the reports for
them. *Christian Missions in Mid-India: A Study of Nine Areas with Special
Reference to Mass Movements* was released in 1938.[13] The study found that
the group-movement approach to evangelism produced healthy church

---

[12]Ibid.
[13]Donald A. McGavran, J. Waskom Pickett and G. H. Singh, *Christian Mission in Mid-India* (Jub-
    bulpore, India: Mission Press, 1938).

growth since it encouraged groups of families to come to salvation without social dislocation.

During this study, a curiosity arose within McGavran's heart and mind that was to focus his ministry for the remainder of his life. He wondered why some churches were growing while others, oftentimes just a few miles apart, were not. He eventually identified four major questions that came to define the church-growth movement: "What are the *causes* of church growth? What are the *barriers* to church growth? What are the factors that can make the Christian faith a *movement* among some populations? What *principles* of church growth are reproducible?"[14]

Another outcome of the study of mass movements was the firm belief among many missionaries that the Holy Spirit was propelling a definite and extensive proclamation of the gospel and that a time of peculiar opportunity for advance was upon them. As secretary of the mission, McGavran gradually became convinced that the missionaries should devote more time to direct evangelism of Indian people. His charge to his fellow missionaries was to devote an hour each day in intercessory prayer for the salvation of the peoples among whom they each worked, seek to win one person to Christ every three months and pledge at least one night a week to do personal evangelism.

McGavran also believed that it would be sound strategy to deliberately seek for mass movements in his area of ministry. The Pentecost experience of three thousand coming to Christ in a single day was common in India of the early 1930s, and McGavran felt he was often walking "knee deep in miracles." Mass movements were the "greatest apologetic Christianity has ever had," he claimed in an article written for the *Christian Evangelist* in 1935. "A religious revival of vast proportions is possible in the India field of the Disciples of Christ," he declared.[15]

As 1936 broke upon his world, McGavran expressed enthusiasm for his life and work.

> It is a good time to be living, lots to do, lots of responsibility devolving on one, lots of scope for activity, health and strength, and the joy of life—what more

---

[14]George G. Hunter III, "The Legacy of Donald A. McGavran," *International Bulletin of Missionary Research* 16, no. 4 (1992): 158; emphasis original.

[15]Donald A. McGavran, "The Coming Revival in India," *Christian Evangelist*, June 13, 1935, 10.

could one ask of God! . . . Our work here goes well. We are living at a time
when the possibility of large groups of men and women, whole castes, coming
to Jesus Christ looms very large.[16]

This happy report glossed over a change, which was to be God's providential
design for an even greater work in McGavran's life in years to come. In 1935
he was not reelected as mission secretary. A report on the annual convention
held in November 1935 said, "This releases Dr. D. A. McGavran for work in
the evangelistic field where he has shown such definite ability in leadership
during the past few years . . . and also for literature work, and for a few
months with Dr. Pickett in the Mass Movement work."[17]

The truth was that many of his fellow missionaries and administrators
were not happy with his emphasis on evangelism and mass movements, so
they voted him out of office. Looking back on this incident fifty years later,
McGavran remembered that in effect the mission said to him, "Since you
are talking so much about evangelism and church growth, we are going to
locate you in a district where you can practice what you preach."[18]

It was all very frustrating, but McGavran went about his new evangelistic
work among the Satnamis with fervor, trusting God was leading him. The
major insight that he felt God had shown him was that people normally
confessed their faith in Christ through a family, caste or tribal group. Reflecting back on this time period, McGavran wrote:

> As I read Waskom Pickett's *Christian Mass Movements in India*, my eyes were
> opened. I suddenly saw that where people become Christians one by one and
> are seen as outcasts by their own people, as traitors who have joined another
> community, the church grows very, very slowly. The one by one "out of my
> ancestral community into a new low community" was a sure recipe for slow
> growth. Conversely, where men and women could become followers of the
> Lord Jesus Christ while remaining in their own segment of society, there the
> gospel was sometimes accepted with great pleasure by great numbers.[19]

The studies Pickett had conducted demonstrated conclusively that winning
people to Christ one by one was an ineffective approach. Since all societies

---

[16]Donald A. McGavran, *Butler Alumnal Quarterly*, January 1936, 253.
[17]Leta May Brown, "Forward—with God—in India," *World Call*, March 1936, 27.
[18]McGavran, "My Pilgrimage in Mission," 53-57.
[19]Ibid., 56.

are made up of more or less homogeneous units, "it is only when a series of individual decisions generate enough heat to lead a whole group to act as a unit and when enough group decisions have been taken to set the caste or tribe alight that the church really grows."[20]

Even in the midst of a depression and war, evangelism and church growth continued to occupy his thought and practice as he evangelized the Satnami people. The war heightened his awareness that the Holy Spirit brings about receptiveness to the gospel at different times for different groups of people. In the difficult times the missionaries were facing, he felt that abundant opportunity existed to establish growing Christian movements throughout India. Though the war years were difficult, he continued to encourage his fellow missionaries and Indian workers that the Holy Spirit had prepared certain people to welcome Christ. It was to those prepared people that evangelistic touring, preaching and prayers were to be extended. He wrote, "Let us not go to people who reject the Gospel, but to those who have been prepared by God to accept His Son."[21] In his call to go to receptive peoples, McGavran did not ignore less receptive areas. "Even in the midst of a world struggle," he explained, "our eyes must be turned toward these unoccupied territories, and our lips and our hearts must seek aid from God that His saving knowledge may be made known to all these who lie in the darkness of ignorance and sin."[22]

A PROFESSOR OF MISSION

With his work among the Satnamis soon ending, McGavran took his vacation in 1951 to begin writing a manuscript tentatively titled *How Peoples Become Christian*. After finishing the manuscript, McGavran thought it focused too strictly on India. So when the McGavran family left for furlough in the United States during the summer of 1954, the UCMS granted a request that he route his travel home through Africa so he could study people movements on that continent. He traveled on a shoestring budget, but it allowed him to study twenty missions and hundreds of churches, evaluating mission policies as they related to church growth. He crossed Africa by plane, rail,

---

[20]Donald A. McGavran, "How Great Races Are Christianized," *World Call*, November 1938, 43.
[21]Donald A. McGavran, "Things New and Old," *United Church Review*, May 1941, 108.
[22]Ibid., 140.

bus, truck, bicycle, foot and canoe, observing firsthand the growth of the church in six countries—Kenya, Uganda, Ruanda (now Rwanda), Congo, Nigeria and Gold Coast.[23]

Arriving in the United States for his furlough, McGavran revised sections of his book, which was published in 1955 as *The Bridges of God*. Reviews of the book lauded his courageous thinking. The *Missionary Digest* wrote that *The Bridges of God* is "the most up-to-date book on new missionary methods of which we know. . . . This book is one of the first to take account of the gigantic movements of the Holy Spirit throughout the world today. Mission-minded people should be deeply grateful to Dr. Donald McGavran for pointing the way."[24] *The Bridges of God* was destined to change the way mission was practiced around the globe, and it became the Magna Carta of the church-growth movement, the primary document from which the movement grew.

Following the furlough, McGavran intended to return to India, but his mission board, intrigued by his church-growth discoveries, decided to send him on several tours of Puerto Rico, Formosa, Philippines, Thailand, Congo and India to study the growth of the church in those lands. Those studies, and many to follow, provided the data and background for a number of books, articles and reports that McGavran would write over the coming decade.

From 1953 until 1961, McGavran's official status was professor in the College of Missions in Indianapolis under special appointment. Throughout those years, he continued to be listed as a missionary to India, but his special appointments often found him studying the growth of churches in other countries, as well as teaching missions courses at Butler University (Indianapolis, Indiana), Phillips University (Enid, Oklahoma), Drake University (Des Moines, Iowa) and Lexington College of the Bible (Lexington, Kentucky).

Those years of travel provided a laboratory for the study of church growth throughout the world. The studies added considerably to Mc-Gavran's understanding, and he published a second book, *How Churches Grow: The New Frontiers of Mission*.[25] *The Bridges of God* showed how the

---

[23]Donald A. McGavran, "A Continent Is Being Discipled," *World Call*, December 1954, 20.
[24]*Missionary Digest*, September-October 1955.
[25]Donald A. McGavran, *How Churches Grow: The New Frontiers of Mission* (London: World Dominion Press, 1959).

church expanded largely through people movements. This new book, however, demonstrated that churches grow in many different ways, depending on the circumstances surrounding each church. The book was the first full expression of his church-growth missiology. One reviewer, Joseph M. Smith of the Christian Theological Seminary, concluded, "This is a book about *one* thing, whose central significance no one can doubt. It will merit careful study, therefore, by all who take seriously the words 'Go . . . make disciples of all nations' [Mt 28:19]."[26]

Questions regarding what McGavran meant by church growth started surfacing from various corners of the missionary world almost as soon as *How Churches Grow* was released. In a letter to Donald Salmon, executive secretary of the department of evangelism of the UCMS, McGavran explained,

> I hold no brief at all for dishonest baptizing or pressuring people into joining the church, under conditions where we know they will not stay in it. I am not in the least interested in an evangelism which is interested in numbers from the sake of the evangelist's professional reputation. But I am enormously interested in numbers for the sake of the salvation of men. No numbers of the saved are ever mere. God is interested in lost sheep. The more brought in and fed and folded, the better pleased is God.[27]

Ross J. Griffeth, president of Northwest Christian College in Eugene, Oregon, expressed interest in calling McGavran to be professor of Christian missions at his college and helping him develop an Institute of Church Growth. The northwest corner of the United States was not the most promising place to begin an interdenominational Institute of Church Growth, but Donald seized it with both hands, particularly since it was his only offer. On January 2, 1961, the Institute of Church Growth at Northwest Christian College opened with one lone student. Over the next four years, fifty-seven missionaries studied at the institute while on furlough.

Reflecting on this time some years later, McGavran noted that the first two building blocks of what came to be known as the church-growth movement were started in Eugene, Oregon. The first was the founding of the Institute of Church Growth, and the second the beginning of the

---

[26]Joseph M. Smith, "Discipling the Nations," *World Call*, May 1961, 39; emphasis original.
[27]Letter from Donald A. McGavran to Donald Salmon, January 14, 1960; Billy Graham Archives, collection 178, box 3.

publication of the *Church Growth Bulletin* (first circulated in 1964), a sixteen-page bimonthly periodical edited by McGavran and published by Overseas Crusades, Inc. The first issue of the *Church Growth Bulletin* was published in September 1964 and proved to be a key communication piece for the burgeoning church-growth movement. By the end of the year, over twelve hundred leaders representing one hundred mission boards in the United States, Europe, Asia, Africa and Latin America were receiving the *Church Growth Bulletin.*

God was at work behind the scenes preparing McGavran for an even larger influence around the world. The years at Northwest Christian College offered opportunities to develop case studies of growing churches, refine lectures, develop reading lists, lead church-growth conferences, refine research methodology and clarify basic terminology, as well as publish early church-growth studies from around the world. Then, as Donald was thinking of retiring to a farm in Eugene, somewhat miraculously Fuller Seminary invited him to begin the School of World Mission in Pasadena, California.

Founding a School

In the spring of 1965, McGavran became aware that the Institute of Church Growth at Northwest Christian College was going to be closed due to a lack of funding. Providentially, David Hubbard, president of Fuller Theological Seminary, extended an invitation to him to move the Institute of Church Growth to Pasadena and establish the School of World Mission as a satellite school of the Fuller School of Theology. McGavran accepted the invitation and emerged from semiretirement at age sixty-seven to become the founding dean of the new School of World Mission and Institute for Church Growth. In September 1965 the school opened with McGavran as dean and Alan Tippett as the second faculty member. Over the next few years, McGavran assembled a world-class faculty who together changed the course of mission practice. He added to the faculty Ralph Winter, who had experience in Guatemala; Charles Kraft, with experience in Nigeria; J. Edwin Orr, an authority on revivals; C. Peter Wagner, with experience in Bolivia; and Arthur Glasser, with experience in China.

Beginning with fifteen graduate students, the School of World Mission grew to become one of the most influential schools of missiology in the world. The growing impact of the Church Growth School was reflected in an article in *Eternity*. Calling McGavran "Today's Expert on Church Growth," Dwight Baker wrote, "Whether speaking against the leaden traditionalism of past mission policies or the heavy pessimism of current theories of mission, his voice is a salutary corrective that needs to be heard—and heeded—today."[28]

Following an illness that nearly took his life, McGavran canceled his travel during the summer of 1968 to put his church-growth ideas into print. As a compilation of wisdom learned from his years of research and insights gathered from his colleagues, *Understanding Church Growth* (1970) received wide attention demonstrating that church-growth theory was an orderly and systematic missiology. McGavran's earlier works had been read by missionaries, but this new book caught the attention of pastors in North America. He cotaught the first church-growth class for North American pastors and denominational leaders with Wagner in 1972, and it launched the North American church-growth movement.

However, what put church-growth missiology on the worldwide map was the Congress of Evangelism held in Lausanne, Switzerland, in the summer of 1974. Over 2,700 people attended the conference, among whom were a number of Fuller alumni who had taken courses in church growth. McGavran, Tippett, Winter and Wagner all presented papers or workshops for the attendees. Following the Lausanne conference, the church-growth movement exploded throughout the world.

McGavran had retired as dean of the School of World Mission in 1971, turning over the role to mission theologian Arthur Glasser, but he continued to teach part time until the 1984–1985 school year. That year the Donald A. McGavran Chair of Church Growth was established at Fuller Theological Seminary. From that time until his death in 1990, McGavran concentrated on writing. He collaborated with Glasser on *Contemporary Theologies of Mission* (1983) and wrote *Momentous Decisions in Missions Today* (1984), *Effective Evangelism: A Theological Mandate* (1988) and *The Satnami Story: A Thrilling Drama of Religious Change* (1990).

---

[28]Dwight P. Baker, "Today's Expert on Church Growth," *Eternity*, August 1970, 45.

INFLUENCE AND LEGACY

By the time of McGavran's death on July 10, 1990, church-growth missiology was well established and highly influential around the world. The movement he founded has waned in the years following his death, but McGavran continues to influence thinking in ten major areas of ministry.[29]

Valuing the Bible. First, McGavran reminds church leaders to hold to the authority of the Bible. In his early writings, McGavran often assumed the importance of biblical authority for effective evangelism. As the years went by, he went out of his way to be clear on the importance of valuing biblical authority. In an interview that may well have constituted his last published words, he said,

> I think that my word would be that all those who seek to proliferate the Christian faith should lean very heavily on biblical authority upon the one hand and on the presence of the Holy Spirit on the other. We cannot spread the Christian faith unless we believe that the Bible is the infallible Word of God. Its authority is based on the fact that it is what God has said. He intends for us to obey. We need to recognize it as authority. We need to let it guide our lives.[30]

This missiological insight continues to influence church ministry in the twenty-first century as missional leaders look to the Bible to establish the rationale, purpose and practice of missiology.

Making disciples. Second, growing out of McGavran's faith in the Bible as God's Word, he continues to press us to remain faithful in obeying the Great Commission. The essential conviction of mission is that God wants his lost children found and enfolded into local churches. Jesus Christ gave his disciples the Great Commission, and the entire New Testament assumes that Christians will proclaim Jesus Christ as God and Savior and encourage men and women to become his disciples and responsible members of his church.

Yet, the Great Commission demands an understanding of *peoples* if it is to be obeyed. Paraphrasing from his favorite passage in Romans 16:25-26, "The Gospel I brought you . . . [is] now disclosed and . . . by Eternal God's command made known to all nations, to bring them to faith and obedience,"

---

[29]Portions of this section appeared in "The Twenty-first Century Relevance of Donald McGavran," *Great Commission Research Journal* 4, no. 2 (2013): 216-24. Used by permission.

[30]Kent Hunter, "An Interview with Donald McGavran," *Global Church Growth* 27, no. 3 (1990): 13.

McGavran reminds us that "the apostle did not have in mind modern nation-states such as India or America. He had in mind families of mankind—tongues, tribes, castes, and lineages of men."[31]

The Great Commission was McGavran's missiological motive for mission, but it meant far more than simply taking the gospel to different lands. It meant taking the gospel to all "peoples"—that is, all families, clans, tribes and units of the human mosaic. The ongoing interest in outreach to unreached people groups is a continuing legacy from McGavran's church-growth missiology.

Prioritizing evangelism. Third, the Great Commission demands that evangelism be the priority over simply serving the physical needs of people. While caring for people's physical, emotional and intellectual needs is part of our Christian duty, doing so is temporal, while salvation is eternal. Logically, the eternal always outweighs the temporal; thus evangelism must be the priority of the church. McGavran asserted, "God therefore commands those of His household to go and 'make disciples of all nations.' Fulfilling this command is the supreme purpose which should guide the entire mission, establish the priorities, and coordinate all its activities."[32]

Within this priority of evangelism, McGavran identified three ways into a church—"biological," "transfer" and "conversion."[33] That the missiological focus is on evangelism means that the best church growth comes from conversion rather than biological or transfer growth. Kenneth Scott Latourette addressed the issue this way: "The primary assignment of missions is evangelism: the proclamation of the Good News and assisting in the emergence of churches which, rooted in the soil and with their own leaders, will be witnesses to the Good News."[34]

Removing the fog. Discovering the facts of church growth through responsible research is a fourth aspect of McGavran's legacy that remains with us today. Responsible research into the causes and barriers to church growth is an ongoing project for many. God has given us a Great Commission, and we dare not assume that all is going well or that we are doing the best that can be done. The Lord of the harvest wants his lost sheep found, and we must be accountable to

---

[31]Donald A. McGavran, *Understanding Church Growth*, 1st ed. (Grand Rapids: Eerdmans, 1970), 62.

[32]Ibid., 51.

[33]Ibid., 87-92.

[34]Kenneth Scott Latourette, quoted in Donald A. McGavran, *The Bridges of God* (New York: Friendship Press, 1955), xiii.

his command. Thus, discovering the degree of growth or of decline, and stating such facts meaningfully, is understood to be an ongoing part of faithful ministry.

Being accountable. Closely related to responsible research is a fifth area of influence—that is, the need for accountability. McGavran felt that "a chief and irreplaceable purpose of mission is church growth."[35] For a church to grow, countable people must be added to its ranks. Since "God . . . is primarily concerned that men be saved, . . . His [church] must also be so concerned. Such mission in today's responsive world demands a theology of harvest."[36] According to McGavran, "Mere search is not what God wants. God wants His lost children found."[37] "When our Lord commands us to make disciples of the nations," McGavran wrote, "He surely does not consider the job success-fully concluded when one in 100 has yielded Him allegiance."[38] While the ultimate growth of the church belongs to God, McGavran contended that God does the work of church growth through his people. How can lost people hear without a preacher? God uses people as his agents to bring about the healthy growth of the church. Thus, as believers, we are accountable to do our best to assist in the growth of our churches and denominations.

Focusing on receptive people. A sixth way that McGavran's missiological insight continues to influence ministry today is by directing our focus to re-ceptive people. McGavran affirmed "the receptivity or responsiveness of indi-viduals waxes and wanes. No person is equally ready at all times to follow 'the Way.' . . . Peoples and societies also vary in responsiveness."[39] He suggested that the main indicator of receptivity was change. Change might come from people migration, national wars or a number of other disturbances. If careful obser-vation finds that people are becoming Christians and churches are being formed, then it is "reasonable to assume that other similar segments will prove receptive."[40] Today we continue to target receptive fields that are "white . . . unto harvest" (Jn 4:35 ASV). This does not mean we abandon resistant fields, but it does mean that we place a priority on winning the winnable.[41]

---

[35]McGavran, *Understanding Church Growth*, 32.
[36]Ibid., 34.
[37]Ibid., 40.
[38]Donald A. McGavran, *How Churches Grow* (London: World Dominion Press, 1959), 14.
[39]McGavran, *Understanding Church Growth*, 216.
[40]Ibid., 228.
[41]Ibid., 229-32.

Using correct methods. McGavran's emphasis on receptive peoples points us to a seventh area of continuing influence: methods. To be effective, McGavran counseled, "let churchmen adopt a pragmatic attitude toward methods."[42] This is not philosophical pragmatism—that is, the belief that something is only of value if it works. Rather, it is simply a reflection of McGavran's common-sense experience. Since God wants his lost children found and brought into local churches, and since he will hold us accountable for results, it is prudent to invest carefully in methodologies that produce the fruit of new disciples.

Targeting specific peoples. Perhaps McGavran's most popular insight is that Christianity travels best over the natural bridges of family, tribe and kinship. This was the main thesis of his first book, *The Bridges of God.* The old mission-station approach most often took new believers away from their natural contexts of family and community, an approach that resulted in limited growth. People movements, on the other hand, came about because new believers were left in their communities, where they could be bridges for others to travel across to meet Jesus. The principle of household evangelism was a crucial missiological insight for effective evangelism of specific groups of winnable people, and this approach is still the primary way people become believers in Christ. Thus, targeting the networks of family, friends and associates is another way McGavran's influence is seen today.

Multiplying churches. The heart of McGavran's missiology is not the growth of single churches but rather the extension of churches into every tribe, clan, caste, family or kinship group in the world. This means that church planting and multiplication constitute the very essence of McGavran's missiological agenda. Even today, the more church leaders research what leads to effective evangelism, the more they see church multiplication as the answer. McGavran advised,

> Perhaps the most immediately practical thing for the specialist is to devote regular time each week to church planting—proclamation and persuasion with the intent that unbelievers should accept Christ and be baptized and added to the Lord in new and old congregations.[43]

---

[42]McGavran, *How Churches Grow*, 90.
[43]McGavran, *Understanding Church Growth*, 61.

McGavran's words still ring true: "Today's supreme task is effective multiplication of churches in the receptive societies of earth."[44]

Making bold plans. Last, McGavran felt it was important to be intentional about growth rather than haphazard. His was a positive view of the future of the church. In his missiological view, the Holy Spirit is active in the world, causing peoples (plural) to become receptive to the gospel. It is our responsibility to do the necessary research to discover them, select the correct methods that will communicate effectively and go forward with much faith making bold plans to proclaim and persuade as many as possible to believe in Jesus Christ alone for salvation and become responsible members of his church. "Church growth seldom comes without bold plans for it."[45] Thus, taking the initiative to set goals and develop bold strategies to win people to Christ and plant new churches is seen in all aspects of church ministry today.

CONCLUSION

The impact of Donald A. McGavran's missiological insights is observable in all areas of missiological practice today. He was convinced that God desires his lost children to be found and enfolded into local churches, and that continues to be a central concern for all Christians in these early days of the twenty-first century. Along with McGavran, we must respond to God's call to "make disciples of all nations" (Mt 28:19). To that, many will say, "God willing." To which McGavran would no doubt respond, "God is willing. The question is, are we?"

---

[44]Ibid., 49.
[45]Ibid., 356.

2

Innovations in
Missiological Hermeneutics

Shawn B. Redford

INTRODUCTION

Mission practitioners and theorists alike have held a variety of opinions and attitudes toward the role of Scripture as it relates to mission. Some, after deciding what their mission action would be, would search the Scriptures to find prooftexts and random indications of a "Bible basis of mission." Others embraced their emerging understanding of the mission set forth in Scripture and shifted from understanding the Bible to be predominantly missionless to allowing the mission in Scripture to further direct the field practices of their day. A few not only understood the fervent missional resolve of Scripture as a whole but found in it needed correctives for the missionary community and the church. When Fuller Seminary's School of World Mission (SWM) hired Arthur Glasser, he was offered the unprecedented opportunity to create a movement within a school of mission in which the presence and corrective voice of the biblical theology of mission have been consistently experienced until the present day. This movement was founded through his teaching, was significantly advanced by Charles Van Engen and was spread by many of those they mentored. Glasser, Van Engen and others developed various hermeneutics that consistently emphasized the missional nature of Scripture: rereading the Bible with missiological eyes. These hermeneutics seek to read the biblical narrative through the lens of God's mission, providing new insight into the text itself while simultaneously reshaping missionary thought and action.

This chapter presents five hermeneutical paths while offering brief case studies illustrating how these hermeneutics transform the relation of Bible and mission for the future.

MISSIOLOGICAL HERMENEUTICS

Missiological hermeneutics has existed as a discipline that seeks to give adequate expression and attention to the mission activity and concepts found in Scripture. Quite often, this requires a mindset of mission coupled with mission experience that allows the interpreter to see how the missional dynamics within Scripture apply to a present-day context.[1] Arthur F. Glasser embodied this ability to perceive present-day mission fields reshaped through Scripture, largely because of his ability to perceive the mission of God in the Bible.

Glasser was famous for walking into a classroom and saying, "I just read this 500-page book on Scripture. It was interesting, but there was no mission!" Glasser, noting the severity of the problem, realized that too often the broader Christian community was writing extensively on the role, nature and purpose of Scripture, but discussion of God's mission was largely absent.[2] Glasser was convinced that the larger theological community too often ignored the mission activity in Scripture, so he dedicated his life to offering a genuine and holistic missional understanding of Scripture using missiological hermeneutics.

In many ways, concerned missiologists and like-minded theologians sensed that biblical interpretation ignored some underlying reality. This may have been the overreaching impact of modernity's fascination with science, or a failure within the larger body of Christ to engage in the mission of God. Scripture consistently conveys God's redemptive concern for humanity, but

---

[1]Those employing a missiological hermeneutic have often perceived mission to be taking place in Scripture where nonmissional interpreters have not seen the same. However, the missionally sensitive interpreter must also avoid any tendency to force on Scripture missionary activity that is not truly present.

[2]That is, unless we were to redefine mission in such broad terms that anything might be considered mission. Van Engen affirms, "With notable exceptions, [biblical scholars'] analysis of Scripture has seldom asked the missiological questions regarding God's intentions and purpose. On the other hand, the activist practitioners of mission have too readily superimposed their particular agendas on Scripture, or ignored the Bible altogether." Charles E. Van Engen, *Mission on the Way: Issues in Mission Theology* (Grand Rapids: Baker Books, 1996), 36.

theological training institutions were largely failing to depict the mission found in the Bible. Despite extensive biblical and theological training, students were too often given the impression that Scripture offered predominantly a message of indubitable transcultural theological truths while having little relevance for mission activity and direction for the present day.

Those who followed Glasser have further developed and taught missiological hermeneutics that address challenges that missionaries face in the field. Those at Fuller who continue to teach and develop some aspect of theology of mission are Charles Van Engen, Dean Gilliland, Robert Gallagher and Shawn Redford. In addition, Alan Tippett, Charles Kraft and Dan Shaw, all anthropologists, have added to this study from another discipline within missiology.

Like many missionaries, Glasser's theology of mission and underlying missiological hermeneutic were molded in the crucible of field service and refined by the continuing need for the world to know the fullness of Christ. Glasser wrote:

> [While serving] in China, I went through the communist revolution. . . . I remember the people being shot, people taken outside the city gates. . . . I was questioned [and] my wife [was] questioned in another room. . . . They were asking the same questions to see if our stories would jibe. This was in the second year after the revolution had taken place in China. . . . Outside there were about thirty guys [with] their arms strapped behind them, [tied to] big canoe paddles [with] Chinese characters written of a particular crime. They were taking guys out and shooting them![3]

The capacity for the Chinese churches to survive in the midst of the ruthless Communist persecution would define Glasser's calling in theology of mission.

> I saw churches just fold up in China, [including] China Inland Mission churches. [These were] good, warm, evangelical [churches], but they had never been taught such things as the kingdom of God. So, when I came here to Fuller, [the] first thing I tackled was this whole matter of the theology of the Christian mission—mission and kingdom.[4]

---

[3] Arthur F. Glasser, "Collection 421—Arthur F. Glasser. T8 Transcript," Billy Graham Center Archives, Wheaton College, accessed August 18, 2015, www2.wheaton.edu/bgc/archives/trans/421to8.htm.
[4] Ibid.

Reflecting on his research published in *Announcing the Kingdom*, Glasser claims,

> We are to be signs of God's tomorrow when the kingdom shall be fully dis-
> played in the world of today. Therefore, the concerns that are on God's heart
> for tomorrow—justice, righteousness, . . . care for the poor—those things
> should be our concern in the world of today. We are to be signs of God's
> tomorrow in the world of today, signs of the Kingdom. . . . The Scriptures
> show how this theme is unfolded.[5]

Glasser's contemporary mission thought dealt with key issues that were
deeply embedded in the Old Testament, such as the character required to
be a witness for the nations.

Case study: the in-breaking of the kingdom of God in Egypt. As one
example of Glasser's concern to empower the missional capacity of the
church, let us consider the in-breaking of the kingdom of God in Egypt at
the time of the exodus, since Glasser's modern-day fieldwork in China had
a number of similar missional dynamics. Glasser never openly mentioned
the failures of the Chinese church in his magnum opus, *Announcing the
Kingdom*. Yet, we hear echoes of his field experience in his writing.

"The church in every age," he affirmed, "must proclaim earnestly the existence of God, the Maker of all things visible and invisible. It must celebrate
his being and rejoice that he rules over all that he has made (Ps. 47–49). It
must confess with humility that nothing deserves to be."[6] The more difficult
field lessons are implied within his thoughts:

> God never ceased to remind Israel, and later the church, of the availability of
> his wisdom and power in his care for his people. Yet they would only know
> of his capacity to intervene powerfully on their behalf when they actively
> looked to him in faith. Unfortunately, both Israel and the church have proved
> to be wayward peoples.[7]

Glasser's ministry in the midst of the Communist revolution gave him
unique missiological lenses with which to interpret the Exodus account of
Egypt's attempt to claim superiority over God's missionary activity.

---

[5]Ibid.
[6]Arthur F. Glasser, *Announcing the Kingdom: The Story of God's Mission in the Bible* (Grand Rapids: Baker Academic, 2003), 32.
[7]Ibid., 34.

It is a fundamental human desire to "make a name" (Gen. 11:4). This tendency exists today in the nationalistic aspirations of peoples. How frequently we have seen nations give way to idolatrous exaltation of themselves and then become hostile toward other peoples. . . . The church that tolerates nationalist tendencies will be defective in its prophetic witness or at best will be paternalistically destructive in its missionary outreach.[8]

How could Israel as an enslaved nation on the brink of collapse break free from the evil yoke of Egypt, the superpower of the day?

> The Egyptians were cruel to the Israelites. . . . If Egypt could be utterly humiliated, its military power completely overwhelmed, and its gods totally discredited as unworthy of human worship, then all Egypt and all nations surrounding Egypt would know that the God of Abraham, Isaac, and Jacob was indeed the true God.[9]

God's purpose is explicitly declared in the book of Exodus, which repeatedly points out that the entire earth will "know that I am the LORD" (Ex 6:7; 7:5, 17; 8:10; 9:14-16; 10:2; 12:12; 14:4, 17-18).[10]

Exodus 9:14-16 in particular displays God's missionary resolve: "If you don't, I will send more plagues on you and your officials and your people. Then you will know that there is no one like me in all the earth. By now I could have lifted my hand and struck you and your people with a plague to wipe you off the face of the earth. But I have spared you for a purpose—to show you my power *and to spread* [סַפֵּר, *sappēr*] *my fame throughout the earth*" (NLT, italics mine). The Hebrew verb סַפֵּר (*sappēr*) meaning "to spread" is the piel verb form of סָפַר (*sāpar*) meaning "to count out, [or] count over again."[11] Prophetically, the nations retold the account of God's hand over Egypt, again and again! The impact of God's actions demonstrated the overwhelming power of God in comparison to Egypt. Furthermore, throughout the ages the nations remembered this single powerful event, properly recognizing that humanity's greatest political and military achievements were no match for God's power.

---

[8]Ibid., 53.

[9]Ibid., 76.

[10]Ibid., 75.

[11]Ludwig Koehler, Walter Baumgartner and Johann J. Stamm, *The Hebrew & Aramaic Lexicon of the Old Testament*, trans. and ed. under supervision of Mervyn E. J. Richardson, 4 vols. (Leiden: Brill, 1994–1999), s.v. "סָפַר."

As the nations recalled God's supremacy over Egypt to new generations in their midst, they indirectly developed their own missional hermeneutic, perceiving anew the limits of humanity and properly perceiving the astonishing authority and capacity of the God of Israel (Ex 18:1; Josh 2:10; 9:9; 1 Sam 6:6; Dan 9:15; Amos 9:7-9).[12] Glasser writes,

> The utter ruin of the Egyptians led the Hebrews to amazement and worship, more than to exultation over their fallen oppressors (Exod. 12:29; 14:26-31). Indeed, the Exodus was totally the action of God. Deliverance came because Yahweh fought for his people. Pharaoh, wind, and sea stood in the way. But all were overcome, not by human activity but by the power of God. There is no other explanation.[13]

Egypt and China were both overruled by God, but in very different ways. Egypt as a superpower could not overcome the physical capacity of God alone. China as a superpower could not overcome the power of the house-church movement in its midst.

Developing a missiological hermeneutic. In tracing the in-breaking of the kingdom of God within the Old Testament and specifically for Egypt, Glasser illustrates some key aspects of missiological hermeneutics. If theology is seeking to know the will and nature of God, then theology of mission is seeking to know the will and nature of the mission of God. Biblical theology of mission and its associated hermeneutics seek to interpret the mission activity found throughout Scripture in order to further question, shape, define, direct, guide and evaluate "our understanding of, and commitment to, our ongoing participation in God's mission."[14] Missiological hermeneutics is an essential skill in biblical theology of mission, founded on a mindset of perceiving the mission activity within a given text.

---

[12]"Note that the word 'earth' (*'ereṣ*) appears in three verses ([Ex] 9:14-16). In all three it surely means 'the earth,' that is, the planet, not merely 'the [local] land,' as it can also mean in many contexts. This passage is something of a *proto-evangelium*, a call to the whole world (even though it is addressed specifically to Pharaoh) to appreciate what the plagues ultimately showed, that there is one God in control of all things and that he alone can save. The world needs to recognize that 'there is no one like me in all the earth' (v. 14) and that the will of God is 'that my name might be proclaimed in all the earth' (v. 16)." Douglas K. Stuart, *Exodus*, New American Commentary 2 (Nashville: Broadman & Holman, 2006), 232.

[13]Glasser, *Announcing the Kingdom*, 77.

[14]Van Engen, *Mission on the Way*, 43.

Employing missiological hermeneutics means that missionaries and biblical interpreters seek to understand the wisdom and values of the biblical mission—analyzing the field situation, the cultural context, the challenges missionaries face, the broader barriers to mission, the bridges for mission, the level of allegiance to God's mission and the response of the nations with respect to the message they have heard. Missional interpreters are not prooftexting Scripture in order to create a biblical basis to justify blindly some currently existing mission practice. Instead, we ask what is happening in terms of God's mission and the missional dynamics of the passage. The vast majority of Scripture speaks to the mission of God, but quite often we need to retrain our minds and our perceptions in order to grasp the mission that has already been recorded throughout Scripture.

How do we go about perceiving and interpreting the mission within the passage? We must draw on our own field experience to consider the deeper implications of what might be happening in terms of mission. To engage in a missiological hermeneutic, we must ask, are there missional elements in the passage? If so, what are they? If not, are there barriers that have caused mission to suffer or be absent entirely? Do we see God's missional intentions embedded within the larger flow of the passage? What is the human response to God's missional intentions? Are the people of God interested in engaging in mission?

In most cases, there are missionary concepts, principles or strategies found within the passage. For example, do we see the development of the people of God or of the church as a missionary entity? If so, how is this taking shape? Is someone or something calling the people of God to engage in mission? Is there concern for the nations? Do the nations respond? Is the mission intentional? Is there a missional "crossing of barriers from Church to non-church," faith to non-faith?[15] Does the theology in the passage support or express a missional concern? Does the author express his or her theology of mission? If so, what missionary field situation or issue was this intended to address?

---

[15]Developed by Stephen Neill and Charles Van Engen, as cited in Charles E. Van Engen, *God's Missionary People: Rethinking the Purpose of the Local Church* (Grand Rapids: Baker, 1991), 28; see also Van Engen, *Mission on the Way*, 26.

Summarizing Glasser's efforts, Van Engen depicted the central driving convictions that shaped the discipline of missiological hermeneutics in his inaugural lecture at Fuller Seminary:

> Glasser's own personal pilgrimage made him deeply aware of the social and political implications of the Kingdom of God that challenges all governments, all forms of racism, all social structures that would seek to deify themselves. Missiology needs Biblical Theology of Mission to keep it from becoming mission studies, or a technical skills center, or a location for inter-faith dialogue, or a meeting place for global churchly conversation. Glasser says, "There is but one acid test that should be applied to all activities that claim to represent obedience in mission. Do they or do they not produce disciples of Jesus Christ?"[16] Here Glasser was echoing Donald McGavran's conviction on which McGavran founded Fuller's School of World Mission.[17]

THEMATIC HERMENEUTICS—THE TAPESTRY OF SCRIPTURE

What Glasser illustrated for mission and the kingdom, Van Engen developed as tools to further shape the role of missiological hermeneutics. Van Engen called on missionaries in training to utilize thematic hermeneutics in order to discover mission theology coursing through Scripture and then to apply the biblical understandings as a means of shaping, guiding and critiquing present-day mission practice.[18] Van Engen sought "an intimate interrelationship of text and new contexts through the vehicle of particular themes or motifs that bridge the text's initial context with today's contexts of mission."[19]

Van Engen likened thematic hermeneutics to a tapestry, as shown in figure 2.1. The vertical threads of the tapestry represent human cultural contexts of the Old and New Testaments. These cultural contexts vary

---

[16]Arthur F. Glasser, "What Is 'Mission' Today? Two Views," in *Mission Trends No. 1*, ed. Gerald H. Anderson and Thomas F. Stransky (Grand Rapids: Eerdmans, 1974), 8.

[17]Charles E. Van Engen, "The Gospel Story: Mission of, in and on the Way," installation address, Arthur F. Glasser Chair of Biblical Theology of Mission, Fuller Theological Seminary, Pasadena, CA, 1996, 3-4. A slightly revised version of this material is found in the front matter of Charles E. Van Engen, Nancy Thomas and Robert L. Gallagher, eds., *Footprints of God: A Narrative Theology of Mission* (Monrovia, CA: MARC, 1999), xxii-xxiii.

[18]It is possible for missiological and thematic hermeneutics to be addressed separately. However, Van Engen always tightly integrated thematic and missiological hermeneutics.

[19]Van Engen, *Mission on the Way*, 42.

greatly throughout Scripture, shaped by factors such as the larger political climate, the societies encountered, the cultural values, the deep-level worldview, the levels of missional intentionality and the missional risks taken by the people of God.

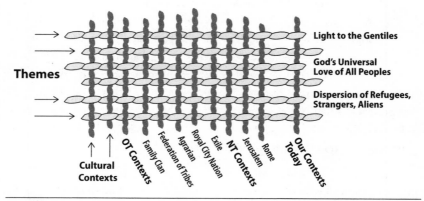

Figure 2.1. The Bible as a tapestry of missional themes in human cultural contexts

The horizontal threads of the tapestry represent missional discernment, concerns, values and actions that repeatedly surface in the cultural contexts of Scripture, giving rise to the development of a theme.

> Interwoven in a word-deed conjunction throughout these radically different contexts are clearly identifiable themes and motifs of God's self-definition of missional revelation throughout human history. To discover them, we must break down the biblical data to focus on specific themes and motifs that course their way through the tapestry of God's mission.[20]

This hermeneutic has challenged many to develop greater depth and understanding of their missiology as they perceive mission in the Scriptures. One of the more powerful benefits of thematic hermeneutics is the ease with which the method can be taught, allowing for a highly repeatable hermeneutic that has significant propagative capacity.[21] Another benefit is that this theme-based approach creates a significant barrier for prooftexting since the hermeneutic naturally avoids fragmenting Scripture. For interpreters to

---

[20]Ibid.

[21]Thematic hermeneutics is aided by concentrated study time, including seminary, but it does not require a seminary degree.

prooftext using a thematic hermeneutic, they would have to distort nearly every passage chosen and forgo the more obvious passages that would challenge their interpretation.

Case study: caring for orphans and widows. Let us consider a brief case study to see the development of thematic hermeneutics. A missionary once told me, "You won't find orphanages in Scripture!" After seeing a different and powerful system of care in Africa, where he had served for many years, this missionary was understandably troubled by the Western tendency to care for orphans almost solely in orphanages. He had often witnessed the African model of caring for orphans in socioculturally appropriate African family systems that were already in existence, cost effective and often the least traumatizing for the orphan. The practice in many African societies is for the orphan and widow to be absorbed into the extended family for ongoing care. In contrast, comparatively expensive Western orphanages provided some orphans good care while others did not due to budget and personnel limitations. Such orphanages also involved separation from the extended family.

Let us briefly employ thematic hermeneutics by tracing the theme of "caring for orphans and widows." The biblical accounts often link widows and orphans because of their common isolation and vulnerability, so adjusting the theme to include both groups will provide a more complete perspective. We will want to consider passages that directly address this topic, such as narratives, direct statements, biblical mission activity, family relationships and more. We can begin by developing an extensive list of passages related to this theme and then narrow those passages according to their relevance and relationship. The repetition of a given theme in the Bible is quite often an indication of the theme's importance to God and the sociocultural tendencies of the people of God. Some passages will naturally hold more weight, even though many passages may have some relevance to the theme. If the theme is too broad, then the larger theme will have significant subthemes that can be developed. In terms of thematic hermeneutics, the subthemes represent passages of greater cohesion. For this case study, a primary goal, which also narrows our theme, is to understand the means and the agents of mission since this is a chief concern for the missionary.

Figure 2.2 shows a number of passages related to caring for orphans and widows. There is not space here to offer a full missional analysis of each passage. Keep in mind, however, that the main concern is to illustrate a thematic hermeneutic so you may quite correctly think of passages with greater weight, relevance or missional dynamics. A strong missional interpreter would also quickly realize that there is much greater missional depth to be uncovered in each analysis.

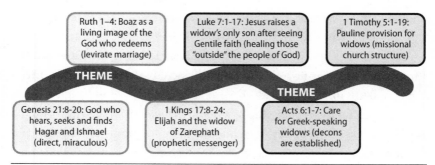

Figure 2.2. Thematic analysis of caring for widows and orphans

Briefly considering the Old Testament passages, in Genesis 21:8-20 Hagar is functionally widowed and Ishmael is soon to lose both his parents or die. God alone is the active agent of mission who hears Hagar's cries and seeks and finds these two. God's missional means is to miraculously save Hagar and Ishmael. By contrast, in the account of Ruth's story (Ruth 1–4), she arrives in Bethlehem as a Moabite widow from outside the people of God, seeking the mercy and kindness of any who will help. Boaz is the human agent of mission who redeems Ruth through the Old Testament custom of levirate marriage. In 1 Kings 17:8-24 the widow of Zarephath and her son are preparing for their last meal. Elijah is the agent of mission, speaking the word of God that literally brings life to the widow and her son through his prophetic message in their time of great despair.

Within the New Testament, Jesus often acts as the agent of mission, for instance, miraculously raising a widow's only son from the dead (Lk 7:1-17), demonstrating the validity of mission to the Gentiles against misconceptions such as avoiding the "unclean" (cf. Acts 10–11). Yet in Acts 6:1-7, the apostles establish deacons as the agents to care for the Greek-speaking widows who were being overlooked in the daily food distribution. The organizational means of incorporating deacons was specifically assigned to support and sustain the apostles' gifts and skills for God's mission (Acts 6:7). Finally, in 1 Timothy 5:1-19, Paul provides a specific set of issues for believers to consider before becoming involved in the care of widows.

A complete missional analysis would require much greater depth and development. However, if we were to devise from these passages a simple thesis, it would be that God has concern for widows and orphans and that God's mission includes a mandate that care be provided for widows and orphans. A deeper and more useful thesis is that throughout Scripture, care for widows and orphans is provided through various culturally acceptable systems without mandating one particular approach.

Developing a thematic hermeneutic. Looking back at our original hermeneutic, the missionary with experience in Africa was arguing from the silence of Scripture. A thematic hermeneutic, however, offers a number of benefits that would help the missionary avoid the same pitfalls as those who see orphanages as the only structure for mission. Foremost, the missionary can affirm that genuine care for widows and orphans through extended families in Africa is just as valid biblically as any other system, including orphanages. Scripture does not presuppose a single method over any other method, provided that care is actually taking place. This is true even of African family structures, which have their own limitations.[22]

Should disease, war or some other factor cause a breakdown of the family, orphans may not receive care even in the midst of long-standing African societal traditions. In Nairobi, there is an orphanage named Nyumbani (Swahili for "home sweet home") that cares for children with HIV/AIDS.[23] In most cases, these "orphans" are children whose parents are both alive and well, but they have been functionally orphaned because of their affliction—most often ostracized as lepers were in Jesus' day. The orphanage takes on the special task of applying for grants in order to provide the children with essential medication for HIV/AIDS. At the same time, the orphanage tries to restore family relationships. In many cases, this does not happen until the children are near adult age. The orphanage offers specialty skills and care

---

[22]This is also true for Boaz and Ruth's levirate marriage, a practice very foreign to Western customs today.

[23]Nyumbani, project of Children of God Relief Fund, website homepage, accessed October 3, 2015, www.nyumbani.org.

when the nuclear families have rejected their own children. The orphanage in this example exists because the African family structure has failed and an alternate structure is required. Consequently, it is equally important that our missionary avoid being overly dogmatic regarding African family structures.

Van Engen's addition of integrated missiological and thematic hermeneutics offered missionaries hermeneutical skills that benefited not only their mission activity but also the mission activity of the newly formed church, due to the inherent nature of this highly reproducible hermeneutic. Glasser and Van Engen were the essential missiologists when it came to developing the skills of missiological hermeneutics at Fuller Seminary. Dean Gilliland added another powerful voice, especially in Pauline theology of mission. Furthermore, other significant areas were developed related to the field of missiological hermeneutics. The most notable of these was ethnohermeneutics.

ETHNOHERMENEUTICS

Ethnohermeneutics is extremely helpful for at least three aspects of biblical interpretation: (1) in-depth understanding of sociocultural values, (2) recognition and appreciation of cultural systems and structures and (3) provision of a self-check to correct for ethnocentric tendencies within biblical interpretation. Charles H. Kraft's *Christianity in Culture* has been a profound work in the field of ethnohermeneutics. Kraft states that "there is a sense in which a new or deepened approach to hermeneutics is the major subject of [*Christianity in Culture*]."[24] Kraft appropriately claimed that the skills developed through the field of anthropology are essential in order "to understand what the authors of Scripture intended" and to discern interpretations that are "as close an approximation as possible to the perception of the original participants."[25] This may sound like an echo of historical-critical hermeneutics, but Kraft is pointing out that anthropologists develop strong skills in understanding society and culture. This missiological training is then solidified through field experience, often working in and communicating with other cultures. In the same way that a skilled poet may have greater appreciation

---

[24]Charles H. Kraft, *Christianity in Culture: A Study in Dynamic Biblical Theologizing in Cross Cultural Perspective*, rev. ed. (Maryknoll, NY: Orbis Books, 2005), 102.
[25]Ibid., 97, 102.

and recognition of the poetic genres of Scripture, missionaries trained and skilled in anthropology have greater capacity to recognize the cultural values found within biblical societies.

Anthropologist R. Daniel Shaw further contributed to this field through his text *Communicating God's Word in a Complex World*, coauthored with Van Engen.[26] Among other concepts, their work expanded on Anthony Thiselton's work, demonstrating that there were at least four cultural frameworks, or horizons, impacting the process of biblical interpretation.[27] These included the sociocultural values of the Old Testament writers, the New Testament writers, the modern-day communicator or missionary, and the audience or community receiving the message for today.[28] These concepts illustrated a further refinement and depth regarding the interplay of cultural anthropology and biblical interpretation. In addition, anthropologist Alan R. Tippett was posthumously published in the field of theology of mission.[29]

Missionaries trained in missiology and engaged in God's mission are quite often more equipped for biblical interpretation than they may first realize, due in part to their skills in the field of anthropology. Their training and experience have tremendous benefit for cross-cultural insights, which provide a deeper sensitivity and perception of biblical societies. Recognizing the cultural values and interpretations of another society reminds any interpreter that the interpreter's societal values are not the norm but simply constitute one of many cultural vantage points. Ethnohermeneutics further helps interpreters to appreciate portions or genres in Scripture that may not have been fully perceived without exposure to another cultural perspective.

Without the field of ethnohermeneutics, interpretations of Scripture are often unconsciously laden with assumptions based on the interpreter's deep-level worldview. Contemplating the product of ethnohermeneutics—that is, ethnotheologies—Kraft perceives Scripture as a set of case studies leading to specific ethnotheological understandings, each embedded in the

---

[26]R. Daniel Shaw and Charles E. Van Engen, *Communicating God's Word in a Complex World: God's Truth or Hocus Pocus?* (Lanham, MD: Rowman & Littlefield, 2003).

[27]Anthony C. Thiselton, *The Two Horizons: New Testament Hermeneutics and Philosophical Description with Special Reference to Heidegger, Bultmann, Gadamer, and Wittgenstein* (Grand Rapids: Eerdmans, 1980).

[28]Shaw and Van Engen, *Communicating God's Word*, 83-95.

[29]Alan R. Tippett and Shawn B. Redford, *The Jesus Documents* (Pasadena, CA: William Carey Library, 2012).

sociocultural contexts and issues of that time. Consequently, each case study helps the interpreter to develop a stronger ability to separate his or her own cultural values and assumptions from those of other cultures, including the cultural assumptions placed on Scripture. Furthermore, Kraft sees the process of developing theologies, or theologizing, as the deeper call of Scripture, which I will address further below.[30]

Various case studies. Some examples of ethnohermeneutics may help illustrate the contributions of this field. In 1 Samuel 4–6, the Philistine diviners are trying to return the ark of the covenant but also attempting to discern if their calamity has been caused by God or is an unfortunate act of nature. They stack the odds in the favor of nature by requiring "two cows that have calved and have never been yoked," placing the calves in a pen, and then having those same cows pull the cart carrying the ark (1 Sam 6:1-13 NIV). When I shared this passage with the Maasai people of East Africa, they had little difficulty correctly discerning the expected outcome of this passage because of their expertise in working with cattle. In contrast, I most often have to explain to Westerners the dynamics in the passage. The Maasai have helpful "interpretational reflexes" in this case because they automatically understand that the typical or natural actions of the cows would be to immediately return to their confined calves rather than pulling a cart in the opposite direction.[31]

Initial perceptions, however, cannot routinely be trusted in biblical interpretation. Because of our scientific worldview, Westerners often gravitate toward didactic commands. This is largely because interpreters tend to value the passages in Scripture that are most easily understood.[32] Thus, Westerners often interpret the father figure in the parable of the prodigal son (Lk 15:11-32) as God the Father because of a scientific tendency toward equivalences, demonstrating that interpretational reflexes can skew the process no matter what our cultural background. However, the use of indirect communication in the passage as a graceful means of admonishment suggests that Jesus is most likely referring to himself as the father figure (cf. Lk 15:1-3, 11).

---

[30]Kraft, *Christianity in Culture*, 239-44.
[31]Ibid., 102-3.
[32]Cf. ibid., 101.

Many cultures are more comfortable with indirect communication such as narratives, parables and allegory because indirect communication is common in these cultures. The Old Testament includes many accounts of communication and theology bound in the cultural values of the day. God's rebuke of David through the prophet Nathan is an excellent example of indirect and direct communication that has significant missional instruction for cultures unaccustomed to utilizing both forms of communication (2 Sam 12:1-13). The account is highly contextual, using terms that David could easily understand, but the story is an indirect form of communication, allowing David to judge the matter with greater objectivity. As David demands justice upon hearing Nathan's fictitious atrocity, the communication quickly changes to a direct admonishment, causing David to see that his actions have been sinful. Most importantly, these are God's words spoken through Nathan. God supplies indirect communication as a face-saving approach for addressing David and quite possibly as a means of protecting Nathan from harm following his delivery of such a difficult message.[33] An ethnohermeneutical grasp of this passage helps the interpreter to understand that theological context and communication can require far greater attention than theological content, which is comparatively straightforward in this instance.

Developing an ethnohermeneutic. Kraft challenges interpreters to consider the levels of cultural information embedded within the passage by contrasting the biblical commands to not steal and for women to wear head coverings.[34] Kraft's anthropological skills help us to see the subtleties in the text as he points out that the Hebraic concept of stealing would likely differ from modern-day definitions of stealing. "In that kind of strongly kinship-oriented [Hebrew] society, it is unlikely that it would be considered stealing if a person appropriated his brother's goods without asking. Nor is it likely that a starving person who 'helped himself' to someone else's food would be accused of stealing (see Matt. 12:10)."[35] This helps us to see that absolutely equivalent perceptions are extremely rare from one society to the next, even though there may be a strong level of overall commonality for a given transcultural concept.

---

[33] I am indebted to the teaching and field experience of J. Dudley Woodberry, and specifically his ability to perceive the missional roles of indirect and direct communication. These ideas were instrumental in developing biblical concepts for the 2001 teaching of Biblical Foundations of Mission.

[34] Kraft, *Christianity in Culture*, 107.

[35] Ibid., 108.

In the case of women wearing head coverings, Kraft's peak concern is the meaning of the practice and the calls for expression of that meaning via a culturally appropriate form in today's societies (1 Cor 11:10-12). The meaning of the passage has many anomalous challenges. If at that time a woman's failure to wear the head covering indicated that she was immoral or disrespectful, then Kraft calls for Christian women today to find parallel cultural forms that express a similar meaning. "The theological truth then—a truth just as relevant today as in the first century—is that Christian women should not behave in such a way that people judge them to be 'out of line' (whether morally or with respect to authority). . . . The same applies to men, of course, though not spoken of in these passages."[36]

Finally, Kraft calls on the field of hermeneutics to perceive the Bible as a developing set of case studies in which the questions and challenges of that day were answered through Scripture. The missional tendency of the Bible is to theologize anew in each context and time in order to offer meaningful ethnotheological understandings that are transformative for those seeking to know God. Kraft is cautious regarding the historical Western tendency to rigidify these experiences and questions, resulting in the same answers being presented out of their context and time frame. This is especially true for those who are attempting to ask a different set of questions while burdened with historical answers for issues that they do not face. Scripture consistently presents a deeper challenge to the West to move from static theology toward theologizing. In effect, Kraft sees a hermeneutical development throughout the time frames of Scripture in which theologizing is the norm, maximizing the relevance, interest and capacity of the Holy Spirit to speak into the sociocultural challenges that each new generation faces. "Theologizing is a dynamic, continuous process."[37]

SPIRITUAL HERMENEUTICS

A fourth area of mission-related hermeneutics developed at Fuller Seminary is spiritual hermeneutics. There is no doubt that any interpreter benefits from understanding a biblical passage within its proper missional, cultural, historical and linguistic contexts, among others. Yet, reading Scripture is

---

[36]Ibid.
[37]Ibid., 228.

not the same as reading any other book. Scripture is the revelation of God given for the purpose of redeeming humanity through Jesus Christ. Furthermore, we serve a living God, a risen Savior, who sees and hears the concerns of God's people. Should Christian missionaries today assume that hermeneutics is bound by the limitations of human reasoning, science, linguistics and a host of other useful disciplines? Not at all. "Hermeneutics is foremost a spiritual act."[38] This must be the affirmation of missionaries and missiologists alike. Like any other part of life, hermeneutics must be open to the in-breaking of the kingdom of God, to the Spirit of God, even to the point where we can affirm God's ability to aid us concretely in the interpretive process.

Spiritual hermeneutics is for the most part not taught at the seminary level. Yet, during the years in which Charles Van Engen and I cotaught biblical theology of mission, I developed this hermeneutic. Missionaries in training were often encouraged to pray and seek wisdom from God regarding their understandings of Scripture and especially regarding difficult or anomalous passages. Students were encouraged to footnote their answered prayers just as they would library resources. This resulted in the occasional footnote related to prayer in student papers. However, spiritual hermeneutics seemed to be difficult for Western interpreters. Did we shy away from this hermeneutic largely because of our Western scientific worldview? In 2010, I began teaching theology of mission in the African context at Nairobi Evangelical Graduate School of Theology (NEGST), now Africa International University. When teaching missional hermeneutics to predominantly African PhD students, one exercise incorporated spiritual hermeneutics, asking the students to join a group of people and pray together over a passage that was difficult or challenging. Even African students struggled with this hermeneutic, largely because of time pressures and the preexisting importation of Western scientific hermeneutics. Spiritual hermeneutics seems to require longer periods of time and contemplation. Yet, John J. Travis, for example, has reported successful implementation of spiritual hermeneutics in Indonesia.[39]

---

[38]Shawn B. Redford, *Missiological Hermeneutics: Biblical Interpretation for the Global Church*, American Society of Missiology Monograph Series 11 (Eugene, OR: Pickwick, 2012), 114.
[39]Discussion with John J. Travis in May 2009.

One common concern regarding spiritual hermeneutics is that this gives a careless interpreter free license to claim that any interpretation is spiritually discerned from God. Any time an interpreter approaches Scripture with a preexisting agenda, this is a problem no matter what hermeneutic is employed. That is, any hermeneutic can be distorted. However, when making use of prayer in spiritual hermeneutics, the interpreter is asked to pray with others as a group. In time, the members of the group can independently share their individual insights to determine if there is consistency and cohesion when seeking God's guidance regarding the interpretation of a given passage. A variety of spiritual disciplines may be employed.[40] These guidelines give shape to the process and offer the interpreter some direction during the interpretation of any hermeneutic.

Case study: spiritual hermeneutics for the Gentiles. In Acts 10, spiritual hermeneutics is implemented as the primary means to overcome a significant first-century missional barrier. The spiritual activities within the account are pervasive and include God-fearing Gentiles respected by the Jews (Acts 10:2, 22), angelic instructions (Acts 10:3, 22, 31-32), a messenger's prayer (Acts 10:9), the use of a trance (Acts 10:10), repetitive visions challenging barriers of the day (Acts 10:11-16), a spiritual "voice" (Acts 10:13-15), the Holy Spirit's guidance (Acts 10:19), the indwelling of the Holy Spirit on the Gentiles (Acts 10:44-45), speaking in tongues (Acts 10:46), praising God (Acts 10:46) and baptism (Acts 10:47-48). All these activities were utilized to help Peter properly interpret a major missional theme already found in the Old Testament—that the people of God were to be a light to the Gentiles.

The amount of spiritual activity in the Acts 10 account is a surprise, but the missional approach is also astonishing. We would normally expect the angel to begin by visiting Peter, who is the witness or missionary in this case. Yet the angelic vision, sent to God-fearing Cornelius, is one sign of the great transformation needed to overcome the deep-seated misconceptions of the time, including the theological concepts of clean and unclean (Acts 10:28-29). Cornelius and his family were seeking greater closeness and understanding of God. Yet they were likely chosen for this account because they so clearly countered the missional barriers that Peter held, bearing in mind that Cornelius

---

[40]Redford, *Missiological Hermeneutics.*

is a military commander of Roman soldiers. Long before meeting Peter, Cornelius and his family exhibit significant levels of spiritual vitality, including generosity to the poor, prayers to God (Acts 10:2), immediate devotion to God's requests (Acts 10:5-8) and respect for the Jews (Acts 10:22).

Acts 10 illustrates the role of spiritually developed understandings that directly challenge missional obstacles. Peter's openhearted attitude was also essential so that he would remain transformative throughout this account. Further in Acts 11, Peter and his fellow Jews realize that the Gentiles are free to accept the gift of salvation through Jesus, which was a significant breakthrough for New Testament missional understandings. These missional barriers seem to have been widely accepted within the first century, in part evidenced by the reactions of Peter's peers (Acts 11:2-3, 18) and the further accounts in Cyprus and Cyrene (Acts 11:20-21). However, it is unclear if they have understood the breadth of this transformation as the Gentiles become fellow workers or co-missionaries in their own right—evidenced by Cornelius's outreach to the poor (Acts 10:2-5).

Developing a spiritual hermeneutic. Peter and his fellow Jews struggled with misconceptions that were deeply embedded in the theological traditions of the day. The root issue was a failure in their theology of mission: the first-century messengers failed to recognize missional themes coursing through the Old Testament, such as being a light to the nations, which would have corrected the hyperextrapolations of clean and unclean, pure and impure. Peter and his peers arrived at a proper missiological understanding of God's concern for the salvation of the Gentiles by way of spiritual hermeneutics. The combination of spiritual forces coupled with mission experience mandated that these first-century missionaries reexamine the tradition they had accepted—one that directly countered the mission of God. The orchestrated spiritual awakening that Peter encountered involved hermeneutical guidance within real-life experience, which helped Peter move beyond the religiocultural misconceptions of his day. Those of us engaging in biblical interpretation today must examine the ways in which our beliefs may become barriers to mission. Realizing that biblical interpretation has never been solely a human effort will help us overcome those barriers. God is available to help the interpreter today, just as has been the case throughout human history.

SCIENTIFIC HERMENEUTICS

When most trained scholars think of hermeneutics, they commonly think of the historical-critical method. This hermeneutic is most often based on a combination of scientific, historical and linguistic research, among other science-based approaches. The historical-critical hermeneutic is the method most often taught in Western seminaries, and this approach has been taught in Fuller Seminary's School of Theology. So many resources are available regarding this method that it is not necessary for me to describe them in detail here.[41]

The method does have significant strengths when it is perceived as one hermeneutic among others. These strengths include depth of historical accuracy, significant original language insights and a strong assessment of the biblical genre. The methodology is well defined by numerous resources in the field. More recently, the method has examined the cultural perspectives of the interpreter, recognizing some subjectivity.

The scientific method also has some weaknesses. First, at times there has been a lack of recognition of the merits of other hermeneutics. Second, this hermeneutic has sometimes been perceived as superior to all others, in part due to a failure to acknowledge its Western bias, such as belief in the superiority of the hard sciences. Third, the scientific method was sometimes thought to be "objective," but it failed to appreciate the presence of subjectivity when interpreting Scripture from either a faith-filled or faith-less perspective. Fourth, this hermeneutic requires seminary-level training and is generally done individually. Finally, the assumption that Scripture is primarily theological in nature typically results in a weak understanding of mission, so most often the theology espoused is nonmissional.

Karl Barth offered the following correctives (paraphrased here) regarding the Western hermeneutic.

> Exegesis begins with the assumption that Scripture is an account of God's revelation, and that Scripture exists because of God's compassion, God's will to speak to us and even God's desire to deal with us. The biblical accounts

---

[41]Some helpful resources include: Thiselton, *Two Horizons*; and Grant R. Osborne, *The Hermeneutical Spiral: A Comprehensive Introduction to Biblical Interpretation* (Downers Grove, IL: InterVarsity Press, 1991). For a modern example-based approach, Dean B. Deppe, *All Roads Lead to the Text: Eight Methods of Inquiry into the Bible: A Template for Modern Exegesis with Exegetical Examples Employing Logos Bible Software* (Grand Rapids: Eerdmans, 2011).

should be understood as actual events based in history but also as events based on God's will and compassion. The historical and the supernatural aspects of Scripture should not be separated. Biblical exegesis is fundamentally an interpretation of God's Holy Scripture. Exegesis cannot try to second-guess whether Scripture is inspired by God. Exegesis explains the biblical witness and proclaims what prophets and apostles have claimed—that Scripture is filled with God's mighty acts.

The science of history has another way of looking at Scripture. It attempts to critically dissect the writer's "intent" and expose the "actual" account, which is then classified into the discrete and limited genres of history, myth, saga and legend. By its very nature, Scripture often does not conform to a strict understanding of "history" and is therefore classified by historians, in their limited understanding of truth, as a myth, saga or legend. The historians' categories have no space for the God who acts in history and who testifies about God's divine nature in history. In spite of the limitations of modern historical scientific method, this method can be helpful for understanding the Bible since the biblical contexts are written within human history.

However, we cannot validate this methodology alone as the only true exegetical method! It should not be seen as anything more than one method among many that can be applied to the Bible. The theologian must take on a different attitude toward the Bible than that of the historian. It is not a problem for theologians to view the Bible historically, but it is a problem if the theologian adopts a limited understanding of truth and forces the text into the historically limited genres of myth, saga or legend. The theologians of the nineteenth century succumbed to the historical way of thinking. They should have rejected this portion of the historical scientific method.[42]

CONCLUSION

Having introduced a handful of hermeneutics, I offer figure 2.3, which depicts the complementary and partially overlapping capacity of five hermeneutics that are helpful lenses in the interpretive process: missiological, thematic, ethnohermeneutical, spiritual and scientific. Each offers unique capabilities that can be utilized or shared with those

---

[42]Paraphrased from Karl Barth, *Credo* (New York: Scribner, 1962), 187-90. Cf. Lesslie Newbigin, *The Open Secret: An Introduction to the Theology of Mission*, rev. ed. (Grand Rapids: Eerdmans, 1995), 83-84.

learning to interpret Scripture. Each requires differing levels of training. Some benefit more from practice and oversight by capable interpreters. Some are better done in groups than individually. As interpreters become more familiar with the imple-

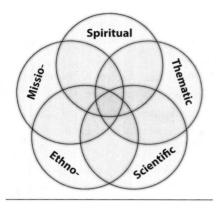

mentation of each, they expand their capacity to bring a wider array of tools to the task.

Within Scripture, we sometimes encounter people or nations trying to interpret earlier portions of Scripture (intertextual hermeneutics), or possibly acts of God. If we were to analyze those passages in terms of the hermeneutics pre-

Figure 2.3. Five hermeneutical lenses

sented here, we might find multiple hermeneutics at work. For example, when the Philistine diviners in 1 Samuel 6 attempt to return the ark of the covenant, they utilize scientific hermeneutics heavily, but they also utilize spiritual hermeneutics because they are open to knowing of God's activity in their midst. They further entertain missional and thematic hermeneutics in their understanding of God's power over Egypt (1 Sam 6:6). Finally, a strong missiological hermeneutic is found in God's concern to reveal God's presence to the Philistines and their diviners.

Often, an interpreter will use only a single hermeneutic. Sometimes, the interpreter will utilize more than one hermeneutic without realizing it. When dealing with difficult or anomalous texts, we are best served by applying multiple hermeneutics to the same passage to determine if each offers some consistent interpretation or outcome. In my own research, I have utilized multiple hermeneutical paths to help solve the anomaly of the leadership requirements presented in 1 Timothy 3:2, 12. I primarily used a combination of missiological and thematic hermeneutics while comparing that to scientific or historical-critical hermeneutics.[43] Utilizing multiple hermeneutics brought greater confidence to the final understanding.

---

[43]Redford, *Missiological Hermeneutics*, 175-85, 216-18.

Despite all these hermeneutics, there is one reality that cannot be escaped. The attitude of the interpreter is the overriding issue in interpreting Scripture. If the interpretation process begins with an agenda, nearly any hermeneutic will be bent toward the predisposed interest of the interpreter. This has been witnessed time and time again, especially when interpreters do not like some fairly obvious aspect of Scripture and they manage to convince themselves that Scripture supports the agenda that they have set out to prove. By contrast, when interpreters come to Scripture as learners with an openhearted attitude, trying to remain free from preexisting agendas, the interpreters have the greatest potential for understanding the genuine concerns of Scripture.

3

....

Seeing with Church-Growth Eyes

The Rise of Indigenous Church Movements
in Mission Praxis

Sarita D. Gallagher

INTRODUCTION

The Binandere evangelists stood with anticipation before the entire population of Kurereda village in Oro province, Papua New Guinea. Just a few months previously, Thomas and Grace Tamanabae prayed about their desire to share the gospel of Christ with their families in the Ioma district. In November 1976, the Binandere believers realized their dream and began their journey back to the urban center of Popondetta accompanied by a small ministry team from their home church of Bethel Center, located in the capital city of Port Moresby. After traveling for several days via dinghy and backcountry trails to the rural village, they arrived in Kurereda, where the tribal leaders invited Barry Silverback, the senior pastor of Bethel Center, to address the community. Peter Igarobae recalls that evening:

> That night Pastor Barry preached a very powerful sermon, and nobody responded because everybody was looking at the chief. So Pastor Barry decided to reach out and let the gift of the Holy Spirit operate, and he had a word of knowledge about [a] grade six young girl. The parents scolded her badly to the [point] that she was embarrassed to stay in the village. So, she packed all her things and hid them under the banana trees, and after the crusade she was [planning] to go on a canoe and paddle down [the river]. That word of knowledge came to Papa Barry. And he said, "If you are that young girl, God is interested in you and what you are doing. And, God wants to help you.

Would you come?" With tears in her eyes [the young girl] slowly walked up. . . . The chief who was sitting there began to think, if God can know what this little girl is doing, how much does God know about men? The same thought was going through all the [people] so when the chief raised his hand, everybody just . . . came, Mums and Dads and children, they all came.[1]

The spiritual revival that was instigated that night in Kurereda village soon extended beyond the Ioma district to the surrounding provinces until it eventually impacted the entire nation of Papua New Guinea. Upon converting to Christianity, the new Binandere believers immediately began preaching the gospel boldly to their neighbors and family members, and soon traveling evangelism teams formed and indigenous churches were planted. During the next twenty years from 1976 to 1987, the indigenous church that developed during this revival established over three hundred and fifty church plants; founded twenty-three Bible colleges in Papua New Guinea, the Solomon Islands, Indonesia, Vanuatu, Fiji and the Philippines; and commissioned and sent thirty-seven national missionaries to Australia, the Solomon Islands, New Zealand, the Cook Islands, Fiji, the Philippines, Vanuatu and Papua New Guinea.[2]

The mass expansion of Christianity that took place during the 1970s and 1980s in Papua New Guinea is not a unique occurrence in Christian history. Instead, it represents a global mission phenomenon that was first documented by the early apostles in the first century as they described the rapid church growth that swept through the Roman Empire from Jerusalem to Rome. While recurrent throughout church history, analysis of church growth and the establishment of indigenous churches only reached the forefront of missiological research in the twentieth century. Leading what later became known as the church-growth movement were missiologists Donald A. McGavran and Alan R. Tippett, who in response to the negative outcomes of colonial mission models sought to develop a new missiology for the postcolonial global Christian church. In the School of World Mission (SWM) at Fuller Theological Seminary, McGavran and Tippett developed their church-growth theory, and an increasingly non-Western orientation for missiology was born.

---

[1] Peter Igarobae, interview by author, Lae, Papua New Guinea, August 3, 2009.
[2] Sarita D. Gallagher, *Abrahamic Blessing: A Missiological Narrative of Revival in Papua New Guinea* (Eugene, OR: Pickwick, 2014), 248-51.

In this chapter, I focus on the innovations of McGavran and Tippett as they contribute to our understanding of missions to and from indigenous cultures. I relate this to my research into an indigenous church's missionary activities in Papua New Guinea. In addition, I suggest ways in which Mc-Gavran and Tippett's innovative scholarship continues to contribute to the global church. In the following sections, I explain McGavran and Tippett's influence on the church-growth movement and their contributions to indigenous mission theory.

THE DEVELOPMENT OF THE CHURCH-GROWTH MOVEMENT

The church-growth movement established by McGavran and Tippett marked a monumental paradigm shift in twentieth-century mission theory and praxis. In highlighting the biblical models of mission, the movement refocused the attention of the global church once again on the central task of evangelism and church planting. Additionally, McGavran and Tippett furthered the missiological understanding of the development of indigenous church communities through their research on people movements, the development of the indigenous church, power encounters and contextualized church planting. In order to understand the significance of the church-growth movement on indigenous mission theory, the genesis and historical development of the movement must be examined.

The church-growth movement in many ways represents the crest of a global wave that began with missiologists Henry Venn (1796–1873) and Rufus Anderson (1796–1880) in the mid-nineteenth century. Forerunners to the future church-growth movement, Venn and Anderson encouraged missionaries to establish native churches that were self-governing, self-supporting and self-extending. In a series of essays addressing the dangers of the missionary-station model and the need for the development of an indigenous church, Venn stressed the importance of training new converts as early as possible "upon a system of self-government, and of contributing to the support of their own native teachers."[3] Venn further asserted that the local church fund should be increasingly supported by native contributions to establish "an indigenous episcopate, independent of foreign aid or

---

[3] William Knight, with John Venn and Henry Venn, *Memoir of the Rev. H. Venn: The Missionary Secretariat of Henry Venn, B.D.* (London: Longmans, Green, 1880), 130.

superintendence."[4] In a letter from the Church of England Mission Committee to its missionaries on June 30, 1868, Venn highlighted the central objective of the mission organization: "As soon as converts can be gathered into a Christian congregation, let a native church be organized as a national institution; avail yourselves of national habits, of Christian headmen. . . . Train up the native church to self-dependence and to self-government from the very first stage of a Christian movement."[5]

Building on Venn and Anderson's scholarship, missiologists such as John L. Nevius (1829–1893), Roland Allen (1868–1947) and Melvin Hodges (1909–1986) also called for missionaries to return to the biblical models of mission and the primary task of making disciples of Christ and planting indigenous churches. The writings of these pioneer missiologists greatly influenced McGavran and Tippett's understanding of church growth, and many of their early missiological concepts were later adapted and expanded on by both scholars. Foundational theories that laid the groundwork for the missiologists' later work include Venn's "three-self" indigenous-church theory, Nevius's church-planting principles and Allen's biblical-mission methodology.[6]

Influenced on the one side by positive missiological voices, McGavran and Tippett's development of church-growth theory was also a response to the mission practices of the recent colonial period. McGavran explained his desire to create a new missiology for the postcolonial era:

> Christian missions in the lands of Asia and Africa are coming to the end of an era. The entire conduct of missions must be thoroughly re-examined. In the minds of too many politically dependent peoples, becoming Christian has been associated with denationalization and with a distasteful dependence upon the dominant whites. How peoples accept Christ in independent countries must be most carefully considered if churches and missions are to meet God's call to help build up these nations.[7]

---

[4]Ibid., 311.
[5]Ibid., 285.
[6]See John L. Nevius, *Planting and Development of Missionary Churches* (1886; repr., Hancock, NH: Monadnock Press, 2011); and Roland Allen, *Missionary Methods: St. Paul's or Ours?* (1912; repr., Grand Rapids: Eerdmans, 1962).
[7]Donald A. McGavran, *The Bridges of God: A Study in the Strategy of Missions* (London: World Dominion Press, 1955), 3-4.

McGavran specifically noted the negative effects of the popular colonial mission-station structure and called for a major transformation in the way that missionaries approached evangelism and church planting overseas.[8] Tippett agreed with this sentiment and, as an anthropologist, felt the need within his research to "work at understanding the cultural voids many colonial evangelists left."[9] Tippett highlighted the problematic philosophy of the previous mission structure:

> The old [colonial] approach to mission was based on a wrong assumption that change was a one-way process. The stronger controlled the weak, the superior the inferior, the adult the child—and likewise the "advanced" people supervised the "child" races. Colonialism was based on these fallacies, and colonial missions consciously or unconsciously went along with them. This was the root cause of our ingrained superiority and our paternalism.[10]

Both McGavran and Tippett endeavored to radically revise mission theory and praxis to reflect a collaborative, globally minded and culturally sensitive approach to evangelism and church planting evident within the initial expansion of the early church.

Instrumental in the development of church-growth theory was McGavran's own foreign mission experience. Having served as a missionary alongside his wife, Mary, with the United Christian Missionary Society in India from 1924 to 1954, McGavran was deeply affected by the lack of church growth throughout the district despite the presence of "eighty missionaries, five hospitals, many high and primary schools, evangelistic work, and a leprosy home."[11] While missionary colleagues concluded that India was resistant to the gospel, McGavran disagreed and dedicated himself to determining which theories of church growth led to the expansion of the church of Christ.[12] Inspired by the research of fellow missionary Bishop J. Waskom Pickett into the Indian "mass movements" to Christianity, McGavran was drawn to the research question, how do peoples become Christian? In the

---

[8]Ibid., 100-106.
[9]Charles H. Kraft, *SWM/SIS at Forty: A Participant/Observer's View of Our History* (Pasadena, CA: William Carey Library, 2005), 87.
[10]Alan R. Tippett, *Introduction to Missiology* (Pasadena, CA: William Carey Library, 1987), 87.
[11]C. Peter Wagner, "Preface to the Third (1990) Edition," in Donald A. McGavran, *Understanding Church Growth*, rev. and ed. C. Peter Wagner, 3rd ed. (Grand Rapids: Eerdmans, 1990), viii.
[12]Ibid., ix.

following decades, McGavran embarked on his own extensive study of conversion, which was later published as *The Bridges of God* (1955). The emphasis on the need for contextualized church planting became a central component to McGavran's and later Tippett's writing on church-growth theory.

After spending several years traveling throughout the United States promoting church-growth principles, McGavran founded the Institute of Church Growth at Northwest Christian College in Eugene, Oregon, in 1961 to support the now burgeoning church-growth movement.[13] Accepting McGavran's invitation to teach anthropology at the recently formed institute, Tippett joined the faculty as a research fellow in 1962. Having served alongside his wife, Edna, in the Fiji islands for twenty years as a missionary with the Australian Methodist church, Tippett shared McGavran's emphasis on the empowerment of the indigenous Christian church.[14] Tippett's experience in Melanesia also mirrored McGavran's people-movement theory and supported the belief that churches should be indigenous from the beginning rather than controlled by foreign mission agencies.

Invited by President David Allan Hubbard of Fuller Theological Seminary to serve as the first dean of the School of World Mission (SWM), McGavran moved the institute to Pasadena, California, in the spring of 1965.[15] Upon the establishment of Fuller's Institute of Church Growth (ICG), McGavran invited Tippett to join the faculty in the fall of 1965 to teach mission anthropology and oceanic studies.[16] In reflecting on this season, C. Peter Wagner, a fellow faculty member in the School of World Mission, notes: "Fuller Seminary . . . became the institutional center of the movement, with the missiological base being the School of World Mission and the application to American churches in the church growth major of the Fuller Doctor of Ministry program initiated . . . in 1975."[17] In addition to McGavran, Tippett and

---

[13]C. Peter Wagner, "Bridges of God," in Moreau, *Evangelical Dictionary of World Missions*, 199.

[14]Robert L. Gallagher, "Alan R. Tippett," in *Encyclopedia of Christianity in the United States*, ed. George Thomas Kurian and Mark A. Lamport, 5 vols. (Lanham, MD: Rowman & Littlefield, 2016).

[15]While at Fuller, Donald A. McGavran and Alan R. Tippett published several seminal texts expounding on church-growth theory, including McGavran's *Understanding Church Growth*, 1st ed. (Grand Rapids: Eerdmans, 1970) and Tippett's *Church Growth and the Word of God* (Grand Rapids: Eerdmans, 1970) and *Verdict Theology in Missionary Theory* (Lincoln, IL: Lincoln Christian College Press, 1969).

[16]Gallagher, "Alan R. Tippett."

[17]C. Peter Wagner, "Church Growth Movement," in Moreau, *Evangelical Dictionary of World Missions*, 199.

Wagner, a number of key scholars also contributed to the development of the church-growth movement during this period, including Arthur F. Glasser, Ralph D. Winter, Charles H. Kraft, Dean S. Gilliland, R. Daniel Shaw, Edmund (Eddie) Gibbs, Charles E. Van Engen and Wilbert R. Shenk.[18]

CONTRIBUTIONS TO INDIGENOUS-MISSION THEORY

While the church-growth movement focused primarily on "understand[ing], through biblical, sociological, historical, and behavioral study, why churches grow or decline,"[19] the movement added substantially to the advancement of indigenous-church theory. These contributions to indigenous-mission praxis and theory included McGavran's development of people-movement theory, the emphasis by both McGavran and Tippett on the biblical foundation of global mission, and Tippett's advancement toward a more nuanced understanding of the indigenous church. In the following sections, I will elaborate on each of these contributions to indigenous-mission theory and praxis.

Development of people-movement theory. Often identified as the birth of the church-growth movement, the publication of *The Bridges of God* by McGavran in 1955 instigated a movement toward a more culturally nuanced perspective of indigenous-church growth. Diverging from the mission-station methodology that drew converts individually to Christ via the "gathered colony approach," people-movement theory reflected the historical pattern of entire tribes, clans and castes accepting Christ collectively within their own cultural contexts. Central to McGavran's research was the concept of "people movements," which he described as a corporate decision for Christ in which "peoples became Christian as a wave of decision for Christ sweeps through the group mind, involving many individual decisions but being far

---

[18]Seminal texts by SWM faculty expounding on church-growth principles include Charles Kraft, *Christianity in Culture* (Maryknoll, NY: Orbis Books, 1979); C. Peter Wagner, *Your Church Can Grow: Seven Vital Signs of a Healthy Church*, rev. ed. (Ventura, CA: Regal Books, 1984); Wilbert R. Shenk, ed., *The Challenge of Church Growth: A Symposium* (Elkhart, IN: Institute of Mennonite Studies, 1973); Arthur F. Glasser and Donald A. McGavran, *Contemporary Theologies of Mission* (Grand Rapids: Baker Books, 1983); Eddie Gibbs, *I Believe in Church Growth* (Grand Rapids: Eerdmans, 1982); Charles Van Engen, *The Growth of the True Church: An Analysis of the Ecclesiology of Church Growth Theory* (Amsterdam: Rodopi, 1981); and R. Daniel Shaw and Charles Van Engen, *Communicating God's Word in a Complex World: God's Truth or Hocus Pocus?* (Lanham, MD: Rowman & Littlefield, 2003).

[19]Thom S. Rainer, *The Book of Church Growth: History, Theology, and Principles* (Nashville: Broadman & Holman, 1993), 21.

more than merely their sum. . . . Each decision sets off others and the sum total powerfully affects every individual."[20] This emphasis on multi-individual conversion contrasted the individualistic approach supported by many Western missionaries. While in the West "individuals [were] able to make decisions as individuals without severing social bonds," a people group preserved their social ties in their decision making.[21] McGavran emphasized the need for mission leaders to understand "the point of view of a people to whom individual action is treachery. Among those who think corporately only a rebel would strike out alone, without consultation and without companions."[22] He explained that within this group context "the individual does not think of himself as a self-sufficient unit, but as a part of the group."[23] Group decisions are not determined by one leader, nor are they "the sum of separate individual decisions"; instead, a people's decision reflects a shared conclusion often sounded out previously through informal conversations.[24]

Highlighting examples of people movements within the New Testament church, Christian history and contemporary culture, McGavran emphasized the continual presence of people movements converting to Christianity. As David J. Hesselgrave has explained,

> The history of the expansion of Christianity is replete with cases where numerous people sharing some common trait(s) have become Christians either simultaneously or within a short period of time. . . . From the time of Constantine through the Middle Ages, tribes and nations of southern, central, and then northern Europe were Christianized as missionaries preached the gospel message and sovereigns prescribed conversion to the Christian faith.[25]

McGavran noted that this pattern is still evident in collective societies around the world, including India, Indonesia, Burma, Formosa, Mexico and the islands of the Pacific. In a prophetic note, McGavran commented that the "list might be made much larger."[26] McGavran's observation was

---

[20]McGavran, *Bridges of God*, 12.

[21]Ibid., 8-9.

[22]Ibid., 11.

[23]Ibid.

[24]Ibid., 12.

[25]David J. Hesselgrave, "People Movements," in Moreau, *Evangelical Dictionary of World Missions*, 743.

[26]McGavran, *Bridges of God*, 76.

confirmed just decades later via the missiological research on global people movements and church growth conducted by scholars influenced by the church-growth movement.[27]

While the people-movement theory has since become accepted by missiologists and embraced as foundational mission theory, the initial reception was mixed. In addition to introducing and developing people-movement theory, McGavran also challenged the concept of evangelism. "He saw evangelism as more than just [the] procla[mation] of the gospel; he insisted that evangelization is incomplete until the person becomes a responsible disciple of Christ."[28] McGavran distinguished between "discipling" new believers and the process of Christians "perfecting" their faith. According to McGavran, the primary task of the church is that of discipling (Mt 28:19), which focuses on "bringing unbelievers to commitment to Christ and to fellowship in the church."[29]

The introduction of McGavran's people-movement theory instigated a dramatic paradigm shift within missiology toward an increasingly global understanding of church growth.[30] Incorporated within McGavran's theory was the recognition that the Western individualistic model of conversion and evangelism was simply one culture's response and approach to the biblical mandate of the Great Commission. In noting the repeated biblical, historical and contemporary pattern of entire peoples accepting Christianity as one unit, McGavran forced his mission contemporaries to rethink mission

---

[27]A significant number of research studies expounded on McGavran's theories of global people movements and church growth, including William R. Read, *New Patterns of Church Growth in Brazil* (Grand Rapids: Eerdmans, 1965); Gordon E. Robinson and John B. Grimley, *Church Growth in Central and Southern Nigeria* (Grand Rapids: Eerdmans, 1966); Roy E. Shearer, *Wildfire: Church Growth in Korea* (Grand Rapids: Eerdmans, 1966); James Canjanam Gamaliel, "The Church in Kerala: A People Movement Study" (master's thesis, School of World Mission and Institute of Church Growth, Fuller Theological Seminary, Pasadena, CA, 1967); Lloyd Emerson Kwast, *The Discipling of West Cameroon: A Study of Baptist Growth* (Grand Rapids: Eerdmans, 1971); Jim Montgomery, *Fire in the Philippines* (Carol Stream, IL: Creation House, 1971, 1975); Gallagher, *Abrahamic Blessing*.

[28]Rainer, *Book of Church Growth*, 17.

[29]Ibid.

[30]Instrumental in this shift was Ralph D. Winter's plenary address, "The Highest Priority: Cross-Cultural Evangelism," at the 1974 Congress of World Evangelization in Lausanne, Switzerland, which launched the church-growth movement internationally. See Winter, "The Highest Priority: Cross-Cultural Evangelization," in *Let the Earth Hear His Voice: International Congress on World Evangelization Lausanne, Switzerland* , ed. J. D. Douglas (Minneapolis: World Wide Publications, 1975), 213-25.

methods, structures and practices. Kenneth Scott Latourette affirms that "to
the thoughtful reader this book [*Bridges of God*] will come as a breath of
fresh air, stimulating him to challenge inherited programs and to venture
forth courageously on untried paths."[31] Indeed, McGavran's research on
people movements has since become foundational to mission theory and
practice and has instigated much additional scholarship.

Biblical foundation of global mission. A second contribution of both
McGavran's and Tippett's scholarship was their renewed emphasis on the
Bible as the foundation of and motivation for mission. In highlighting
the sovereignty of God's mission, the *missio Dei*, McGavran argued, "The
problems of mission should be viewed in the light of [God's] revealed
will. Being the kind of God he has shown himself to be in Christ, what
kind of mission does he desire?"[32] In addition to providing the impetus
and guidelines for mission praxis, Tippett identified the Bible as the
"frame of reference" for missiology. He explained:

> In missiology we find our frame of reference in the Bible. . . . It is a written
> record which preserves the words of our Lord, by which He commissioned
> His followers to mission, in the world and to the world. . . . It reveals the
> precise context of that commission. It records the basic information about the
> Person who is central in Christian mission, the nature of His own mission to
> mankind and the authority in which He commissioned His followers. It tells
> of the purpose and scope of the world mission. It is natural that we should go
> back to these things for testing the mission as we practice it ourselves.[33]

It was this concept of "testing the mission" according to biblical principles and
Christ's teaching that later proved imperative to the church-growth movement.

In reviewing the Hebrew Scriptures, two missional themes emerged for
the church-growth theologians: (1) the nations and (2) "the responsibility of
the people of God towards the nations."[34] In the New Testament, Scriptures
such as the Great Commission in Matthew 28:19 and Christ's commission
to Paul in Romans 16:25-26 emphasized Christ's imperative to "go . . . and
make disciples of all nations" (Mt 28:19). McGavran noted that the Greek

---

[31]Kenneth Scott Latourette, "Introduction," in McGavran, *Bridges of God*, xiv.
[32]Donald A. McGavran, *Understanding Church Growth*, 3rd ed. (Grand Rapids: Eerdmans, 1990), 20.
[33]Tippett, *Introduction to Missiology*, 14.
[34]Ibid.

phrase "*panta ta ethnē*, 'all nations,' should read 'all peoples.' [As] the apostle did not have in mind modern nation-states . . . [but] cultural groupings—tongues, tribes, castes, and lineages."[35] He continued that "the biblical mandate to bring the *ethnē* to faith and obedience falls on [the church] with particular force" as in this age "not only is there the command, but God has provided the opportunity."[36] Church growth, McGavran argued, was directly connected to the church's obedience to Christ's call to the nations. He noted, "Only where Christians constrained by love obediently press on, telling others the good news of the Savior, does the church spread and increase. Where there is no faithfulness in proclaiming Christ, there is no growth."[37] Additionally, "There must also be obedience in hearing. Churches do not multiply and spread across a land or through a city unless among the multitudes who hear there are many who obey and—loving Christ more than father or mother—deny themselves, take up their crosses daily, and follow him."[38] For both McGavran and Tippett, the making of disciples was the foremost task of all missionary endeavors.

While humanitarian aid and educational advances are valuable, both scholars emphasized that the church's primary task was evangelism. Wagner explained that during a "time when liberal Christianity was in its heyday . . . [and] advocating conversion to Christianity was widely frowned upon as being manipulative proselytism . . . McGavran countered this by advocating that the central purpose of missions was to be seen as God's will that lost men and women be found."[39] Tippett agreed with this focus on evangelism and warned against the watering down of the mission of Christ:

> Of course, there could still be many Christian projects serving those in need, training the undertrained, fighting for social justice and so on. This is all part of the Christian duty, but it is an accompaniment of mission and not a substitute for it. They are scripturally conceptualized as two different ministries of the one Church. The ministry of the Church in the world is thereby a partial thing and this idea clashes with the Scripture presentation of the Church. We could indeed perform this half-service and be Universalist or even Hindu.

---

[35]McGavran, *Understanding Church Growth*, 40.
[36]Ibid.
[37]Ibid., 6.
[38]Ibid.
[39]Wagner, "Church Growth Movement," 200.

What we would have is a humanitarian ministry . . . but there would be nothing distinctively Christian at all—and certainly no mission.[40]

McGavran argued that the "primary goal of missions is discipling (winning people to Christ)" while "'perfecting,' or assisting those already saved with schools, hospitals etc. is not the foremost goal."[41] He emphasized that "evangelism . . . [was] not just . . . proclaiming the gospel whether or not something happened"; instead, it involved actively "making disciples for the Master."[42]

While emphasizing the biblical mandate of making disciples, McGavran and Tippett also embraced the integrative nature of missiology. Darrell L. Whiteman explained:

> Tippett saw missiology as an interdisciplinary field of study and brought to that field competencies in anthropology, history, and theology. He was driven by the conviction that missiology must be holistic and interdisciplinary, always striving for synthesis out of analysis and that one area of its development must not occur at the expense of another's neglect.[43]

In their missiological research, both scholars emphasized "the importance of employing the social and behavioral sciences as missiological instruments."[44] As an anthropologist, Tippett saw his academic discipline as "providing the tools and resources by which the missionary can direct change without ignoring the human context," which in turn "helps to show us how we can better perform our role in a responsible manner." He explained that "anthropology does not bring individuals to Christ, but it shows missionaries how they may be more effective and less of a hindrance in doing so."[45] In "the conscious application of cultural anthropology to evangelistic strategy," both McGavran and Tippett sought to share the good news of Christ effectively via culturally appropriate methods.[46]

---

[40]Tippett, *Introduction to Missiology*, 16.

[41]Kraft, *SWM/SIS at Forty*, 79.

[42]Wagner, "Church Growth Movement," 200.

[43]Darrell L. Whiteman, "The Legacy of Alan R. Tippett," *International Bulletin of Missionary Research* 16, no. 4 (1992): 165.

[44]Ken Mulholland, "Donald A. McGavran," in Moreau, *Evangelical Dictionary of World Missions*, 607.

[45]Tippett, *Introduction to Missiology*, 28.

[46]Wagner, "Preface to the Third (1990) edition," x.

Toward an understanding of the indigenous church. Another significant contribution to missiology was Tippett's research on the nature of the indigenous church. Building on Venn and Anderson's definition of indigenous churches as self-supporting, self-governing and self-propagating, Tippett extended this limited framework to include a more holistic ecclesiological understanding. Whether founded by national or foreign missionaries, Tippett defined the indigenous church as an empowered and fully functioning member of the body of Christ:

> A church is indigenous: when it is culturally a part of its own world; when its witness is relevant in meeting the needs of its congregation and the world about it; when its message is meaningful in the context where it belongs; when its physical form and operating structures are suitable for the culture; when it acts on its own initiative in the service ministries arising from local needs and crises and in missionary outreach; and above all, when it is aware of its own theological identity—in other words, it sees itself as the Body of Christ ministering the love of Christ, the mind of Christ, the Word of Christ, and His ministry of reconciliation and comfort in the location where it is set in the world.[47]

While noted for his compartmentalized analysis of indigenous-church characteristics, Tippett emphasized that each category should be understood as organically interrelated within the "total entity" of a church community. In proposing a more intricate understanding of the indigenous church, Tippett endeavored to move beyond the limited emphasis on "self-support," which he noticed was often overemphasized by mission leaders and in turn "sometimes led to tragic mistakes in policy."[48]

Tippett highlighted six central characteristics or "marks" of an indigenous church: self-image, self-function, self-determination, self-support, self-propagation and self-giving.[49] The first mark, self-image, refers to whether a Christian community sees "itself as *the* Church of Jesus Christ in its own local situation, mediating the work, the mind, the word, and the ministry of Christ in its own environment."[50] The second characteristic, self-functioning,

---

[47]Tippett, *Introduction to Missiology*, 86.
[48]Ibid., 378.
[49]Ibid., 378-81.
[50]Ibid., 378; emphasis original.

characterizes a church that operates with its members serving in different roles and performing a variety of tasks but functioning together as the body of Christ. Self-determination refers to the indigenous church's freedom to make and enforce decisions apart from outside influences. Self-support indicates that "the Church carr[ies] its own financial burdens" and "adequately finance[s] its own service projects."[51] Tippett's fifth characteristic is self-propagation, which develops as a "Church see[s] itself as being directly addressed by the words of the Great Commission." The final mark, self-giving, emanates from a church that "fac[es] and allevi[ates] the social needs and problems of the local world in which it lives."[52]

In identifying the marks of an indigenous church, Tippett acknowledged that church communities face challenges as they move toward indigeneity. He claimed that due to "the imbalance of much mission policy over the years, many emerging Churches will reflect the consequences of that balance." Existing external financial support structures, Western theological frameworks and foreign denominational governance structures are just some of the potential challenges facing indigenous churches. Despite these challenges, Tippett emphasized that "the truly indigenous Church is an ideal for which we strive—something truly a Church and truly indigenous."[53]

In the years following the first publication of Tippett's "six marks" definition,[54] research on the indigenous church continued to advance.[55] A further mark, self-theologizing, was later accepted as an additional characteristic of the indigenous church.[56] David J. Bosch, noting this adoption, remarked: "It was finally recognized that a plurality of cultures presupposes a plurality of theologies and therefore, for Third-World churches, a farewell

---

51 Ibid., 379.

52 Ibid., 381.

53 Ibid.

54 See Tippett, *Verdict Theology in Missionary Theory*.

55 Additional research has significantly expanded on the concept of indigenization, including the following seminal texts and articles: Kraft, *Christianity in Culture*; Paul G. Hiebert, *Anthropological Insights for Missionaries* (Grand Rapids: Baker Academic, 1985); Andrew F. Walls, "The Gospel as the Prisoner and Liberator of Culture," in *Landmark Essays in Mission and World Christianity*, ed. Robert L. Gallagher and Paul Hertig (Maryknoll, NY: Orbis Books, 2009), 133-45; Wilbert R. Shenk, "Recasting Theology of Mission: Impulses from the Non-Western World," in Gallagher and Hertig, *Landmark Essays*, 116-32; and Simon S.W. Kwan, "From Indigenization to Contextualization: A Change in Discursive Practice Rather than a Shift in Paradigm," *Studies in World Christianity* 11, no. 2 (2005): 236-50.

56 See Hiebert, *Anthropological Insights for Missionaries*, 195-96, 215-19.

to a Eurocentric approach."[57] Paul G. Hiebert explained the process and importance of self-theologizing:

> Theologizing must be led by the Holy Spirit, who instructs us in the truth. We need also to recognize that the same Holy Spirit at work in us is also at work in the lives of believers in other contexts. Theologizing must also affirm the priesthood of all believers and recognizes that they must and will take the universal message of the Bible and apply it to their own lives and settings.[58]

The topic of indigenization continues to be a relevant issue within missiological research and conversation. As A. Scott Moreau remarked: "The fact that evangelical missiologists continue to generate proposals framed by indigenous principles . . . demonstrates the continuing vitality of indigeneity as a guiding concept for evangelicals in contextualization."[59]

THE INDIGENOUS CHRISTIAN REVIVAL CRUSADE (CRC) CHURCH MOVEMENT IN PAPUA NEW GUINEA (PNG)

In the following sections, I explore the development of the PNG CRC church movement of the 1970s and 1980s as it relates to the missiological research of McGavran and Tippett during the same period.[60] While separated geographically, the missiological theories of McGavran and Tippett were exemplified on multiple levels within the PNG CRC revival narratives. In this section, I focus on three such missiological parallels: (1) the PNG CRC revival as a people movement, (2) the biblical foundation of the PNG CRC missionary endeavors and (3) the emergence of the PNG CRC church as an indigenous-church movement.

Development of a PNG people movement. Upon joining the Bethel Tabernacle CRC church in Port Moresby in 1976, Thomas and Grace Tamanabae prayed for the salvation of their family members, both in the surrounding

---

[57]David J. Bosch, *Transforming Mission: Paradigm Shifts in Theology of Mission* (Maryknoll, NY: Orbis Books, 1991), 452.

[58]Paul G. Hiebert, *Missiological Implications of Epistemological Shifts: Affirming Truth in a Modern/ Postmodern World* (Harrisburg, PA: Trinity Press International, 1999), 101.

[59]A. Scott Moreau, *Contextualization in World Missions: Mapping and Assessing Evangelical Models* (Grand Rapids: Kregel, 2012), 126.

[60]This research is based on ethnographic interviews conducted by the author from May to August 2009 in Papua New Guinea and Australia. During this field research, the author conducted thirty-four interviews with PNG pastors, national leaders and Australian missionaries involved in the 1970s–1980s Papua New Guinea CRC revival movement.

city and in Oro province. Along with Marilyn Teague, an Australian missionary, the Tamanabaes "often called their [relatives'] names to the Lord in
prayer, interceding for their salvation and deliverance."[61] The faithful group's
prayers were answered as one by one each member of their family living in
the city converted to Christianity.[62] Inspired by their answered prayers, Tamanabae and several of his newly converted family members returned to Oro
province later that same year to share the Christian message with their relatives. It was during this initial evangelism trip to Kurereda village in the Ioma
district of Oro province that the Binandere-speaking community experienced an outpouring of the Holy Spirit. "Immediately, God began working
in the village as people started turning to Christ, finding supernatural healing
and delivery from demonic oppression."[63] As the Binandere evangelists
preached the gospel, a people movement as described by McGavran began.

Led by the clan's chiefs and elders, each community upon hearing the
gospel message and witnessing the signs and wonders of God rejected their
dependence on traditional sorcery and turned collectively to worship and
follow Christ. In Kurereda village, for example, the two chiefs of the Tamanabae clan, Daniel Tamanabae and Graceford, publicly terminated the
community's dependence on traditional witchcraft and sorcery and declared "that Jesus Christ would be the Lord of the clan."[64] The chiefs replaced
the villages' three sources of spiritual power with the Father, Son and Holy
Spirit and professed the three persons of the Trinity as the clan's God and
that of their children and children's children. Remembering this momentous
occasion, Peter Igarobae, a member of the Binandere tribe and university
student at the time, recalls the chief's declaration that "serving the Lord will
be family, clan business." The community responded in unison by burning
all the artifacts of witchcraft and sorcery present in the village.[65]

Although there was no official strategic ministry plan, Christianity spread
organically through kinship groups in Oro province and later throughout
the nation of Papua New Guinea. After the Binandere evangelists preached

---

[61]Marilyn Teague, "The Outpouring of the Holy Spirit in Papua New Guinea (1965–1978)" (pho-
tocopy of unpublished report, Adelaide, Australia, May 2005).
[62]Thomas Tamanabae, interview by author, Popondetta, Papua New Guinea, July 23, 2009.
[63]Gallagher, *Abrahamic Blessing*, 141.
[64]Igarobae, interview by author, August 3, 2009.
[65]Ibid.

in the Ioma district, they traveled into the Kokoda, Afore, Oro Bay, Higaturu, Tufi and Popondetta districts of Oro province, and entire families and clans came to Christ just as they had done among the Binandere tribe.[66] As the Binandere evangelists traveled throughout the region, family after family, clan after clan and village after village converted to Christianity. As the Christian revival expanded, it soon shifted from a clan movement to a tribal movement and then to a national movement.[67] John Togawata explains this communal model of church growth:

> If you receive the Holy Spirit, you go to . . . your village [and] you start [a] fellowship with your family. Your family accepts the Lord Jesus and they receive the Holy baptism. They build the . . . fellowship, then the others join you [and] they all join. Then the village now has a church. But then other people want [a church] in the next village. So they go . . . into the next village and when they start their fellowship they don't want to come here to us. It's too long for them to walk here or they have to drive so they said no we'll start ours here. You guys come and sing to us and visit us. This is the way it happened in the Book of Acts.[68]

This collective model of evangelism "enabled the good news to travel rapidly throughout kinship systems, spreading the gospel to wider and wider social circles."[69] In reflecting on this missional expansion, Igarobae notes: "Looking back the Holy Spirit used that pattern" of talking first "to chiefs or landowners who have some sort of influence over the villages. And village after village was coming to the Lord. . . . I believe that [the] Lord used the family, clans, and tribes to break through in the urban areas."[70] Togawata also acknowledges God's role in the collective expansion of Christianity during the PNG CRC revival. In summarizing the revival period, he explains: "The Pentecostal Movement . . . was just like a fire. It would burn one corner of society. It goes to the next village and then if they stop[ped] there it would come out to another village somewhere else. And it would stop there. And then it start[ed] somewhere else. It happened that way."[71]

---

[66]Numba Puri, interview by author, Lae, Papua New Guinea, August 2, 2009.

[67]Richmond Tamanabae, interview by author, Port Moresby, Papua New Guinea, July 13, 2009.

[68]John Togawata, interview by author, Port Moresby, Papua New Guinea, July 13, 2009.

[69]Gallagher, *Abrahamic Blessing*, 181.

[70]Igarobae, interview.

[71]Togawata, interview.

Biblical foundation of the PNG CRC mission. In addition to exemplifying McGavran's people-movement theory, the PNG CRC revival embodied McGavran and Tippett's emphasis on the importance of preserving a biblical foundation of mission. This emphasis was expressed through several means during the Melanesian revival, including the evangelists' motivation for mission, the message shared and the manifestation of the Holy Spirit experienced during the revival. First, "although there were many motivations that led the PNG Christians into ministry, the principal motivator during the revival period was God. Whether it was God . . . leading his mission through visions or dreams, or directly orchestrating the events through the Holy Spirit, it was evident that [the] respondents gave God the credit for establishing the revival."[72] Margaret Sete explains the power of God's call on her life, which in turn led her to full-time ministry:

> During one of the Easter conferences up at Ukarumpa, YWAM's [Youth with a Mission's] team was speaking on world missions. They were speaking from Genesis 12:1-3 . . . [and] I felt God calling me. . . . When [Kalafi from Tonga, a YWAM leader] was speaking about brown-skin missionaries going out and *Deep Sea Canoe* missionaries who came in our shores, I felt compelled. I felt challenged to go. . . . I felt like the Lord just swept down the aisle and stopped where I was and said, "Yes, Margaret, I know what you're thinking. What if I asked would you go for me?" And [with] that kind of question, you can't pass the buck. You have to answer that yourself.[73]

In addition to calling the revivalists into ministry, God's hand was clearly evident throughout the "growth and establishment of [the] CRC in PNG."[74] Togawata explains: "Our lives [and] our movement w[ere] all directed by God. We never really saw it then, but boy it was so clear to us. Looking back now . . . we now recognize so clearly [that] God was in every turn. He commanded and he directed everything."[75]

The revivalists were also motivated by a sincere concern for the salvation of their families, villages, provinces and nation. Sete describes her own

---

[72]Gallagher, *Abrahamic Blessing*, 164.
[73]Margaret Sete, interview by author, Port Moresby, Papua New Guinea, August 8, 2009.
[74]Richmond Tamanabae, interview.
[75]Togawata, interview.

motivation for mission: "Like the Bible says about finding a pearl, I couldn't keep this to myself. I had to tell it; to share it with others."[76] Barnabas Tabara similarly states:

> Between 1980 and 1983 I must have read the whole Bible from Genesis to Revelation a dozen times. . . . So that deep hunger for the Word of God [developed]. Man, I had never seen that before. Straight after my water baptism I had that hunger. That was one of my personal experiences in the Word. . . . We knew there were changes, but we were not preaching for that purpose, we were just preaching for souls. That's all. All we were interested in was just [the] salvation of souls. Witness and bring them in.[77]

Tamanabae also experienced this strong desire to share the gospel of Christ. He explains:

> As far as motivation is concerned, in those days it seemed like everything in the world meant nothing to you . . . and [you] didn't really care what was happening around. Money, those things meant nothing. And what I would say is that I really fell in love with the transformation that I saw in the lives of the people. If anything that was the thing; I did it out of love. To see the transformation of the people.[78]

Just as in the first-century Christian church, miraculous signs and wonders accompanied the preaching of the gospel in Papua New Guinea. From the impetus of the revival in Kurereda village, the evangelists healed the sick, cast out demons and prophesied through the power of the Holy Spirit, witnessing the signs and wonders of God. In Kurereda village, for example, the entire community received the baptism of the Holy Spirit during the first evangelistic outreach in 1976. Igarobae, who was in attendance that evening, recounts the narrative:

> Pastor Barry led them in [the] sinners' prayer and then he turned around to me and said, "What's next?" And I said, "Let's get them filled with the Holy Spirit." . . . So we took them out on the oval and I shared on . . . the baptism of the Holy Spirit. And I said, "Who wants to receive this Holy Spirit?" Then the whole village put their hands up and Pastor Barry came up and said, "You

---

[76]Sete, interview.
[77]Barnabas Tabara, interview by author, Mount Hagen, Papua New Guinea, June 30, 2009.
[78]Richmond Tamanabae, interview.

have to ask them again. I don't think they really . . . understand." So, this time Richmond [Tamanabae] explained everything and said "Okay, who wants to be filled with the Holy Spirit?" The whole village went down to the oval. We asked them to all raise their hands and Pastor Barry prayed. As he was praying, it was like a cool breeze from the mountains came, but the mountains are far away. Every one of us felt this cool breeze going through. . . . When we opened our eyes nobody was standing, they were all on the grass speaking in tongues.[79]

As the CRC revival unfolded, the parallel with the book of Acts became increasingly evident. In reflecting on the revival during the interviews, the PNG missionaries often highlighted the parallel, remarking as Togawata did: "People got healed. People [were] filled with the Holy Spirit. Miracles [like] what was written in the Book of Acts [took place]. Signs and wonders follow[ed] the proclamation of the gospel. [It] literally happened the way . . . it [did] in the Bible."[80]

Toward an understanding of the PNG indigenous church. From the impetus of the CRC revival, the church movement was uniquely Papua New Guinean. Due to the geographical distance between Bethel Center in Port Moresby and the new church plants in Oro province, the Binandere churches relied primarily on local Christian leadership, ingenuity and missional vision. Consequently, the national churches embodied Tippett's defining characteristics of ecclesiastic indigeneity: self-image, self-function, self-determination, self-support, self-propagation and self-giving. As the PNG CRC church grew, the indigenous churches felt ownership of the revival movement and local evangelism:

> Young and old, urban dwellers and villagers alike felt personal responsibility to share the good news that they had received. Although God did raise key families and leaders up in the revival areas, there was an overwhelming sense that each individual had the power to change the fate of their family and friends by sharing with them the blessing of God.[81]

A major turning point in the development of the PNG CRC church movement was the corporate call heard by the Papua New Guinean church to global mission. As recipients of missionary advances for decades, the

---

[79]Ibid.
[80]Igarobae, interview.
[81]Gallagher, *Abrahamic Blessing*, 217.

Melanesian leaders initially regarded the PNG church as the mission field, not as a missionary-sending community.[82] However, during the decade following the revival, the PNG CRC church increasingly found its identity and purpose in the missionary call of Christ to the nations (Acts 1:8). Explaining this shift, Tamanabae emphasizes:

> Up until [the 1980s], the world regarded PNG as a mission field. So, our mission effort was only confined to PNG. But, there was a shift in that; that we should now start sending missionaries, because the Bible says we should be witnesses in Jerusalem, Judea, and Samaria, and to the uttermost [regions of the world]. . . . We should not see ourselves as [a] mission field and remain in PNG . . . but we should begin now to see ourselves as missionaries.[83]

In speaking of her own paradigm shift toward global mission, Sete realized that "wok mission i no long waitman tasol" (mission work is not the task of white people alone). Sete expounds:

> As a mature church we have a responsibility. *Mipela no olsem ol pikinini* [we are not like children]. We are not babes. We are not *sucking su su olgeta taim* [nursing infants]. As a mature church we also have an obligation. We also have to be responsible to the call of God to go out there to evangelize the world. . . . We were just getting fat. Fed over and over. And what right did we have to hear the name of Jesus more than one hundred times when somebody else didn't hear it once. So, those were the challenges that came to me. And one of the things that I used to struggle with was if I went who would support me. But the message that came across on the call of Abraham that morning was very clear. It was a command to leave. Not when you feel like it. Not when all the conditions are right. It's a . . . [command]. It's loving Jesus. It's a *mark bilong yu* [characteristic of you] about how you obey him.[84]

Central to the PNG church leaders' paradigm shift was Bethel Center's preaching on cross-cultural mission by Pastor Silverback.[85] Additionally instrumental for Sete was Tippett's text *The Deep Sea Canoe: The Story of Third World Missionaries in the South Pacific*,[86] which recounted the

---

[82]Richmond Tamanabae, interview.
[83]Ibid.
[84]Sete, interview.
[85]Igarobae, interview.
[86]Alan R. Tippett, *The Deep Sea Canoe: The Story of Third World Missionaries in the South Pacific* (South Pasadena, CA: William Carey Library, 1977).

narratives of the Polynesian missionaries who first carried the gospel message across Micronesia and Melanesia to Papua New Guinea.[87] Inspired by Tippett's account, Sete dedicated her life to joining the global church in its fulfillment of the Great Commission.

As the contemporary global church continues to participate in the mission of God, McGavran and Tippett's missiological theories prove to be as relevant today as when they were first presented. As a missionary in Papua New Guinea, one of my first tasks was to retype *The Deep Sea Canoe* for local distribution. Decades after Tippett wrote this monumental text documenting the pilgrimage of Polynesian missionaries to Melanesia, it remains one of a few published accounts of non-Western missionaries to the islands. While the Christian church has moved forward in embracing indigenous expressions of Christianity, there is still more work to be done. As Tippett foresaw, "the notion of indigeneity has changed from a half-baked strategy to a full-orbed theology, and this is one of the greatest changes emerging in the era of post-colonial missions and a sign of greatest hope for the future."[88]

---

[87]Sete, interview.
[88]Tippett, *Introduction to Missiology*, 87.

4

···

A "Fuller" Vision of God's Mission and Theological Education in the New Context of Global Christianity

Wonsuk Ma

INTRODUCTION

This study identifies three priority issues in Christian mission, exploring each of them through two lenses. The first lens is that of the development of the School of Intercultural Studies (SIS) of Fuller Theological Seminary over the previous half century; the second is the contemporary shift of global Christianity. Three agenda items are, I believe, important issues for the purpose and mission of SIS and of critical significance to future Christian mission. They are (1) the expansion of global Christianity, (2) shaping of the understanding of Christian mission and (3) preparation of mission players. This study will conclude by bringing the discussion into the life of SIS as a learning and research institution.

Discussion in each section begins with the formative years of the School of World Mission (SWM) through the 1980s, when the institution experienced a significant change. This coincides with the time when global Christianity became a religion of the Global South, for the second time in church history.[1] When necessary, time is spent in a closer look at the shaping of the "received" mission thinking and paradigm through the Christendom legacy. The discussion will examine the future of global Christianity with its challenges and possibilities.

---

[1]Todd M. Johnson and Kenneth R. Ross, eds., *Atlas of Global Christianity 1910–2010* (Edinburgh: Edinburgh University Press, 2009), 52-53.

In the discussion of global Christianity, trajectories and numbers presented by the *Atlas of Global Christianity* will be used. In spite of debates around specific numbers contained in the book, I found the book useful in identifying trends and movements. The other useful source to the development of SWM/SIS is Kraft's almost eyewitness record.[2] The image of the institution I have for this study is that of global mission leadership. I speak as a member of the "Southern" church, and my understanding of global Christianity bears this perspective.

GROWTH OF GLOBAL CHRISTIANITY

Christians share the unique mission of Christ: to preach the good news of eternal life. Therefore, the growth of Christianity is not only the natural outcome of this missionary lifestyle but also the commitment of each believer.

When SWM was founded . . . The period when SWM was established (in 1965) was a significant time for global Christianity. According to the trajectory of the statistical center for global Christianity, the steady southwestward move since the sixteenth century gained serious southward momentum in 1950.[3] This was, without a doubt, caused by the growth of African Christianity, especially its indigenous or independent families. Equally evident is a strong eastward pull from this period, accelerated two decades later (1970) in the growth of Christianity in Asia. This move has been steadily sustained until now and is expected to continue in the foreseeable future. Unfortunately, we all know that this drastic development reflects not only growth in the geographical south and the east, but also decline in the north and the west.[4] This general trend in the middle of the twentieth century has been statistically supported in various studies. There is no doubt that SWM has sailed on this unique "trade wind," although it was not always predictable and smooth.

---

[2] Charles H. Kraft, *SWM/SIS at Forty: A Participant/Observer's View of Our History* (Pasadena, CA: William Carey Library, 2005). Henceforth *SWM/SIS*.

[3] Todd M. Johnson and Sun Young Chung, "Christianity's Centre of Gravity, AD 33–2100," in Johnson and Ross, *Atlas of Global Christianity*, 50-51.

[4] Patrick Johnstone has offered us a stunning visual presentation of past and projected continental changes in Christian demography between 1900 and 2050. The contrast between the growing continents and declining ones is striking. Patrick Johnstone, *The Future of the Global Church: History, Trends and Possibilities* (Colorado Springs, CO: Global Mapping International, 2011), 95.

Therefore, it is almost natural for the first evangelical school dedicated to world mission to be exclusively focused on the expansion of global Christianity (or "church growth," to use McGavran's passionate term) as its top priority. One of two motivations, as observed by Charles Kraft, was the sharp focus on evangelism and church growth, which mainline (or conciliar) churches and their institutions had abandoned.[5] In the age when the missionary movement was losing its appeal, especially among mainline churches, as an imperialistic and colonial enterprise, Fuller's commitment to intentionally begin SWM was a historic decision. McGavran's missional optimism, that the missionary sun was not setting but rising, provided inspiration and motivation.[6] This conviction, coupled with a commitment to "workable mission knowledge," made the institution more than a wind chaser: it now set the agenda and direction of Christian mission.[7] The opening of numerous schools of mission or evangelism in the ensuing decades, both in North America and throughout the world, attests to the prophetic foresight and the trendsetting mission leadership of the institution.

The institution's immediate target group was career missionaries during their home service (or on missionary sabbatical). The main purpose of McGavran's Church Growth Institute in Oregon, which later became the School of World Mission, was for "experienced missionaries . . . [to] study the growth and non-growth of the churches in which they worked."[8] The immediate priority was to equip evangelists to be effective in their work. The primary clientele was Western missionaries, and the space of this church-growth enterprise was the "mission field," presumably in the non-Western world. It was C. Peter Wagner who brought church-growth study to North America in later years. This small but burgeoning institution was preoccupied with the urgent task of world evangelization. Evangelicals seemed to have felt a historic call to inherit this missionary mantle, so prominent in the 1910 Edinburgh Missionary Conference but slowly abandoned by

---

[5]Kraft, *SWM/SIS*, 64, quoting an insightful reflection of Wilbert Shenk on the missional context of the 1960s.
[6]Ibid., 78.
[7]Mark A. Noll, *The New Shape of World Christianity: How American Experience Reflects Global Faith* (Downers Grove, IL: InterVarsity Press, 2009), 77-93, presents the surge of the evangelical missionary movement in the United States and its impact on the world.
[8]Kraft, *SWM/SIS*, 13.

mainline missiology in the first half of the twentieth century. Furthermore, McGavran's "fierce pragmatism"[9] and missionary experience led him to study and facilitate "people movements." Urgency of evangelism also led him to develop "harvest theology," which argued for the deployment of resources where the missionary iron was hot for a maximum gain.[10]

The 1980s saw a drastic change in the life of SWM, when the balance of global Christianity tipped toward the South, beginning in 1981 according to the *Atlas of Global Christianity*.[11] The demographic changes in global Christianity in that period and the following decades have been staggering. The growth of African Christianity, with the growth of nonmissionary churches, often called African Independent (or Initiated) Churches, is particularly noteworthy. Chinese Christianity returned with a strong sign of presence and strength, to a much-surprised world-mission watcher. Pentecostal-type churches have proliferated and energized growth globally.

Following this growth, the composition of SWM's student body shifted from midcareer Western missionaries to national church and mission leaders from various parts of the world. The focus of the school moved from a single emphasis on church growth to diversified specialties, to which we can turn later. One question that can be asked is, did SWM contribute to this global growth of Christianity? It is hard to ascertain the answer to this question without any firm evidence, but the SWM community was definitely caught up in this colossal change and probably played an important, or even key, role in the growth. One thing is clear however: the school was diligent in gathering data from various parts of the world, analyzing and drawing patterns and lessons to be applied elsewhere. Again, the study of church growth, the main bread and butter of the school, found new areas (such as the spiritual dimension) through the watchful eye of Peter Wagner.[12] This, by the way, demonstrates that SWM was and is not afraid of new approaches if they prove to contribute to the expansion of God's kingdom.

---

[9]Ibid., 70.

[10]Ibid., 78.

[11]Johnson and Chung, "Christianity's Centre of Gravity, AD 33–2100," 50–51.

[12]A series of shifts began when he noticed a Pentecostal dynamic in church growth, then the dimension of spiritual warfare, followed by the new apostolic movement, each of these not without much controversy. See, e.g., C. Peter Wagner, *Churchquake! How the New Apostolic Reformation Is Shaking up the Church as We Know It* (Ventura, CA: Regal, 1999).

The one-third challenge and possibility ahead. Missiologically speaking, in the preceding century we witnessed changes, shifts, growth, decline, wars, new nations and much more, perhaps far more than in all the previous nineteen centuries combined. We celebrated the expansion of global Christianity as observed above. However, the same growth can also be presented in a challenging way: the proportion of Christians in the world population has declined in the last hundred years. In fact, the time around the 1910 Edinburgh Conference records the highest watermark of world Christianity throughout its entire history: 34.8 percent of the world population! Indeed, this was the very first, but brief, time in church history when Christianity crossed the line of one-third of the world population. There was clear optimism that the presentation of the gospel to the world at that time could be easily achieved, which would lead to a further expansion of Christian faith. Except for the eastern part of Asia, much of the world was either already Christian or under Christian (colonial) rule. The development of Christian and mission since the Edinburgh Conference has been complex. And yet, one thing is sure: more efforts, research, missionaries, funds, institutions and mission societies/boards/agencies were established for mission in the twentieth century than in all the previous centuries. The net result has been the decline of world Christianity, which slid below the one-third line (or 33.2 percent in 2010). This happened in spite of an unprecedented level of effort and resources poured into world evangelization in the last hundred years!

Before going any further, I would like to ask a two-millennium-old question: Can global Christianity grow beyond the one-third line of the world population for the first time (in a true sense) in our generation? What signs point to this possibility? What role are we called to play to ride this wave of possibility? To tackle the first question, let's return to the growth in the southern continents (or Global South) in the twentieth century. In 1910, slightly more than 18 percent of world Christians lived in the Global South, which had close to 70 percent of the world's population at the time. In 2010, more than 60 percent of world's Christians were found on these continents, whose population grew to 84 percent of the world total. Although the decline of Christianity in the northern continents has seriously contributed to the rate of the shift, the very fact that Christianity has significantly grown in the places with higher numbers of people gives us hope for the future. The south and southeastward move of the centers of global Christianity reflects the sustained and significant growth that has been recorded in both Africa and Asia.

In particular, Asia holds the most important key to this global prospect. Its population is more than 60 percent of the world's total, yet its rate of evangelism is only 8.5 percent, about a quarter of the world's average. Once the main culprit for the under-one-third state of Christianity, now Asia can lead the world church toward this historic one-third breakthrough and keep it beyond the line. China and India, the two mega-nations, each with a population over one billion people, have recorded an impressive growth of Christianity; similar growth has been recorded in the Philippines, Indonesia, South Korea, Malaysia, Myanmar and other Global South countries. Since the 1980s, equally importantly, some of these churches have emerged as prominent missionary powers. The Korean and Filipino churches are good examples. Koreans, however, have more or less followed the established pattern of mission, and close to 60 percent of its mission forces work in Asia.[13] On the other hand, Filipinos, perhaps because they host large numbers of immigrant workers, have shown creative engagements that suggest new ways of mission.

The other powerhouse for this global prospect is Pentecostal/charismatic Christianity. A good portion of the growth of Christianity in the previous century, especially in Africa, Asia and Latin America, was among Pentecostal churches. Some of them are African Independent Churches, Chinese churches and "new evangelicals" in Latin America. Much of the exponential growth in Africa, for example, is attributed to the emergence of nonmissionary indigenous Spirit churches. It is projected that by 2050 one-third of Christians and one-tenth of the world population will be composed of various Pentecostal families.[14] In Asia, 51 percent of Christians are Spirit-Christians. Their role is important in the expansion of Christianity for two reasons. First, they tend to have dynamic faith in God's role in life, and this makes them more ready and zealous (and sometimes more effective) soul-winners. Particularly effective are their experiences of healing, exorcism and other miracles, which

---

[13] As of 2014, 57.7 percent of Korean missionaries work in Asia. For a more detailed analysis, see Timothy K. Park, "The Missionary Movement of the Korean Church: A Model for Non-Western Mission," in *Korean Church, God's Mission, Global Christianity*, ed. Wonsuk Ma and Kyo Seong Ahn, Regnum Edinburgh Centenary Series 26 (Oxford: Regnum Books, 2015), 24-26.

[14] Johnstone, *Future of the Global Church*, 125.

have a great appeal in the Global South, where one's religion is expected to include such experiences (while traditional Christianity fails to deliver them). Second, their churches, in addition to being a part of the well-known mega-church movement, tend to proliferate and reach small communities. For example, in Burkina Faso, the Assemblies of God denomination has 1.1 million members in 7,100 congregations, while the Catholic Church has 1.9 million members in 2,420 churches. The average number of people for each church or congregation is 155 for the Assemblies of God and 785 for the Catholic Church. This shows how the Pentecostal church has saturated the nation, reaching out to small villages as well as urban centers.

We are a historically blessed generation that has experienced an incredible development of Christian mission (since the Edinburgh gathering) and are now living with the one-third possibility before us. The focused and dedicated attention of the SWM/SIS to church-growth missiology in its half-century history, therefore, has put the school at the center of the Holy Spirit's agenda in our generation. Its contribution to the expansion of world Christianity is significant. This discussion also suggests unprecedented possibilities before us and several places we all (including SIS) need to look at very closely.

MISSION: ASSUMED VERSUS SUPPOSED TO BE

The birth of SWM in 1965 is a prime example of the powerful impact of American evangelicalism on the rest of the world. As Mark Noll argues forcefully, in the twentieth century evangelicalism was and still is the most powerful Christian influence in the shaping of global Christianity and its mission.[15] The SWM was not the first of its kind in North America: there were countless ministry and missionary training programs among evangelicals, Pentecostals and fundamentalists. Mainline churches also ran well-structured programs in mission studies, such as the Kennedy School of Missions of Hartford Seminary Foundation. Its closure in 1967, two years after the birth of SWM, was part of the growing crisis of mission-studies programs in Europe and North America.[16] The mantle of Christian mission was passing

---

[15]Noll, *New Shape of World Christianity*, 13, helpfully lists six characteristics of American evangelicalism.

[16]Wilbert Shenk, "Missiology," in *Encyclopedia of Protestantism*, ed. Hans J. Hillerrand (New York: Routledge, 2003), quoted in Kraft, *SWM/SIS*, 64.

from historic (mainline and Catholic) churches to evangelicals. Although viewed as radical, McGavran's insistence on evangelism and church growth proved to be an appropriate response to an accurate assessment of the demise of the missionary work among mainline churches.[17] The development of the school and its emphases over the years also accompanied a change in the understanding of mission and now provide a useful window to enlighten our understanding of mission in its own context.

The understanding of mission then. Within the American evangelical vision of new world mission leadership (SWM as the institutional expression), several elements are identified as components of an understanding of mission at that time. The first is SWM's sharp focus on evangelism and church growth. It was partly a reaction against the prevailing conciliar missiology, which, according to McGavran, was concerned with many "good works" but left out the "most important" (i.e., evangelism) along the way.[18] This naturally takes unevangelized or underevangelized places as the target for mission. In the context of the 1960s in North America, it meant primarily Asia and Africa (and also Latin America). The second characteristic of this understanding of mission was that it consisted of something taking place "out there." A popular language in the mission world was "foreign" mission, which later evolved into "world" mission. The third characteristic, an emphasis on the Great Commission and its message of "go . . . and make disciples of all nations" (Mt 28:19), often serves as the starter for the whole process of mission engagement. This intentionality of mission is an important part of mission thinking. At the end, once we put all these together, a small number of specially committed and trained people from the West are expected to carry out this important task of the church in the rest of the world. We call them missionaries. The SWM's call was to equip the churches and mission workers so that they could be more effective in the field. And it did exceptionally well.

These characteristics of mission seemed to be quite natural and normal, even normative. Was this really the case? In order for us to explore this, we will need to dig deep to trace the shaping of mission thinking in the West.

---

[17]To avoid a danger that "essential mission gets lost"; see McGavran's note to Hubbard, February 26, 1965, cited in Kraft, *SWM/SIS*, 57.
[18]Kraft, *SWM/SIS*, 57.

It is commonly agreed that an intentional missionary era began in the sixteenth century with the appearance of the Jesuit order as part of the Counter-Reformation process, and its members received special status and support along with specific training and commissioning. In fact, the words *mission* and *missionary* as we use those terms today also began to be used at that time. This radical move was motivated by, among other things, the discovery of new lands, where people needed to be evangelized. Jesuit missionary explorations were truly groundbreaking in South America and in East Asia, for example. This creation continued into the era of Protestant mission after Christendom was broken into smaller religious states, primarily in Europe. Starting in the eighteenth century, special missionary societies undertook the missionary mandate of European Christians and churches in their colonial territories.

In the second half of the second Christian millennium, this development of a missionary paradigm was a natural creation of the social contexts: (1) The world was divided between Christian and "heathen."[19] The unevangelized were found far "out there," as "home" was understood to be fully evangelized: Christendom. (2) Because the mission "fields" were radically different in weather, culture, language, people and level of civilization, a small group of chosen people was trained, sent out and supported under special arrangements. (3) As a result, the church at "home" was kept away from mission. These churches supported and prayed for those who were "doing mission." Consequently, mission became an elitist movement, left to the hands of experts.

This unique shaping of the understanding of mission had serious consequences.[20] Particularly, this restriction of mission to the trained elite dictated how mission was carried out and by whom. In the end, unfortunately, the church has theologically become deprived of the call to mission. The church today has inherited this distorted picture of mission, not only in the

---

[19]This is the first characterization of Christendom according to Stuart Murray, *Post-Christendom: Church and Mission in a Strange New World* (Milton Keynes, UK: Paternoster, 2004), 83.

[20]For further discussion, see Wonsuk Ma, "'Life' in Theological Education and Missional Formation: A Reflection for a New Christian Era," *Transformation* 32, no. 4 (2015): 223-37. Also helpful is a Catholic reflection by Stephen Bevans, "Theological Education and Missionary Formation," in *Reflecting on and Equipping for Christian Mission*, ed. Stephen Bevans et al. (Oxford: Regnum, 2015), 94-96.

West but in the whole world. Passionate and honest as it was, the founding mission statement of SWM reflects this understanding of mission: for "experienced missionaries . . . [to] study the growth and non-growth of the churches in which they worked." It really meant, at least to a mission mind from the global South, that specifically selected, trained and commissioned Western missionaries were to move from the West to the "rest" to evangelize people in the non-Western world.

Changes experienced by SWM in the 1980s during the Dean Paul Pierson era also reflect not only a change in the global Christian landscape but also a questioning of received mission thinking and practices. The increasing number of non-Westerners in the student body was a clear sign of this. Signs of decline in American Christianity accelerated this trend. The diversification of academic emphases of SIS was a clear sign of the widening understanding of mission, mirroring the change in global Christianity. However, it seems likely that the pragmatic ethos hindered the community's ability to intentionally reflect on the wider context and its implications.

The democratization of mission: the present and future agenda. The revision of Christian mission in our time can be summarized as democratization, or even liberation, of mission. *Democratization* is a theological concept referring to a process through which a privileged status or call, initially granted to a small group of select people, is eventually expanded to include the whole community of God's people. For the democratization of mission as an important agenda for reforming mission, three considerations are required: (1) the Christendom process that resulted in an elitist and narrow conception and practice of mission must be reexamined, (2) contemporary social contexts where mission was practiced have changed and (3) the ideal of mission as taught by Jesus, and the glimpse of it we have in the records of the early church, must be reconsidered. These are three areas that will have to be considered for Christianity to be relevant and to be effective in the new era and world.

The first requires the democratization of missionary-sending and missionary-receiving places. In the 1960s, the movement of Christian mission was more or less unidirectional: from the West to the rest. This historical phenomenon was shaped by the reality that the West was Christian and the rest heathen, either in reality or by perception. This was further reinforced by the removal of "world" and mission target from Christendom theology and church life. Once the territories controlled by the Western world were brought under Christian domain, the "world" was thought to have been successfully brought under the kingship of Christ. Thus, the mission objects/targets were found in faraway lands, and the mission model was to recreate Christendom societies by introducing Christianity, civilization and commerce.

We began to hear a new popular expression, especially among the Lausanne circles: "mission from everywhere to everywhere." This may have been an outcome of a serious theological reflection on mission, but it was the steady demographical changes in global Christianity that forced us to rethink the West-rest binary. When SWM was established in the 1960s, the elitist and unidirectional mission was not questioned but was assumed as a norm. Thus, naturally the objective of the school was to equip Western missionaries for the expansion of Christianity in the "rest." By the 1980s, or the Pierson era, the balance of global Christianity was tipping toward the Global South. This shift had two sides: growth in the South paralleled by decline in the North. This decline was experienced among the mainline churches and eventually spread to the evangelical churches in the States. The United States was no longer a "Christian" nation, and new generations were growing up without the influence of Christianity. The world was at the doorstep of the church, but soon it would be surrounded by the forces of the world. This has certainly challenged the notion of mission that's "out there." We are not talking just about non-Christian immigrants but also about our own generation in the West, who cannot be assumed to possess Christian faith. Now, Jesus' sending out of his disciples "into the world" (Jn 17:18) can be ours in a true sense, as finally the world has been restored in our Christian life and theological thinking. The rise of new missionary-sending churches from the Global South has also had an impact on this thinking. For example, the South Korean church began to send its missionaries en masse from the late 1970s, and soon it became the second largest missionary-sending church among the Protestants. Before the turn of the century, missionaries from the non-Western churches outnumbered those from the traditional Western churches. The rise of mission consciousness among Christian migrants in the North and throughout the world further contributed to the erosion of

the old two-tiered divide of the world.[21] Then it was the turn for the theological world to restore this in theological construct and theological formation both in churches and in institutions.

The second move toward democratization was in the domain of mission.
Evangelism as mission was a universal understanding as observed in the
1910 Edinburgh Conference theme: "Evangelisation of the World in Our
Generation." However, in the subsequent decades, mainline Protestant missiology was shaped first by the International Missionary Council and then
by the World Council of Churches. Their close attention to social contexts
resulted in a radical missiology, such as liberation theology, which betrayed,
to the evangelical eyes, the Edinburgh commitment to evangelism. When
SWM was established, mission thinking was clearly divided between evangelical and conciliar missiologies, leaving almost no middle ground. Interestingly, this extreme dichotomy roughly corresponds with the Cold War
period. The SWM has certainly led a critical evangelical campaign not only
to restore evangelism as the center of Christian mission but also to bring
this mission thinking to a credible academic engagement through graduate
programs and research. At the Lausanne Congress in 1974 the academic
community of evangelical mission, less than a decade old, played a significant role in affirming and setting the evangelical mission agenda.

However, in that very affirming meeting an important voice, later known
as "radical evangelicals," was also heard representing churches in the Global
South. Based both on the reading of the Gospel texts and the reading of the
social contexts of many countries in the Global South, Christian mission,
they argued, must take the daily struggles of ordinary people as a valid
mission agenda. To distinguish themselves from conciliar missiology, they
affirmed their commitment to the authority and full message of the Bible.
This holistic vision of mission was clearly noticed in the 1980s (or the Pierson
era). Kraft observes that during Dean Paul Pierson's leadership (1980–1992),
the single focus on church growth (and evangelism) with anthropology as a
corollary soon grew into multiple emphases in mission studies. This time,

---

[21] An in-depth study of African Pentecostal/charismatic immigrants to Germany shows a strong
missionary consciousness. See Claudia Währisch-Oblau, *The Missionary Self-Perception of Pen-
tecostal/Charismatic Church Leaders from the Global South in Europe: Bringing Back the Gospel*
(Leiden: Brill, 2009), esp. 254-62. Cf. a critical and reserved view by Paul Freston, "Reserve
Mission: A Discourse in Search of Reality?," *PentecoStudies* 9, no. 2 (2010): 103-74.

regular faculty posts included professors of Islam, leadership, communication, Bible translation, spiritual dynamics and others.[22] In this period, the
majority of the student body changed from career (Western) missionaries on
their furloughs to non-Western national leaders and perhaps "pre-field" missionaries, those preparing for their first assignments.[23] We need to take note
of the appearance and steady increase of the national church and mission
leaders and workers in the SWM/SIS student body. The steady rise of new
missionary churches from the Global South and their engagement with challenging social contexts have challenged evangelicals to think of and act on
mission holistically. It is important to remember that the new missionary
churches do not have to cross borders to find the world to evangelize: they
are *already* in the world, surrounded by religions, corrupt political systems,
poverty, exploitation and many signs that oppose the kingdom of God. The
organization of the International Fellowship of Mission Theologians in the
Two-Thirds World (INFEMIT) in 1987 and the opening of the Oxford
Centre for Mission Studies in 1983 provided a strategic avenue for "radical
evangelicals" to network, train and research.[24] By the time the Lausanne
Movement had its Cape Town meeting in 2010, the holistic nature of life, the
gospel and Christian mission were taken as certainties or givens. What a
change in less than four decades!

The third area of mission democratization has to do with the agents of
mission. Until recently in Europe, it was largely either missionary orders
(of the Roman Catholic Church) or mission societies (of Protestant
churches) that carried out missionary programs. Although some mission
boards continued the model of mission societies in the United States, soon
denominations began to establish their mission programs, encouraging
their member congregations to commit themselves to denominational
mission programs. Parallel to this church-based missionary approach, specialized mission agencies emerged at a fast rate, further encouraging local
churches and believers in mission participation. American Christianity,
free from any burden of a state-church alliance, was able to bring Christian

---

[22]Kraft, *SWM/SIS*, 195-96.

[23]Ibid., 195.

[24]Al Tizon, *Transformation After Lausanne: Radical Evangelical Mission in Global-Local Perspective* (Oxford: Regnum, 2008).

mission one important step away from the Christendom paradigm and one large step forward toward the democratization of mission. However, we still face a challenging question: how can the whole church—both North and South—fully participate in mission?

If every believer is called by God, empowered by the Holy Spirit and sent to the world for God's mission, what should mission be like? We have come to agree that *missionary* is one of the most problematic words in today's mission thinking. In addition to the historic perception of power, especially in the context of the colonial era, it conveys an elitist notion that mission is a call applied only to a few specialists. In order to shape "mission for the rest of us," it will require, first of all, adding the everyday world to the mission field, which has been understood, until now, as the faraway ends of the earth. Second, daily work needs to be understood as itself a mission engagement such that the workplace becomes a mission field. Professions then become valuable mission tools. Third, this can provide a firmer basis for every believer to be seen as a missioner. Fourth, a holistic view of life can be fostered so that Christian mission may be seen as bringing God's rule over both "life before death" and "life after death."[25] Fifth, the believer's life becomes a living testimony to the saving grace of God in addition to words and works. Sixth, Christians will begin to engage with various elements of the world, with a balanced theology of the world—presently under the enemy's domain but yearning for the day of redemption. After all, God so loved the world!

This repositioning of Christian mission will have significant implications for spiritual and theological formation, both in the local churches and in formal theological institutions. Everyone, both North and South, will need to contribute to this effort. The North is able to critically evaluate the legacy of Christendom and share its learning with the world church. The new churches in the South should be critical in continuing what is the received missionary paradigm by offering a close reading of the Scriptures and the contexts. One consensus has already surfaced: mission cannot go on as business as usual. It requires a serious re-envisioning at this opportune time, when the church badly needs global mission leadership. Who knows but that SWM/SIS has been prepared for such a time as this?

---

[25]Julie C. Ma and Wonsuk Ma, *Mission in the Spirit: Towards a Pentecostal/Charismatic Missiology* (Oxford: Regnum, 2010), 264-65.

EQUIPPING AND NURTURING MISSION COMMUNITIES

The initial purpose of SWM was for "experienced missionaries . . . [to] study the growth and non-growth of the churches in which they worked," and we have spent sufficient time in deciphering its deeper meaning. As the third main agenda for mission, this old purpose statement is revisited, but with important adjustments. The discussions above revealed several key components in need of serious rethinking. The present discussion revolves around an urgent and practical question: how can the churches, both in the South and in the North, be equipped and prepared for the new era of Christian mission?

The expansion of Christianity has been set as a priority goal of mission, especially with the goal that in the near future global Christianity may embrace more than one-third of the world population. Even a conservative Pew report predicts that Christian growth will roughly correspond to the rate of the population growth.[26] Considering that world Christianity reached a historic watermark around the time of the 1910 Edinburgh Conference (34.8 percent of the world population), it has receded since then to the present level (less than one-third in 2010). The Pew forecast suggests that the decline has hit bottom. Its rise beyond the population growth rate is the common task for all Christians. With this unprecedented opportunity and possibility, the focus must be on how to prepare the majority churches in the Global South. Two immediate challenges are faced by these churches. First, they have not had much history of, or experience in, mission. In fact, they have been, and some still are, receiving mission gifts from elsewhere (traditionally from the West), even if many churches are richer in human and spiritual resources than the benefactors. Second, the majority of them do not have sufficient financial resources to undertake a missionary enterprise. Unless alternative approaches are developed for and taught to them, mission is likely to remain outside of their lives. This is where the second discussion is necessary: how to re-envision Christian mission. The first discussion attempted to lay a foundation for the "majority" churches to become aware of their missional call. This section ponders the ensuing question: how can the growing churches in the South, as well as the waning churches in the North,

---

[26]Pew Research Center, "The Future of World Religions: Population Growth Projections, 2010–2050," April 2, 2015, www.pewforum.org/2015/04/02/religious-projections-2010-2050/.

be prepared, equipped and empowered for mission? My discussion will explore two major missionary paradigms found throughout church history.

The mission approach, then. North American mission began to take global leadership in the twentieth century, as already noted in the discussion of John R. Mott's leading role in the Edinburgh Conference and its ensuing development. When mainline churches adopted more socially inspired missiology, it was American evangelicals who carried the mantle of the global leadership role in mission. The establishment of SWM can be understood in this context. Its contribution to the American evangelical mission movement and soon to the global mission movement is well attested by the composition of the student body and its enduring efforts in training mission workers and leaders. For example, the rise of the modern missionary movement in Korea was directly and indirectly influenced and aided by SWM. Ralph Winter played an important role in training early Korean missionaries through David Cho's East-West Center for Missionary Research and Development starting in 1960. Soon, a throng of Korean missionaries and mission leaders received their training through SWM. Especially from the 1980s, the institution's contribution to the growth of churches and mission movement throughout the world is generally and appreciatively recognized.

We have already discussed some of the issues related to the missionary paradigm. In this discussion, I am using the concept of power as an important element characterizing mission approaches. Perhaps without any intention, the Christendom shaping of Christian mission resulted in a definite mission paradigm: mission with power. Before going any further, I would like to make two comments on power. First, power produces effects not only on the subject wielding it but also in the perception of the object. In a mission setting, a Western missionary, even if extremely careful not to exhibit any behavior or attitude of power, can still be viewed as having power, or having privileged position or status. Therefore, this discussion is not to undermine the sacrificial and genuine dedication of most Western missionaries. Second, as our attention is now on the non-Western or majority churches in the Global South, the perspective of this particular discussion is of the majority and Southern churches.

The perception of mission with power has been shaped in several areas. The first is the political superiority of traditional missionary-sending nations.

Since the sixteenth century, this political power with corresponding military might was permanently etched in the minds of the Global South through colonial experiences. Christianity was thus perceived by nationals as the religion of the powerful. As a consequence, embracing Christianity was also viewed as a path to power, though this generalization may not apply to East Asia, where the colonial power was not Christian. The net result, to the eyes of the Global South, is that mission is a privilege limited only to the politically powerful nations. The second perception related to mission is economic power. Although the colonial powers exploited natural resources, their advanced societies were undergirded and supported by superior economic power. This point is important for later discussion. The third perception of mission relates to the power of civilization, often expressed in governance, education, law, human rights, arts and medical advancements. Although the Global South boasted several rich and ancient civilizations, in the modern era it was Euro-America that became a benchmark of civilization. The fourth and the net power is a perception of "superior race." It was no one's intention, but the historical reality was of white people preaching the Christian gospel to the "others." Under this general perception, to the majority eyes, mission was a privileged call for the powerful, and power is unfortunately perceived as a prerequisite for mission. How do we know this? Ask a thriving church in Asia or Africa in a Christian majority nation if their church is doing mission. Most likely the answer will be "no, because we do not have money."

As part of the American evangelical mission movement, SWM inherited this paradigm as a child of its age. Its contribution to and leadership over global Christian mission needs to be assessed within its own context. At the same time, from the beginning, the school has paid keen attention to how the Holy Spirit works in a specific context. This was where church-growth study met anthropology! Its eye was on the right place, and its openness was a rule, though still within the limitation of the era. Perhaps it could have taken advantage of experiences and resources found in the churches among the student body. For example, Mennonites and Catholics might have been particularly helpful.

Mission with weakness: possible? Going back to the question at hand, can we develop a mission paradigm that the "new" churches in the Global South can embrace, with its political, religious, cultural and economic challenges? If mission is perceived to be a work of the powerful or, worse, if power is perceived as the prerequisite for mission, the logical alternative is the other end of the continuum: a paradigm of mission with weakness or from a position of weakness. Then where can one look for models of mission with or in weakness? I suggest at least three places for our exploration: (1) the life of Jesus and his early church as recorded in the Bible, (2) missionary models in the first Christian millennium and (3) contemporary cases that point to the paradigm of weakness.

My reading of the Gospels is strikingly counter-Christendom. Jesus' incarnation is often characterized as a process of kenosis (emptying), and Paul admonishes early Christians to imitate his life (Phil 2:5-8):

> Let the same mind be in you that was in Christ Jesus,
> who, though he was in the form of God,
>> did not regard equality with God
>> as something to be exploited,
> but emptied himself,
>> taking the form of a slave,
>> being born in human likeness.
> And being found in human form,
>> he humbled himself
>> and became obedient to the point of death—
>> even death on a cross.

It is not through miracles and demonstration of divine power (as clearly seen, for example, in his temptation) but through dying on the cross that he fulfilled his call. His voluntary assumption of weakness is the way of mission, and we are called to follow his way.

The early church was a persecuted community. These early believers were both Jews and Greek-speaking as well as political, social and religious underdogs or even personae non gratae. The only thing Paul can boast is the foolishness of the cross. In the short life history of the Jerusalem church, there may have been a notion of professionalism of mission; that is, the apostles and the deacons were called to preach. When persecution scattered the believers, unknown believers were responsible for the establishment of the church in Antioch as they preached the risen Lord everywhere they went

(Acts 11:19-21). Their minority status, hardship and persecution left them with only one option: mission with, or in a position of, weakness. Although no church is perfect, weakness is definitely not a handicap but a favorite means that God uses for his mission.

In the first millennium of Christian development, among the best mission forces were Syriac Christians, who were credited with reaching India and China. They were subjected to Persian persecution and later to Islamic oppression. Even after the Roman oppression of Christians ceased in the fourth century and the religion eventually attained a privileged position of power, Syriac Christians continued their marginalized life because they followed Nestorian teachings. Their mode of mission was their embedded life in new places. Although an example in the extreme, the story of Frumentius, the first Ethiopian bishop, is an illustration of the missionary life of Syriac Christians. Rescued and then enslaved in Ethiopia, when he was eventually freed, he decided not to return home but converted Ethiopia to Christianity.

In our day, it is argued that the total number of Muslims converting to Christianity through Filipino maids in the Middle East outnumbers the total converts brought about by the efforts of missionaries.[27] If this is true, then why? To begin with, these migrant women work away from their families and sometimes leave children behind to earn enough money to support their families. They are neither recognized as missionaries nor trained or commissioned to these Islamic nations. Perhaps many struggle to live (and work) each day, let alone continue a conscientious Christian life or fulfill a missionary call. Their lives of service to others manifest their Christian witness. It is mission with, and in the position of, weakness.

These are examples of mission from weakness in several time periods. This discussion comprises more anecdote than argument, but the Bible clearly presents this model of mission. Consequently, we stand at the crossroads of two major mission paradigms: mission with power and mission with weakness. Both paradigms have been shaped by the locus of the church in society, and both are valid approaches to mission. The paradigm of

---

[27]This was first pointed out by Melba Maggay at the International Symposium on Asian Mission, although her published chapter records only the significant presence of Filipino Christians in the Arab Peninsula. Melba Padilla Maggay, "Early Protestant Missionary Efforts in the Philippines: Some Intercultural Issues," in *Asian Church and God's Mission*, ed. Wonsuk Ma and Julie C. Ma (Manila: OMF Literature, 2003), 39.

weakness is a paradigm that the church today needs to recover, to be added to the paradigm with strength and resources. I would call global mission circles to diligently collect cases illustrating how these paradigms are tried and how they work in various communities. Perhaps both paradigms may merge into workable and healthy models of mission in practice.

LOOKING AHEAD: WHAT IS A CALL FOR SIS?

The opportunity open before us is unique, rare and unprecedented. Three aspects of the new era of mission have been discussed; many more can be added. In conclusion, let us explore the question, what role does SIS have in this new era of Christian mission if we are going to see a radically new era of world Christianity and its mission? Two areas will be examined as the institution shapes its future role.

The SWM/SIS has undoubtedly exercised its leadership in the shaping of mission thinking and practice, both regionally and globally. With a radically new era of mission open before us all, however, intentional leadership is called for more than ever. One may ask why, in the era of the Global Southern Christianity, an institution in the West is expected to take on this leadership. This will require considerable discussion, but I would argue that this is one special gift the West can offer at this point of history in global Christianity. I would like to specifically mention two areas where SIS is called to serve the world church through such leadership.

Re-visioning mission and its agenda setting. What is required in the thinking and practice of mission is a global collaboration and joint efforts among mission thinkers, practitioners and leaders. It will take experience, input and reflections, both from the growing South and the waning North. The North has a long history of mission engagement, human knowledge and financial resources. With its long history of Christianity and mission, only the North can provide self-analysis and discernment of the received mission thinking and practices.

The SIS has proven its ability to call for or convene a global space of exchange, learning and dialogue to be able to facilitate a global process in reshaping global Christianity and its mission. Regional theological institutions and mission networks can be part of the process. This convening power exists partly because American evangelicalism is relatively free from colonial baggage. Also, churches in the Global South resonate with SIS's commitment to evangelism, which is why a good number of Christian leaders and mission practitioners are attracted to Fuller's program. Equally important is SIS's ethos, shaped by what transpires in mission. It is true that often the main emphasis of the school has been shaped by a championing faculty member, be it church growth, anthropology or spiritual warfare. At the same time, the school has demonstrated its openness to experiment with new subjects and approaches that are useful for mission.

With these unusual gifts, SIS can intentionally draw on global stake-holders in mission, including major regional institutions, and begin to chart tomorrow's Christian mission. But change will require far more than a discussion of methodologies; evaluation of mission and plans for the future will need to begin with the very foundation of mission.

In order for SIS to take up this historic and challenging leadership call, it will have to overcome several important obstacles. Among others, it will have to learn to think about and recognize what the Holy Spirit is doing from a global perspective. Leaving an American evangelical perspective is hard, particularly with its own institutional stakeholders, whom the seminary is initially called to serve. It may take much convincing. The SIS needs to seek genuine global voices, such as an African voice—not an American missionary who once worked in Africa but an African insider. Equally importantly, it will need to act ecumenically to rightly represent its student body but hold firmly to evangelical conviction. For example, SIS's unique place in mission thinking was hardly present at the Edinburgh 2010 process, in the conference or in the extensive thirty-six-volume publication. Finally, intentionality in its awareness of a call for global mission leadership is critical, knowing that leadership is fulfilled by serving so that others can fulfill their God-given calls.

Creation of mission knowledge. From the beginning, SWM/SIS insisted on the creation of knowledge, as shown in its top-ranked position in every ten-year survey of the production of dissertations on mission.[28] It broke new ground by bringing social science, anthropology in this case, to mission studies. In addition, its insistence on training mission practitioners through

---

[28]Robert J. Priest and Robert DeGeorge, "Doctoral Dissertations on Mission: Ten-Year Update, 2002–2011 (Revised)," *International Bulletin of Missionary Research* 37, no. 4 (2013): 195-202.

its programs resulted in the creation of knowledge-based practices. However, as Kraft's concluding reflection suggests, the training of mission practitioners is both an enduring commitment and a challenge to sustain. This emerges from a lingering dichotomy between professional degrees, such as doctor of missiology, and the academic one, namely, doctor of philosophy (PhD) in North American higher education.

The quandary, then, is how SIS can remain a thought leader, especially in the reshaping of mission perception and practice, while maintaining the training of mission practitioners as a priority. The creation of new knowledge will definitely require a continuing strength in the PhD program. Is there a way to bring practices (thus, practitioners) to the PhD regime? My answer is a definite yes, and two models may provide helpful guidance. One is a model from other disciplines, especially the social sciences. Field data often form the most critical research base, and mission studies cannot be an exception. In fact, the list of SIS PhD dissertations, I believe, already proves this. The other model may come from several other successful PhD programs in mission studies, such as the Oxford Centre for Mission Studies, perhaps the largest PhD provider in Europe in mission studies, which has crafted its PhD delivery system mostly based on field experiences and data.[29]

Making a change in mission studies comes with several challenges, but also unique advantages. The first challenge SIS will have to face is the typical PhD structure in the United States. If its program is realigned to make it more conducive to midcareer mature leaders with rich experiences of mission engagement, then it will have to make part-time study readily available. The second challenge, however, is more formidable: full-time resident course work, the most onerous requirement for many would-be candidates. Although building a general and broad knowledge base is essential for the candidates, since many of them come with rich experience both in practice and reflection, perhaps this can be negotiated with the accrediting body. There are strong arguments that, because of their experience, they come with varying levels of preparedness and deficiencies. Perhaps the course work could be customized to meet the

---

[29]D. P. Davies, "The Research Contribution of OCMS," *Transformation* 28, no. 4 (2011): 279-85.

unique needs of each candidate. (My individually and custom-designed study at the School of Theology was an example.) The third, and perhaps most difficult, challenge is for SIS to radically expand its supervisory capacity beyond its traditional faculty resources. Again, this has been successfully done elsewhere. This way, SIS can continue its programs in professional doctorates as well as the master-level training, especially to serve its immediate constituencies.

Each generation is called to discern the needs and God-given opportunities for its own time. We live in a remarkable time, and we will all stand to be judged if we have been faithful stewards of opportunities. Of those to whom more has been given, more will be expected, and SWM/SIS is a program that has been given more in our time.

5

Who Is Our Cornelius?

Learning from Fruitful Encounters at the Boundaries of Mission

Pascal D. Bazzell

INTRODUCTION

Jalal-ad Din Muhammad Rumi, a thirteenth-century Sufi scholar, wrote: "Truth is a mirror that falls from the hand of God and shatters into pieces. Everyone picks up a piece and believes that that piece contains the whole truth, even though the truth is left sown about in each fragment."[1] As I reflect on this poetry, I keep wondering how church history with its mission expansion would have looked if it had been marked by the apostle Paul's words that as believers we now see only through a mirror dimly and, even though we have received the fullness through Jesus Christ, we understand that we do not have the wholeness. Even though the truth is given freely to the recipients from God, Reinhold Bernhardt notes that this does not mean the wholeness of truth is imparted, as the giver, in this case God, is always greater than his revelations.[2] Rumi's assertion recognizes that there are truths that extend beyond their own social locations and contextual understandings. Furthermore, the fact that Rumi discerns that others too are bearers of truths related to God means that they have been led to discern particular truths.

---

[1] Quoted in Lloyd Ridgeon, *Makhmalbaf's Broken Mirror: The Socio-Political Significance of Modern Iranian Cinema* (Durham: University of Durham Centre for Middle Eastern and Islamic Studies, 2000), 14.

[2] Reinhold Bernhardt, "Coordinates for Interreligious Discernment from a Protestant View: Transcendence—Freedom—Agape—Responsibility," in *Criteria of Discernment in Interreligious Dialogue*, ed. Catherine Cornille (Eugene, OR: Wipf & Stock, 2009), 59.

Similarly, in Christian theology today there is a general understanding that from the beginning God has been in dialogue with all people and therefore, "a ray of that Truth"[3] and the "seeds of the Word"[4] are found in other religious and cultural traditions.[5] Or as Amos Yong has argued, the Spirit of God has been poured out on "all flesh" in the last days (Acts 2:17), and therefore pneumatological symbols of divine presence and divine activity are to be found not only in our Christian tradition but also in other faiths.[6]

On the other hand, the construction of religious boundaries has always served to secure the essential identity of a particular faith—the unique truth that has been revealed from a "higher power" or "God" and the resulting horizons that separate one group of religious adherents from another. These boundaries of exclusion are built to ward off the intrusions of the religious other, and they serve practically to protect the purity of one's faith, the truth revealed by God. At the same time, mission as a human endeavor is imperative for many religions in which the bearer of truth moves beyond the boundaries of exclusion to become a witness to what was divinely revealed.[7] This mission activity then invites the seeker of truth inside of a faith's circle of exclusions.

This is a seemingly contrary situation, which, on the one hand, rightly requires exclusionary boundaries in order to identify one's faith and yet, on the other hand, acknowledges and seeks to participate in God's mysterious work outside of faith's boundaries. However, within this apparent contradiction, the Spirit of God paves a third way, or what some have

---

[3]Second Vatican Council's *Nostra Aetate*: "Declaration on the Relation of the Church to Non-Christian Religions, *Nostra Aetate*, Proclaimed by His Holiness Pope Paul VI on October 28, 1965," par. 2, www.vatican.va/archive/hist_councils/ii_vatican_council/documents/vat-ii_decl_19651028_nostra-aetate_en.html.

[4]Second Vatican Council's *Ad Gentes*: "Decree *Ad Gentes* on the Missionary Activity of the Church," par. 11, accessed October 1, 2015, www.vatican.va/archive/hist_councils/ii_vatican_council/documents/vat-ii_decree_19651207_ad-gentes_en.html.

[5]See Antonio M. Pernia, "The State of Mission Today," *Verbum* 55, no. 1 (2014): 12.

[6]Amos Yong, "The Holy Spirit, the Middle Way, and the Religions," *Evangelical Interfaith Dialogue* 2, no. 2 (2012): 8.

[7]Of course each religion has its own understanding of what *mission* means (as there is not one common understanding even in Christianity). However, *The Oxford Dictionary of World Religions* defines *mission* as "the sense of obligation in all religions to share their faith and practice with others, generally by persuasion, occasionally by coercion." John Bowker, ed., *The Oxford Dictionary of World Religions* (Oxford: Oxford University Press, 1997), 646.

called an "in-between space."[8] I will be using the Peter and Cornelius story (Acts 10:1–11:18) as a framework to elaborate on how this in-between space takes the church beyond itself into the mission work of the Spirit to connect with the stranger, the neighbor, the other. It is in this space that one encounters the Spirit's mysterious presence in the other in a manner that enables mutual transformation.

As we celebrate the fiftieth anniversary of the School of Intercultural Studies (SIS) at Fuller Theological Seminary, we want to be particularly aware of the various historical events that shaped mission today. The SIS has participated in and led many historical events that catalyzed paradigm shifts in mission practice and theology. The early days of the School of World Mission could be characterized as marked by concern for Christian mission *to* every people. Donald McGavran and Ralph Winter's prophetic voices sought to mobilize for church planting and led to catalytic movements into "unreached people groups."[9]

Later, key scholars such as Charles Kraft, Paul Hiebert, Charles Van Engen and R. Daniel Shaw helped us rethink doing Christian mission *among* the people where the gospel is communicated appropriately and where theology and church are biblically faithful and culturally appropriate.[10] Building on this foundation, I see SIS currently nurturing a new orientation in understanding mission and missiology from *missio ecclesiae* to *missio Dei*,[11] or what I also refer to as Christian mission *with* the people.

Christian mission *with* the people attempts to move beyond, or at least to emphasize, a dimension of mission that was undervalued in both the sending-receiving model of mission (Christian mission *to* the people) and the current model of Christian mission *among* the people. This current model emphasizes that God's chosen people are holding the truth, and as

---

[8]Volker Küster calls this an interstitial space in his *Einführung in die Interkulturelle Theologie* (Göttingen: Vandenhoeck & Ruprecht, 2011), 16. Homi K. Bhabha refers to this in-between space as "Third Space," in *The Location of Culture* (London: Routledge, 1994), 22; and Hans-Georg Gadamer claimed this "in-between space" to be the "true locus of hermeneutics," in *Truth and Method*, 2nd rev. ed. (London: Bloomsbury Academic, 2004), 293.

[9]See Michael Pocock, Gailyn Van Rheenen and Douglas McConnell, *The Changing Face of World Missions: Engaging Contemporary Issues and Trends* (Grand Rapids: Baker Academic, 2005), 10.

[10]See also Jonathan Tan, *Christian Mission Among the People of Asia* (Maryknoll, NY: Orbis Books, 2014).

[11]Even though, of course, the *missio ecclesiae* should reflect the *missio Dei*.

they give the truth to the local believers, those local believers rearticulate or adapt its meanings in local contexts. Christian mission *with* the people frames a new approach of doing Christian mission in today's pluralistic contexts, not to diminish the former paradigms, as context may determine their usefulness. Rather, we seek to complement some of their inadequacies. This reframing is necessary because mission history reveals that context shapes the perceptions of the gospel; therefore, in each historical epoch there is a need to realign the dominant paradigm of Christian mission with the *missio Dei*. Inherently in the current reframing there is an attempt to recognize God's saving grace evident in the other—including the religious other—while holding on to the truth that God has been revealed fully in Jesus Christ. In this task we need to be reminded that there is no "pure" gospel[12] and that in today's pluralistic world the gospel has often been tainted. Where initially the missionary was challenged to not bring a double-sided gospel—the gospel of Jesus Christ and one's own culture—today's challenge includes not affirming the negative historical and contextual connotation of the gospel in a particular locale. The gospel today has been embedded in many cultural and religious traditions, though often only partially and sometimes misleadingly; yet, the gospel of Jesus Christ is enculturated.[13] Not affirming this reality only reinforces some of the negative neocolonial connotations that have attached to the gospel. Even though today's context may determine a different frame for Christian mission, the beauty of Scripture is that there is not one expression of doing Christian mission but rather a plurality of expressions.

Christian mission *with* the people is a radical embrace of the divine in the other. This approach attempts to discern and participate in God's mission *with*

---

[12]David J. Bosch, *Transforming Mission: Paradigm Shifts in Theology of Mission* (Maryknoll, NY: Orbis Books, 1991), 297.

[13]In practical terms this would mean, for example, Christian mission *among* the people would see a Muslim view of Jesus Christ as a mere prophet and seek to point out the rest of the truth of Jesus Christ, just as Paul did mission *among* the Athenians. Yet, we need to be reminded that Paul did not face an audience that experienced a gospel that has been tainted but rather heard the gospel about Jesus Christ for the first time. On the other hand, Christian mission *with* the people would come alongside and affirm that Jesus Christ is a prophet in order to learn from and communicate with those of other faiths. In many Western societies the role of prophet no long exists. Therefore, there is much one can learn from Muslim friends who might have a much closer biblical understanding of Jesus Christ as a prophet, and there is much to learn about who Christ is from that understanding. Of course, in that journey together, seeking and proclaiming who Christ is, Christian missionaries can fill in aspects that their faith tradition has revealed about Jesus Christ.

the people as they move beyond the one piece of the mirror—the truth that we are holding so dearly—toward recognizing that even though we have the fullness, our search should be for the wholeness. This is a shift in mission thinking from a superiority position of mission to understanding mission as humility. Mission then is understood as entering into the triune God's redemptive work in the other. The other may also minister to the missionary in order to move beyond the boundaries that we have set before God that limit our own missional engagement. This is what we read in the story of Peter and Cornelius, the pivotal point of the Gentile mission as Luke tells the story in Acts.

In the encounter of Peter and Cornelius we see how the early church learns to embrace God's Spirit at work in the other. The unfolding story of God's revelation in this passage becomes a prophetic corrective for Peter and the early church. The encounter, and Peter's openness to the Spirit, changed church policy, mission practice and theology. Building on this, I will discuss implications for discerning and participating in God's mission in today's pluralistic world. To frame this discussion, I have identified three main stages that characterize and define a Cornelius encounter: (1) a receptive individual encounters the divine, (2) the receptive (now enlightened) individual encounters a parallel yet "other" enlightened individual and (3) post-encounter (now twice enlightened) individuals interact with their respective (responsive) communities.

RECEPTIVE INDIVIDUAL ENCOUNTERS THE DIVINE: THE CORNELIUS ENCOUNTER IN THE SELF

Mission history was changed as two men, Peter and Cornelius, set aside time to seek God in prayer. Mission flows out of this intimacy with God. However, traditionally, mission has been understood primarily as the activities of the church and our spirituality as a separate part of our faith. Rowan Williams reaffirms this by noting that usually we "think of 'mission' and 'spirituality' as pointing in different directions—the communication of faith and the cultivation of faith."[14] However, if we understand today that mission is about who God is,[15] then missions and spirituality are formed in the discerning of and participating in the *missio Dei*.

---

[14]Rowan Williams, *A Ray of Darkness: Sermons and Reflections* (Cambridge, MA: Cowley, 1995), 221.
[15]Pernia, "State of Mission Today," 11.

Fuller's leading practitioners and scholars, such as Jude Tiersma Watson[16] and L. Paul Jensen, are articulating new practices in Christian spirituality that shape Christian mission. In the increasingly hurried pace of today's lifestyles in our urban pluralistic society, it is important to be reminded again how Christian spirituality and Christian mission are inseparably linked. Jensen rightly observes in Scripture and church history that an "empowered inward spirituality is correlated with transforming outward mission."[17] Christian mission should be marked by a contemplative presence with the people that then shapes our engagement.[18]

Mission is about God and his people participating in the redemptive mission of God in this world. Mission theology should describe not only the horizontal dimension of God's redemptive work but also a vertical dimension of being in intimacy with God. We see the *missio Dei* at work in Cornelius's prayer as God gives him the truthful message that he needs to seek a certain truth; therefore he becomes a bearer of truth as well as a recipient. The next day, God reveals to Peter another truth, a truth about purity and impurity, which he has a hard time accepting. Although divided by the faith boundary, Peter and Cornelius have parallel experiences, and in the end they are both moved to a new middle ground. Both have visions; both reach across the cultural division between Jew and Gentile, crossing social boundaries. In the end, Peter compares and identifies with Cornelius's household ("just as we," Acts 10:47) instead of contrasting with them.

Therefore, for Peter, the Cornelius encounter meant facing a Roman centurion with greater social status and power, a representative of the government that had long oppressed his own people, the Jews, and also an individual who challenged his core religious beliefs regarding an unclean heathen. As I will share later in this essay, my first missional Cornelius encounter, which cast me as the privileged person encountering a mother who

---

[16]See articles by and interviews of Jude Tiersma Watson at Fuller's website Urban Youth Ministry Self-Care Toolkit, accessed January 27, 2016, https://fulleryouthinstitute.org/urban/toolkit.

[17]L. Paul Jensen, *Subversive Spirituality: Transforming Mission Through the Collapse of Space and Time* (Eugene, OR: Wipf & Stock, 2009), 260.

[18]For an example of mission as spirituality or how spirituality is shaping missional practices, see Pascal D. Bazzell and Amelia Ada-Bucog, "Subversive Urban Spirituality in Asian Cities: Transforming Spiritual Discipline and Missional Practices," in *Walking with God: Christian Spirituality in the Asian Contexts*, ed. Charles Ringma (Quezon City, Philippines: OMF Literature, 2014), 194-204.

was facing homelessness. Thus, one can experience a Cornelius encounter in relation to a person or community of any social status, culture or religion other than one's own. In such an encounter, a conversion takes place on both sides, not only in Cornelius, as is traditionally recognized, but also in Peter, who undergoes a change of heart that broadens his understanding of God's mission. Even though Peter had the fullness of the truth that was given to him by Christ, he needed the encounter with Cornelius to show him where he had put boundaries that limited his engagement in the *missio Dei*.

THE CORNELIUS ENCOUNTER BREAKING DOWN LANDSCAPES OF EXCLUSIONS: RECEPTIVE (NOW ENLIGHTENED) INDIVIDUAL ENCOUNTERS A PARALLEL YET "OTHER" ENLIGHTENED INDIVIDUAL

A missiology that attempts to discern the work of the Spirit outside our sociocultural, theological and ecclesiastical boundaries must allow room for the infinite in the finite other, even the infinite in the religious other. In so doing, we do not deny our Christian faith but rather engage in a truth-seeking endeavor with the other for the purpose of mutual edification.

Fuller has been at the forefront in discerning that the unifying work of the Spirit does not operate only within the boundaries of our Christian communities. Just as the Holy Spirit helped Peter cross cultural and theological boundaries, so today the Holy Spirit seeks to break down our own landscape of exclusion. The Holy Spirit continues to create these in-between-space encounters that challenge some of our boundaries and may provoke resistance and division in Christian communities. However, these encounters often result in an embrace of crucial paradigm shifts in order to participate in the unifying eschatological fruit of God's kingdom.

While Peter bridged a greater gap for Cornelius, Cornelius also bridged a gap for Peter. God used with Peter the image of a sheet holding unclean foods as a metaphor. Then Cornelius and Peter are placed in a similar metaphoric relation, having been led to this relationship by their respective revelations. They are unlike but related as recipients of differing revelations. A new, unique meaning arises as they are juxtaposed. This is where the Holy Spirit locates his work, between the actors, not in or to

Peter or Cornelius alone.[19] Missional fruitfulness paralleling this account rests on revelation that arises first between individuals and God; this fruitfulness is increased as revelation arises between inspired individuals and other inspired individuals. The mistake for mission would be to assume falsely that either all revelation is equal or that no revelation at all may exist on the other side of our extension with the gospel. The task of missiology is to discern the degree and kind of revelation that is in play on both sides of the mission frontier.

Mission, then, is entering into and participating with the triune God's ongoing dialogue that is taking place in the space between God's self and the other. This creates a complex dialectic space. Once it is perceived that we stand between God and the other, we can see that dialogue extends simultaneously between God and us, between God and the other, and between us and the other. The other always stands in the gap between God and us, just as we stand in the gap between God and the other, even though our bridging may be to varying degrees.

Discerning and participating in the unifying work of the Spirit outside our boundaries is not always easy, as language and categories often differ from what we are used to in our Christian communities. However, to announce the king's arrival, Scripture tells us that God used a variety of prophetic means. God sent angels to the shepherds (Lk 2:8-20). Scripture also tells us of "wise men" whose religious practices included astrology, which they employed to learn the mysteries of the universe. Their discernment led them to the star and then to the king of the Jews, whom they worshiped (Mt 2:1-12). We even see God describing a pagan king as "my servant King Nebuchadrezzar" (Jer 43:10) and the Persian Cyrus as "[my] anointed" (Is 45:1). Amos Yong points out that "if the glory of the new heaven and (new) earth will be constituted in part by what kings and nations bring into the New Jerusalem (Rev. 21:24, 26), it is

---

[19]Paul Ricoeur points out that metaphor holds unlike objects or ideas in relation and that, when it does, a unique meaning arises in the space(s) between them in a way that cannot be articulated without using the metaphor. Metaphor requires participants that differ from each other since, if they are the same, no metaphor develops. See Paul Ricoeur, *The Rule of Metaphor: The Creation of Meaning in Language / Uniform Title: Métaphore vive*, English Routledge classics (London: Routledge, 2003). I learned a lot from Adam Ayers's discourses on Ricoeur and the concept of meaning arising in this in-between space from his SIS doctoral dissertation, "In Search of the Contours of a Missiological Hermeneutic" (PhD thesis, Fuller Theological Seminary School of Intercultural Studies, Pasadena, CA, 2011).

inconceivable that such will be bereft of the beauty found in other faiths."[20] Hence, we need a missiological theology of discernment that attempts greater affirmation of the awareness of God's presence in others. Hopefully this nurtures a spirit of humility that recognizes the importance of the other and qualifies a tendency toward an excessively triumphalist spirit that still exists in some mission practices and theologies. Mission today should be marked by humility as we come to understand that mission is God's alone and not ours.

With this new understanding, we don't do biblical missiology that assumes a unified mission practice and theology for each context, but we do missiology that is biblically informed or formed. I do not advocate producing a blurry syncretism or emphasizing context over Scripture, but I do wish to address the prevalent word-flesh and spirit-flesh dichotomies in contemporary missiology. Where the former (Christian tradition based on the Word of God) attempts to theologically frame the latter (the winds of the divine), whose very nature is that it "blows where it chooses" (Jn 3:8), tension is created in our mission practices and theology. However, the strength of the discipline of missiology is that if it is rightly applied, it is able to dance between both, between being rooted in Scripture and traditions and discerning and participating with the *missio Dei*, and the *missio Spiritus* more specifically, in each local context. If missiology is able to hold this tension together, then it can be truly "the mother of theology" as it has not only been the mother of the New Testament but also becomes the mother of the church and theology today.[21]

Missiology inherently involves study to discern the presence, activity and even absence[22] of the *missio Dei*. However, discerning "genuine works of God" is not always easy because ideologies might just look like the work of God, as Scott W. Sunquist has pointed out.[23] Part of missiology's disciplinary mandate,

---

[20]Amos Yong, "Missiology and Mission Theology in an Interfaith World: A (Humble) Manifesto," *Evangelical Interfaith Dialogue* 5, no. 2 (2014): 6.

[21]Scott W. Sunquist, *Understanding Christian Mission: Participation in Suffering and Glory* (Grand Rapids: Baker Academic, 2013), 10.

[22]Amos Yong has written extensively on how the Holy Spirit can be present and absent in contexts. See Amos Yong, *Discerning the Spirit(s): A Pentecostal-Charismatic Contribution to Christian Theology of Religions*, Journal of Pentecostal Theology Supplement Series 20 (Sheffield, UK: Sheffield Academic Press, 2000), particularly 127-29, and Amos Yong, *Beyond the Impasse: Toward a Pneumatological Theology of Religions* (Grand Rapids: Baker Academic, 2003).

[23]Sunquist, *Understanding Christian Mission*, 145.

then, entails looking beyond the development of strategies or models intended to precipitate Cornelius events while also discerning existing Cornelius encounters in the witnesses of the biblical writers, in church history and in the voices of others around the globe today. Attuning missiology's discernment toward discerning Cornelius encounters empowers missiology to recognize within a broad spectrum of others' experiences God's mysterious work of redemption, and it strengthens missiology's fulfillment of its disciplinary vision. Further, just as it did in the apostles' day, responsiveness to God's revelatory work in the other provides a safeguard for the church against the kinds of well-intentioned yet excessive exclusionary or doctrinaire theological articulation that may hinder Christian mission's divine purpose. The strength then of missiology may not reside in its maintenance of creedal formation and theological doctrines but in its ongoing practice of learning to discern the *missio Dei* as God's redemptive work. From the past to present, we continue to seek ways to participate in his mission.

My Cornelius encounter: seeking the divine in the excluded. I had my first Cornelius encounter as a grad student in a class titled Theology of the City. One of our tasks was to do an urban ethnography of our city. Although I had lived in that Asian city for many years, I was surprised to find that, instead of some individual beggars or street kids living on the streets, we found whole communities that had made the streets their home, some even for decades.[24] Being moved by their many stories, I believe under the prompting of the Holy Spirit, we decided to continue our visits on the streets beyond our class requirements, a mission that I ended up serving full time for ten years.

After just a few months of regularly visiting the streets, I had my Cornelius experience with Mary, a homeless mother of seven children. I remember well the shock I felt when I heard that Mary's daughter, Joy, was missing. Fond memories of playing with her just the night before prompted feelings of fear and concern. Joy was only three years old. She had the kind of personality that made her unforgettable—a little girl with a big smile, full of joy. When she saw you across the park or sidewalk, she would run to you

---

[24]I describe an ethnography of such a community in my book, Pascal D. Bazzell, *Urban Ecclesiology: Gospel of Mark, Familia Dei and a Filipino Community Facing Homelessness*, Ecclesiological Investigations 19 (New York: Bloomsbury T&T Clark, 2015).

and whole-heartedly embrace you. Joy had lived all her life on the streets with her mother and other siblings. When she went missing, we started looking for her. The police got involved, posters were put up and emergency prayer requests were sent out around the globe.

Three days later, I sat down with Mary, and she recounted her experience. Devastated that Joy could not be found, as you can imagine, Mary was totally panicked, hysterical, crying all the time. Then, on the evening of the second day, at 6:00 p.m., she told me that the "peace of the Lord" came upon her. She knew Joy was okay. She got up, showered and sat down at the city park where she was living with her children. At 8:00 p.m. the police brought Joy back to her. When she asked them when they found her, they told her that it had been at 6:00 p.m.

I had just started my missional engagement with the urban poor, and this experience nurtured a crucial shift in me. From the outside, Mary appeared to be anything but a believer. She had had seven children with three husbands; the children were neglected, dirty and struggling. Yet, in this incident I learned that Mary, while living on the streets, had many experiences with God that opened my eyes further to God's mysterious work. Scripture talks about an assurance of Christ's presence not only among those who confess him and his second coming but also among the poor (Mt 25:31-46).[25]

The narrator of Peter and Cornelius's encounter points out explicitly that Cornelius was a devout and God-fearing man: he prayed regularly, and he had a generous heart toward those in need. To be able to discern the *missio Dei* in today's pluralistic world, one has to be attentive to the cries of the oppressed. Because Christ promises his presence among the destitute, and the *missio Spiritus* aims to always point toward that presence, the voice of the *missio Dei* is often best heard in those marginal communities.

Our Cornelius encounter: finding the divine with the excluded. Christian mission *with* the people is attentive to the divine in the excluded. It was clear for Peter, the apostles and the early church that if a Gentile would embrace the gospel, then he or she must surely first become a Jew. This was black and white; no unclean Gentile would ever have eternal life and become part of God's people. Even when Peter had a vision from God,

---

[25]Jürgen Moltmann, *The Church in the Power of the Spirit: A Contribution to Messianic Ecclesiology* (Minneapolis: Fortress, 1993), 122-23.

he resisted change: "[Peter] saw the heaven opened and something like a large sheet coming down, being lowered to the ground by its four corners. In it were all kinds of four-footed creatures and reptiles and birds of the air. Then he heard a voice saying, 'Get up, Peter; kill and eat'" (Acts 10:11-13). Still Peter's response was, "By no means, Lord!" Scripture tells us that "this happened three times" (Acts 10:16).

We don't know why Jesus' main ministry on earth was to minister to the Jews only. For Peter and the early church, it seemed obvious that if the excluded Gentiles would like to follow Christ, they were to become like Jews. Philip F. Esler points out that Jews in the first century CE "were zealous in keeping themselves apart from the Gentiles by means of definite boundaries which were perceived as originating in the Mosaic code."[26] Jesus had broken down many religious boundaries and social taboos during his time, but never under the guidance of the Spirit did he embrace Gentiles the way Peter and the early church did. However, it was clear that the work of the Spirit was leading Peter, even after years with Christ, to think differently. For Esler, then, the story is much more than the gospel being preached to the Gentiles. Peter's choice to enter an unclean house and eat with Gentiles had great ethnic and social implications.[27] The church in Jerusalem took issue not with Peter baptizing the uncircumcised but with his presence in table fellowship with them. Therefore, vănThành Nguyễn is right to note that the Peter and Cornelius story "is not the legitimacy of the Gentile mission or admission into the church but the legitimacy of complete integration of Jews and Gentiles in the Christian community which included table fellowship."[28] Antonio Pernia points out that

the primary image Jesus used for the kingdom was table fellowship, the subject of many of his parables and the object of many meals he shared with outcasts and sinners. Through this image Jesus announced that God . . . was inviting everyone—everyone without exception—to communion with him.[29]

---

[26]Philip F. Esler, *Community and Gospel in Luke-Acts: The Social and Political Motivations of Lucan Theology* (Cambridge: Cambridge Press, 1987), 84.

[27]Ibid., 93.

[28]vanThanh Nguyen, *Peter and Cornelius: A Story of Conversion and Mission* (Eugene, OR: Pickwick, 2012), 80.

[29]Antonio M. Pernia et al., *The Eucharist and Our Mission*, Following the Word 7 (Rome: SVD, 1996), 38.

Most churches have some kind of boundaries or exclusions to their table fellowship. Even Jesus initially excluded the Syrophoenician woman from table fellowship but was then confronted by the woman's faith, creating an in-between space that only the Holy Spirit could create. The encounter contributed to breaking down Jesus' social marker, extending God's healing and the offering of deliverance to the excluded.[30] As noted earlier, boundaries are not bad; they give a sense of belonging and identity, protecting the purity of one's faith, and yet the challenging question is, what are boundaries that need to be re-evaluated, negotiated or even reimagined? Ongoing self-critique and self-awareness can serve to ensure that we don't exclude where we are supposed to participate with the other in the *missio Dei*.

POST-ENCOUNTER (NOW TWICE ENLIGHTENED) INDIVIDUALS INTERACT WITH THEIR RESPECTIVE (RESPONSIVE) COMMUNITIES

Meeting Mary and her community has been truly transformative for my own missional journey. This journey has deepened my understanding of God and his mysterious work among us. I remember well, on one of our community visits, Mary told us that her husband had been killed. With horror I looked into her daughter Joy's teary eyes as this three-year-old girl showed me on her own body where her father had been stabbed when she saw him. As we asked a street-living community of around two hundred people how they would respond to this tragedy of losing a member, they shared that they wanted to meet every Tuesday and start praying for protection for their community. Another time, knowing that some of us were pastors, they asked us if we would baptize one of the newborn babies. In my book, *Urban Ecclesiology: Gospel of Mark,* Familia Dei *and a Filipino Community Facing Homelessness*, I describe how one ecclesial practice after another became part of Mary's community.[31] However, when I have examined works on ecclesiology, church planting and homeless populations, I have found little that could help me in my journey. In the literature,

---

[30]See also Pascal D. Bazzell, "A Marginal Asian Reading of Mark 7:24-30: An Inter-Faith Homeless Ecclesial Community's Encounter with the Syrophoenician Woman," in *Pathways for Inter-Religious Dialogue in the Twenty-First Century*, ed. Vladimir Latinovic, Gerard Mannion and Peter C. Phan (New York: Palgrave Macmillan, 2015), 231-43.

[31]Pascal D. Bazzell, *Urban Ecclesiology: Gospel of Mark,* Familia Dei *and a Filipino Community Facing Homelessness* (New York: Bloomsbury T&T Clark: 2015).

there is an extensive dialogue regarding ecclesiology, church planting and the poor. However, as soon as the discussion turns to those facing homelessness, the approaches are focused primarily on commodity-based benevolence with a rescue and rehabilitation mentality.

Doing Christian mission *to* those facing homelessness (service provider) and being *among* them (sharing the gospel) have often diminished the ecclesial communal work of the Holy Spirit (a communion-in-between). The Spirit of God directs not only toward the *imago Christi* but toward each other in order to embody the gospel of Jesus Christ among real relationships, known as the church. The story of Peter and Cornelius reveals that the inaugural mission to the Gentiles did not focus merely on Cornelius; it included his whole household. As we reflect on mission today in our pluralistic world, we need to ask ourselves, where are the spaces in our neighborhoods, our nations that we traditionally might exclude? Or in the case of Mary's community, which could be seen as a traditional target group, we might ask how we are missing the pneumatological work of the communion-in-between and, hence, missing participation in the *missio Dei* in that place.

From a theological perspective, one can easily justify excluding other forms of faith communities. However, if we embrace the *missio Dei* in the other—doing Christian mission *with* the people—then the church is not limited by the boundaries that prevent engaging with the other. The church enters into the *missio Dei* as if on a pilgrimage, constantly negotiating and reimagining its existing boundaries with actual neighbors. This is the beauty of Scripture: it does not provide one definition of church as a static and fixed entity. Instead, it imagines a church that exists in missional engagement with the church's physical neighbors. One of the fundamental issues, then, in the twenty-first century will continue to be an exploration of the role of the church in this in-between space. How will the church embody the gospel with actual neighbors and neighborhoods influenced by globalization, migration (including undocumented immigrants and refugees) and technology?

Christian mission seeks a relationship that invites us to discern the *missio Dei* in the actual neighbor. Walking together, the journey becomes an opportunity to seek the wholeness of God's truth. This in-between space transforms church theology and mission practices as we discover new dimensions of God's leading spirit. When we talk, for example, about the fruit of the Spirit (Gal 5:22-23), these fruits are best discerned in oppositions. It is one thing to demonstrate "love, joy, peace, patience, kindness, generosity, faithfulness, gentleness, and self-control" in many of our homogenous churches, although even that is sometimes difficult. But it is another thing when we experience these fruits in the context of grave difference. Discerning the *missio Dei* requires being attentive to the unifying and reconciling work of the Spirit of God, which we can experience anew if we allow ourselves to journey with our actual neighbors. Mission, then, is not about what the church does but about discerning and participating with the mystery in the other—the mystery of the triune God who is actively involved in the midst of all humanity.[32]

In order to grasp the significance of what transpired between Peter and Cornelius, we need the community of believers to be fully engaged in the process of discernment. The church as a hermeneutical community is an integral component of mission theology. Yet, the church in Acts does not interpret unilaterally. It interprets in and across the space between itself and others. As Peter and Cornelius interact with each other, they also must interact with their communities. As Paul Ricouer's work with metaphor has pointed out, unique meaning arises in the space between the identities involved in juxtaposition.[33]

In the case of Peter and Cornelius, the Holy Spirit generates special meaning between the individual actors and between their communities. One metaphor arises between them as individuals, another arises between each and his respective community, and still another arises between the communities. This robust kind of revelation reaches its peak in the truth that arises throughout the complex of interactions involving Peter and Cornelius as inspired individuals and their representative communities, and it arises as they share the fruits of their individual and group encounters with their communities. The Spirit's unique revelation emerges in this type of encounter when (1) a receptive individual encounters the divine, (2) the receptive (now enlightened) individual encounters a parallel yet "other" enlightened individual and (3) post-encounter (now twice enlightened) individuals interact with their respective (responsive) communities. As we

---

[32]See also Pernia, "State of Mission Today," 20.
[33]Ricoeur, *The Rule of Metaphor.*

look for Cornelius encounters, we should keep in mind that it is crucial for all to participate and to see the moment through to its end. All three stages of relating must proceed effectively if new revelation is to arise in a way that sets precedent and transforms movements (and mission). Even though good can result from proceeding through any stage, it is most fruitful to follow through all stages successfully. This is when major breakthroughs in mission history occur.

WHO IS OUR CORNELIUS? EMBODYING TRUTH IN RELATION WITH THE OTHER

Who is our Cornelius? This is the penetrating question of this essay. This is not an abstract question that should guide us into a philosophical inquiry concerned with otherness. The question—who is our Cornelius?—is about our actual neighbors with whom the local church is or should be in relation. It challenges our claim of truth to embody this truth in relation with the other.

While in Asia recently, I had another Cornelius encounter with Muslim followers of Jesus Christ. I asked them, "Where do you see the divinity in Jesus Christ?" I assumed it would be in Jesus' healing ministry, the miracles, maybe the exorcism, his preachings, or even his resurrection and ascension. However, one interviewee answered me with the following reflections:

> I see His divinity when he was crucified. I really did not like that part in the beginning of my faith. But I saw how submissive he was. He did not have to go through it, but he did. . . . He really showed his divinity through full submission to the Father and dying on the cross for the sins of the world. He is showing the world that we should be submissive as he, being Christ, submitted to the Father, so should we submit to the will of God. . . . Hence, I see the divinity in Christ's submission. Christ submitted to the perfect will of the Father by dying on the cross. He could have said no, because he is all-powerful. He is showing us an example as he perfectly submits to God's will.[34]

---

[34]Interview 35 in the Philippines. This is part of my current postdoctoral research, titled "Inter-religious Christology: An Intercultural Theology of Southeast Asian Muslims," which is funded by the Swiss National Science Foundation. For more information, please see http://p3.snf.ch/project-155138, accessed January 27, 2016.

That Muslim follower of Christ concluded his reflection stating, "Islam means submission; that is why Isa is Islam" (P-35). In line with this Islamic teaching on submission, another Muslim follower of Christ pointed out that he sees Jesus' divinity in his ability to fully and perfectly commit himself to the will of God. This interviewee stated: "Christ's divinity manifested in the prayer Garden: not my will but yours be done" (P-37). This person concluded with the following statement: "No human can ever do that except God, and hence Isa, Jesus Christ, is God" (P-37).

Until that moment I had never reflected on Jesus' humanity and the concept of submission. It truly opened my eyes to see in Scripture how submissive Jesus truly was and to recognize that his obedience is a central message of the gospel. Whereas my traditional christological interest lay in how God became human, my Muslim brothers emphasized Jesus' being the perfect human and thus sought how as humans we can become more human (see 1 Jn 4:1-3). If interreligious theology is "the future shape of theology," as German theologian Perry Schmidt-Leukel has argued at the renowned 2015 Gifford Lectures in Scotland (forthcoming) and in other writings,[35] then missiology, as a discipline that attempts to discern and describe God's historical redemptive work in the other, provides a unique and important contribution to contemporary global theological discourses. This concept has missiological implications for the church as it aims to cross boundaries and seeks to achieve mutual transformations.

Christian mission *with* one's neighbors requires entering into this in-between space on a relational level, not for the purpose of producing a metareligion or metatheology, but in order to attest to our statements of truth. An example would be to demonstrate our claim that Jesus Christ is the only way, truth and life by living out tangible tensions with our actual neighbors in our neighborhoods—the imam, the rabbi, the monk, the prostitute, the businessperson. Christian mission *with* the people holds our claims within the tensions of universality and particularly for the sake of seeing the gospel fleshed out in the cultural human media of our contemporary world. In so doing, we might augment the contents of those

---

[35]See, e.g., Perry Schmidt-Leukel and Reinhold Bernhardt, eds., *Interreligiöse Theologie: Chancen und Probleme* (Zürich: Theologischer Verlag Zürich, 2013).

theological statements[36] that we have received, as both they and we are being gradually revealed, each uniquely, that we may with all the saints comprehend a bit better who this Jesus Christ is that we call Lord and Savior. In this approach, mission theology in our contemporary pluralistic societies is best done when truth is articulated not exclusively from inside our own religious boundaries but in the dynamic, tangible in-between, taking into consideration the truth of the other.

The story of Peter and Cornelius leaves the church and missiology today with a deep challenge. Who is our Cornelius? This question is a challenge to embrace the Holy Spirit's guidance, which may invite us to be defiled, to become unclean, in the eyes of fellow believers in order to discover more fully the divine in the excluded. In conclusion, Christian mission *with* the people is about being co-pilgrims in faith with the other, together seeking and proclaiming who God is. Consequently, mission is not only about *giving* but also *receiving*, not only about *evangelizing* but also *being evangelized*. Mission becomes sharing *to* and hearing *from* the mystery work of the triune God in the other in order to participate *with* God's mission.

---

[36]For example, in ecclesiology, to avoid an abstract and idealistic view of the church, we need to examine the theological statements we have received concerning the ecclesiality (essence of the church) in the local church (empirical ecclesiology). Ecclesiality is about the indispensable ecclesial markers (see Bazzell, *Urban Ecclesiology*, 47-71). However, these ecclesial markers (i.e., marks of the church) are neither static nor fixed, and a fixed definition would merely promote a "perfect" nature of the church that the historical and empirical reality of the church would not be able to reach; hence, it would produce an abstract ecclesiology that has little bearing on the local churches. Therefore, I argue for a rereading of the ecclesiality embodied in the locality that unpacks an empirical understanding of the essence of the church that contributes not only to "a deeper understanding of the substance of the church, but also gives a needed realigning of its shape and missional output." Pascal D. Bazzell, "Towards an Empirical-Ideal Ecclesiology: On the Dynamic Relation Between Ecclesiality and Locality," *Ecclesiology* 11, no. 2 (2015): 235.

Rethinking the Nature of Christian Mission

A South Korean Perspective

Moonjang Lee

INTRODUCTION

While we celebrate the dawning of a global Christianity through the cross-cultural expansion of the gospel during the last two centuries, today we also find ourselves in the midst of great changes and even in a crisis in global Christianity. Now we say that Christian mission is at a crossroads. The modern Western missionary era has ended, and a new paradigm for global mission has not yet been devised. Although various aspects of the colonial paradigm for Christian mission have undergone revisions in order to negotiate with the changing environment in global contexts, we might say that we are still trapped in an old habit of thought and practice in Christian mission that needs radical adjustment and modification. In this chapter I will seek to add a new ingredient in our search for a breakthrough in Christian mission in rapidly changing global contexts.

GLOBAL CHRISTIANITY

In the history of Christianity, the last two centuries were unprecedented as the gospel was delivered to all the nations in the world. In 2010 we celebrated the centennial of the 1910 Edinburgh World Mission Conference, and, in the wake of this monumental occasion, the *Atlas of Global Christianity* was published. The use of the phrase "global Christianity" in the title was intended to emphasize that Christianity has become a global phenomenon. We do not hesitate in acknowledging that world Christianity was the fruit of the modern missionary movement of Western churches. Western churches and missionaries have done a marvelous job in bringing the gospel to the nations. Their labors and sacrifices were the very foundation of the churches in the non-Western world.

F. F. Bruce used the title of *The Spreading Flame* (1980) to describe the rise and progress of early Christianity, highlighting the fact that the expansion of the early churches was rapid and successful.[1] The modern missionary movement during the last two centuries was a similarly spectacular phenomenon in bringing the gospel to the whole world, like a spreading flame.

We find another similarity between the early Christian expansion and the modern Western missionary movement in that both progressed side by side with colonial expansion. While the early missionary outreach was expedited by *via Romana*, the modern Western missionary movement cashed in on the colonial expansion of European imperialism. Wittingly and unwittingly, the expansion of Christianity during the colonial period was done hand in hand with the Western colonial conquest. As a result, Christian mission has been intertwined with the image of Western colonial dominance. Ironically, the historical association of Western Christian mission with Western colonialism eventually served as one of the causes for the retreat of Western mission.

A CHANGED REALITY: THE END OF THE COLONIAL ERA

While Western colonialism served as one of the most significant contributing factors for the global expansion of Christianity, the end of Western colonialism also exerted an enormous impact in modern Christian history. The end of Western colonialism symbolized the sunset (using Donald McGavran's metaphor) of Western missions, and we are expecting that a new sun will rise for global mission sooner rather than later. In this postcolonial era, we have come to realize that the business-as-usual attitude does not work any longer and that we must deal with the colonial legacy of Christian missions, including the pattern of colonial mission, the image of Christianity and the colonial understanding of the nature of Christian mission.

---

[1] Cf. F. F. Bruce, *The Spreading Flame: The Rise and Progress of Christianity from Its First Beginnings to the Conversion of the English* (Milton Keynes, UK: Paternoster, 1980).

By and large, Western missionaries came to the colonized lands as allies of the colonial process in the early stage of Western expansion. They worked under the aegis of the colonial powers, and their missionary engagements were facilitated by what we call "Western premium" as they brought commerce and civilization to Africa and Asia, along with Christianity. So it is said that Western missionaries brought three Cs (commerce, civilization and Christianity) to the primitive colonized world. Part of their task as missionaries was to help the local people upgrade their standard of living, providing them with advanced educational institutions and medical facilities. Therefore, Western missionaries were perceived as coming from rich countries to poor, remote and primitive regions to impart the benefits of civilization.

With the changing climate in the postcolonial season of Christian mission, the demand to find a new direction or a new paradigm for mission became essential, and mission scholars (including practitioners) were busy devising new mission strategies relevant to the changing postcolonial milieu. So the churches began to scrutinize various presuppositions and practices readily accepted during the colonial era. One of the new perspectives is related to the direction of Christian mission.

The direction of Christian mission in the New Testament was from a small, less civilized Palestinian country called Israel to a more civilized Roman Empire and to its burgeoning cities. Although the Jewish people might have felt proud of their own cultural heritage, the Roman culture and civilization were much more advanced and highly sophisticated from a secular standpoint. Moreover, Israel was one of the Roman occupations. The direction of the early Christian mission from a poor, less civilized and colonized country to the rich, highly civilized Roman Empire contrasts starkly with that of the modern Western mission. The early Christian mission could never enjoy the support of the colonial empire. Rather, the colonial power ruthlessly cracked down on the missionary movement. The apostle Paul was a good example. In his relentless missionary outreach Paul did not have any political power supporting his work. No identifiable rich sending church provided mission funds for him. Paul supported himself through his tent-making business. He did not bring with him an education team or a medical team from Israel to help enlighten and upgrade the living standards of the local people within the Roman Empire. Such a thing was neither imaginable nor realistic. Paul had to rely solely on

the power of the gospel, which he delivered boldly, even in the face of opposition and persecution. We might say that Paul brought three *P*s: poverty,
power of the gospel (in the power of the Holy Spirit) and persecution.

This seemingly simple observation implies that we may urgently need to
restore the very nature of Christian mission in the twenty-first century.
Christian mission in the twenty-first century faces the hostile world without
such premium factors as commerce and civilization. The most essential element for Christian mission will be the power of the gospel. The missionaries
might be from poor African or Asian countries to rich and affluent Western
countries and vice versa. In this regard, the Christian mission in the coming
decades will become multidirectional, from everywhere to everywhere. This
reflection demands that we discard the old presuppositions or habits of
thought in Christian mission as these were formed in the colonial framework.

GLOBAL DE-CHRISTIANIZATION

As early as 1976 Andrew Walls pointed out that the modern Western missionary movement brought about a shift in the center of Christian gravity
from the West to Africa, South America and some parts of Asia. Walls wrote
that within the last three centuries Christianity has grown from a "tribal
religion of the Caucasian peoples" to a world phenomenon.[2] Lamin Sanneh
has suggested that Christianity might have become a non-Western religion.[3]
Christendom in the former centers of Christianity collapsed, and new
centers of Christianity emerged at what were once considered the periphery.
However, ironically enough, what we observe in the postcolonial world is a
kind of global de-Christianization.

The Western countries have been the heartland of Christianity. That's why
Christianity has been perceived to be a Western religion. However, Western
societies can no longer be characterized as Christian. It is widely recognized
that the West has become post-Christian—secularized, reflecting the waning
of the Christian influence in society in general. Walls said that Christianity in
the West, in Europe in particular, is "in marked recession, losing in adhesion,

---

[2]Andrew Walls, "Towards an Understanding of Africa's Place in Christian History," in *Religion in
a Pluralistic Society*, ed. J. S. Pobee (Leiden: Brill, 1976), 180.
[3]Cf. Lamin Sanneh, *Whose Religion Is Christianity?: The Gospel Beyond the West* (Grand Rapids:
Eerdmans, 2003).

respect and influence."[4] As the churches decline, it is said that Christianity has become a nocturnal religion in that churchgoers prefer to remain anonymous in religious practice and feel ashamed to expose their Christian identity in public. This de-Christianization of the Western societies may also be described as implying a de-Westernization of Christianity. The implications of this fact need further reflection.

The situation in places where the newly emerging Christian centers are located is not all that favorable. The de-Westernization of Christianity does not necessarily mean the Christianization of the non-Western world. The non-Western world has not been Christianized yet. In fact, it may be safe to say that the non-Western world is still a pre-Christian world. In the case of South Korea, one of the places in Asia where the churches grew remarkably in a short period of time, it would be more legitimate to say that South Korea is now a post-Confucian society. The shift in the Christian center of gravity is a phenomenon observed within Christian circles, and the newly emerging churches in the non-Western world exist mostly as minority groups within their respective wider secular arenas.

Moreover, there are several factors working as stumbling blocks for evangelism in the new centers of Christianity in the non-Western world. The first is the resurgence of other traditional religions like Buddhism and Islam. The second is the postcolonial ethos and the rise of neonationalism. The third is related to the second: the globalization of the anti-Christian sentiment or global hostility against Christianity. The fourth is the image of Christianity as a Western religion. The fixed image of Christianity as a Western religion acts as a hindrance for evangelism in many parts of Asia.

New Initiatives

Regardless of the enormous contributions of Western churches in the spread of global Christianity, some negative aspects of the colonial pattern for mission continue to receive criticism. One of those aspects has been the exclusivist approach of Western missionaries to local indigenous cultures. In the African context, Edward Fasholé-Luke expressed this aspect of Christian mission during the colonial era as follows:

---

[4]Walls, "Towards an Understanding of Africa's Place."

Western missionaries stressed aspects of discontinuity between Christianity and
African cultures and traditional religion to such an extent that they excluded the
aspects of continuity between Christianity and African cultures and traditional
religion. They condemned without proper evaluation African religious beliefs
and practices and substituted Western cultural and religious practices.[5]

This exclusivist approach of Western Christian missionaries has been under
critique in many parts of the non-Western world. There is one phrase being
circulated in Asian Christian circles that captures the negative sentiment of
Asian people toward the exclusivist and triumphalist approach of Western
Christian missions: "One more Christian, one less Chinese."[6]

There were many attempts to rectify this exclusivist approach by Western
mission scholars who grappled with the issue and tried to devise culturally
appropriate mission strategies enhancing the cross-cultural communication
of the gospel. The discourse of contextualization demonstrated this desire.
Some of the pioneering efforts were published in works by Eugene Nida,
Louis J. Luzbetak, Charles Kraft and Paul Hiebert.[7]

At the same time mission scholars noticed a significant change in the field
of missiology. As a result, a number of authors engaged in an exhaustive
search for a theology of mission that would be relevant and appropriate to
that changing reality.[8]

---

[5]Edward Fasholé-Luke, "Introduction," in *Christianity in Independent Africa*, ed. Edward
Fasholé-Luke, Richard Gray, Adrian Hastings and Godwin Tasie (Indianapolis: Indiana University Press, 1979), 357.

[6]There has been a slight controversy over the origin and authenticity of this phrase. See Darrell
Whiteman's answer to David M. Stowe's question in "Author's Reply," *International Bulletin of
Missionary Research* 21, no. 3 (1997): 106.

[7]Cf. Eugene Nida, *Customs and Cultures: Anthropology for Christian Missions* (New York: Harper
& Row, 1954); Louis J. Luzbetak, *The Church and Cultures: An Applied Anthropology for the Re-
ligion Worker* (New York: Orbis Books, 1976); Charles Kraft, *Christianity in Culture: A Study in
Dynamic Biblical Theologizing in Cross-Cultural Perspective* (New York: Orbis Books, 1979); and
Paul Hiebert, *Anthropological Insights for Missionaries* (Grand Rapids: Baker Academic, 1985).

[8]Gerald H. Anderson and Thomas F. Stransky, eds., *Mission Trends No. 1: Crucial Issues in Mis-
sion Today* (Grand Rapids: Eerdmans, 1974); idem, eds., *Mission Trends No. 2: Evangelization*
(Grand Rapids: Eerdmans, 1975); idem, eds., *Mission Trends No. 3: Third World Theologies*
(Grand Rapids: Eerdmans, 1976); William Jenkinson and Helene O'Sullivan, eds., *Trends in
Mission: Toward the Third Millennium; Essays in Celebration of Twenty-Five Years of Sedos* (New
York: Orbis Books, 1993); David Bosch, *Transforming Mission: Paradigm Shifts in Theology of
Mission* (New York: Orbis Books, 1994); James A. Scherer and Stephen B. Bevans, eds., *New
Directions in Mission & Evangelization* (New York: Orbis Books, 1992); Vinay Samuel and Chris
Sugden, eds., *Mission as Transformation: A Theology of the Whole Gospel* (Oxford: Regnum,
1999); James F. Engel and William A. Dyrness, *Changing the Mind of Missions: Where Have We*

In the wake of these great shifts in the mission environment and because of the sense of crisis in Protestant Christian mission, Donald McGavran founded the School of World Mission (SWM). McGavran and his associates called for new initiatives, new ways whereby the Christian church could be contextually appropriate among vastly different cultures.

A SOUTH KOREAN EXPERIENCE

Let me share stories of Christian history in South Korea as the churches there have experienced firsthand both this amazing expansion and de-Christianization. Korea is a country where traditional and folk religions like Buddhism, Confucianism, Taoism and shamanism have permeated the very fabric of people's everyday lives for thousands of years. Buddhism was the state religion on the Korean peninsula from the fourth century up to the end of the fourteenth century; Confucianism replaced Buddhism during the Chosun dynasty (1392–1910); and shamanism has formed the core of the religious consciousness of the Korean people since time immemorial.

The history of the Protestant churches in Korea is well over a century old now, and during the twentieth century Christian faith and practice became familiar to the Korean people. The introduction of Christianity to Korea in the late nineteenth century (1884) coincided with the collapse of the Chosun dynasty and the subsequent disintegration of traditional Confucian society. The introduction of Christianity to the Korean people was perceived as a providential arrangement in two respects. First, as the control of traditional society began to disintegrate, Korean people became disillusioned with and lost confidence in their traditional religions and were given the space to change their religious affiliations and practices without the organized persecution from the government that they had experienced in the eighteenth century. Second, those who delivered the gospel to the Korean people were not from Japan, which had colonized Korea. Many Korean people joined this new religion in the hope that they would defeat the Japanese colonial power and rebuild Korean society on the teachings of Christianity. In this regard, many Western missionaries

---

Gone Wrong? (Downers Grove, IL: InterVarsity Press, 2000); and Michael Pocock, Gailyn Van Rheenen and Douglas McConnell, *The Changing Face of World Missions: Engaging Contemporary Issues and Trends* (Grand Rapids: Baker Academic, 2005).

had done a tremendous job in enlightening and transforming the whole society by bringing Western civilization. So, the modern history of Korea cannot be told without the impact of Christianity.

The twentieth century for the Korean peninsula was a time of great upheaval and radical changes that would be characterized by modernization and Westernization. Every aspect of Korean society had to undergo a restructuring, and the church contributed significantly to the building of a new nation. Korean people responded enthusiastically to the positive role of the church in its early manifestation in Korea, and Christianity was able to penetrate Korean society. As a result, the church grew remarkably.

During the same period, the traditional religions looked dormant in the drive toward modernization, industrialization and Westernization. The explosive growth of the church gave the impression that Christianity now emerged as a new leading religion in Korea. Some Christians even expressed confidence that evangelization of the entire Korean society was just around the corner.

Entering the twenty-first century, however, we notice a significant change in the religious geography of Korean society. Too frequent immoral and unethical behavior among church leaders began to damage the integrity of the church, and the image of Christianity in Korea began deteriorate. Today, Korean people express more openly their negative and hostile sentiments against Christianity. Some even say that the church has become the main obstacle for evangelism. Today the anti-Christian sentiment is becoming stronger, and churches are losing members.

Another phenomenon we see is the resurgence of the traditional religions. Some years ago an autobiographical book by an American Buddhist monk titled *From Harvard to Hwa-gye Temple* became a bestseller in Korea. Many intellectuals who became disappointed or disillusioned with Christianity have turned to traditional religious teachings. In addition, as South Korea has developed into an industrialized, modernized and technological society, she has become more secularized, causing Korean people to lose interest in religious affiliation.

At this juncture the big issue for the Korean church is whether the churches can draw Korean people to Christianity. Korean Christians are pressed to discover how to renovate or reinvent Christianity in South Korea.

They may have to seek rather urgently a viable way for Christianity to negotiate its presence in the religious and spiritual milieu in Korea, competing with other traditional religions in the religious marketplace.

Can the churches in Korea be the primary source of hope for the Korean people again? Can the churches regain their spiritual authority to lead and influence the collective life of the Korean people? Korean Christians no longer feel optimistic about the future of the church in Korea. They may have to wage an uphill battle to restore the lost credibility of the church and to reinvent the once positive image of the church in the Korean society.

On a positive note, the strong anti-church sentiments of the Korean people may serve as an impetus for the Korean churches to pause and reflect seriously on ways to influence the religious consciousness of the Korean people and to upgrade the public image of the church.

IDENTIFYING THE MISSION: BECOMING CHRISTLIKE

We need to diagnose correctly the nature of the current situation of global Christianity. If we see global Christianity as prospering, we might continue to do business as usual. If we see global Christianity as being in crisis, we may have to find remedies to fix the situation. When a person is diagnosed with cancer, the doctor cannot give a prescription only to relieve the pain. Likewise, the way we diagnose the current situation of the church around the globe may dictate the way we devise remedies either to repair or to reformat Christianity. What, then, might be a correct diagnosis of the current situation in global Christianity? On the one hand, we celebrate the dawning of global Christianity in terms of the geographical spread of the gospel. On the other hand, we see global Christianity getting more ghettoized and relegated to its own sacred canopy, losing a sense of reality in the global theater and facing serious challenges from many different sides. If the latter is the case, we need to go beyond talking about strategies or methodologies of mission. A discourse of contextualization and cross-cultural communication is necessary. But we may need to find new ways to innovate or renovate Christianity.

The rise and progress of Christianity, like the spreading flame in early Christian history, was possible because the bearers of the gospel were authentic followers of Jesus Christ. The authority of the Christian churches was affirmed as church members practiced the teachings they had received from Jesus Christ. We know of Paul's exhortation to his Christian brothers and sisters in the city of Corinth: "Be imitators of me, as I am of Christ. I commend you because you remember me in everything and maintain the traditions just as I handed them on to you" (1 Cor 11:1-2). It is correct to say that the most effective and crucial element for evangelism in the early church was the quality of the messengers who demonstrated the true picture of disciples of Jesus Christ.

Here it may be meaningful to recall the so-called Tiger Woods effect. One reporter once wrote: "The number of people taking up the game of golf had increased at a rate of 5% a year since Tiger came on the scene. The annual rate of increase was only 1% before Tiger turned pro in 1996. That's one way to tell a mere star from a true icon: The former draws people to his games, but the latter draws people to *the* game."[9]

We need to produce or raise up Christians who will live Christianity on a different level. Those who truly embody or personify the Christian teaching will draw people to Christianity. So what really matters is the quality of Christians and of the churches.

In this regard, what the late John Stott said in his last sermon at the Keswick Convention in England also rings true for us in our search for ways to restore Christian influence in this secularized world.

Why is it, you must have asked, as I have, that in many situations our evangelistic efforts are often fraught with failure? Several reasons may be given and I do not want to over-simplify, but one main reason is that we don't look like the Christ we are proclaiming. John Poulton, who has written about this in a perceptive little book entitled, *A Today Sort of Evangelism*, wrote this:

The most effective preaching comes from those who embody the things they are saying. They are their message. Christians need to look like what they are talking about. It is people who communicate primarily, not words or ideas. Authenticity gets across. Deep down inside people, what communicates now is basically personal authenticity.

That is Christlikeness. Let me give you another example. There was a Hindu professor in India who once identified one of his students as a Christian and said to him: "If you Christians lived like Jesus Christ, India would be at

---

[9]Brad Herzog, "The Tiger Factor," *Sky Magazine*, May 2007, http://www.bradherzog.com/tiger.html.

your feet tomorrow." I think India would be at their feet today if we Christians lived like Christ. From the Islamic world, the Reverend Iskandar Jadeed, a former Arab Muslim, has said "If all Christians were Christians—that is, Christlike—there would be no more Islam today."[10]

What the late John Stott said couldn't be more true in that the quality of the messenger comes before any strategies or methods for evangelism. Unless the quality of a product is guaranteed, any marketing strategy or sales technology would be of no avail in the end. Related to this observation, we remember what Mahatma Gandhi once said about the historical churches: "I like your Christ; I do not like your Christians. Your Christians are so unlike your Christ." Although Gandhi accepted the teachings of Jesus Christ and put them into practice personally, he did not accept the historical churches, because they failed to embody the teachings of Jesus. We may safely argue that Gandhi's critical perception of the historical churches might apply to the churches in general in the global context.

In his excellent book on Chinese philosophical traditions and teachings, Fung Yu-Lan wrote: "The ultimate purpose of Buddhism is to teach men how to achieve Buddhahood—a problem that was one of the most vital to the people of that time. Likewise, the ultimate purpose of Neo-Confucianism is to teach men how to achieve Confucian Sagehood."[11] *Sagehood* refers to an "ideal man." One of the core teachings in Hindu tradition is to help people achieve freedom through inner renunciation.[12] Can we also say that the ultimate purpose of Christianity is to teach men and women how to achieve Christlikeness?

In the Asian religious milieu, where other religious traditions encourage their followers to cultivate their spiritual growth to the level of their masters through the practice of inner renunciation and self-denial, Christians are expected to present themselves as the genuine embodiment of their master Jesus Christ in denying themselves, taking up their own crosses and following Jesus. We have to realize anew that unless Christians and the churches can impress the Asian people with their Christlikeness, the Christian missions in the Asian theater might become "mission impossible."

---

[10]John Stott, "The Model: Becoming More Like Christ" (sermon at Keswick Convention, July 17, 2007), available at www.cslewisinstitute.org/Becoming_More_Like_Christ_Stott.

[11]Fung Yu-lan, *A Short History of Chinese Philosophy* (New York: Free Press, 1948), 271.

[12]Cf. Roger Marcaurelle, *Freedom Through Inner Renunciation: Sankara's Philosophy in a New Light* (Albany: State University of New York Press, 2000).

AN ASIAN SUGGESTION

We need to remember that Christianity was a late arrival in the Asian religious marketplace. Other traditional religions have nurtured the minds of Asian peoples for thousands of years. So it is not surprising to observe that in those countries where the presence of traditional organized religions remains strong, Christianity has almost failed to make any inroads.

For several decades, Asian Christian scholars and missiologists have been grappling with the issues and questions we have surveyed above. Their proposals complement those initiated by their Western counterparts, including, for example, Donald McGavran and his successors at SWM/SIS, but perhaps those initiatives are also suggestive of alternative paths forward not heretofore considered in the present ferment. I would like to reflect on two areas where concerted efforts should be made for the future of Christianity in Asia and beyond.

Making Christianity an Asian religion. Simply put, we need to find a way to make the teachings of Jesus an actual belief of Asian people. In other words, we must make Christianity an Asian religion. Buddhism, Hinduism, Confucianism, Taoism and Islam are said to be authentically Asian religions. Although Buddhism originated from India, it was imported to many Asian countries. Asian countries like China, Korea and Japan would say that Buddhism is one of their traditional religions. However, there would be very few who would say that Christianity is an Asian religion.

As we enter the postcolonial era, Asian churches have an uphill battle in attempting to create a public image of Christianity as a non-Western religion. That is, the de-Westernization of the image of Christianity in Asia is now a crucial challenge for the future of Asian Christianity.

An important aspect of this challenge would be to make the teachings of Jesus Christ permeate the everyday life of Asian people, providing the living principles or codes of conduct to replace the existing influence of other religions. This is a huge challenge but vital for the future of Christianity in Asia. Therefore, Christian scholars in Asia and also in the West need to join hands and gather wisdom together, seeking to devise ways to make Christianity an Asian or an African religion by making the teachings of Jesus (and of the Bible) their actual belief.

One area calling for rather immediate attention in this struggle is restoration of the religiosity of Christianity. In Asia Christianity is perceived to be less religious. Before the introduction of Christianity in Asia, Asian people were nurtured by other religious traditions for thousands of years. On the surface, Western civilization, culture and values made inroads into the private and public sectors of many Asian countries. However, the influence of the traditional cultures with their respective religious elements did not die out. These influences are very much alive in the religious consciousness and subconsciousness of Asian people. Informed by sustained religious elements in their cultures from a long history with other religions, Asian people have their own standards and also expectations regarding viable religious practices, lifestyle and the ethical role a religion has to play within the society.

If a religion loses its religious integrity and impact as a religious tradition and practice, then its raison d'être may evaporate. In this regard, the point John Mbiti made in his article "Theological Impotence and the Universality of the Church" should be acknowledged in theological circles around the globe.[13] At the same time it should be emphasized that the recent works of Charles Kraft on spiritual warfare make perfect sense to Asian and African people.[14]

The churches on Asian soil have not been quite successful in gaining the hearts of Asian people. It is difficult to affirm that the practice of self-denial of church leaders is superior to the self-discipline of other religious practitioners.

Reconfiguring theological education. The renovation of theological education has been a topic for many decades, and no noticeable breakthrough seems to have been made thus far. Once, the CEO of Samsung Group asked all his employees to change everything except their wives. Probably we must change everything as well—the way we conduct theological education, the way we play Christianity. We may need to change everything except the gospel.

The limitations and relevance of Western theologies and Western theological education have been analyzed and evaluated by Christian scholars from many different angles. About four decades ago Walter Wink asserted that in the field of biblical studies the historical-critical method of interpreting the

---

[13]John Mbiti, "Theological Impotence and the Universality of the Church," in Anderson and Stransky, *Mission Trends No. 3*, 6-18.
[14]Cf. Charles Kraft, *The Evangelical's Guide to Spiritual Warfare* (Minneapolis: Chosen, 2015).

Bible was defunct because it was incapable of achieving the purpose of biblical studies, which he identified as personal and social transformation.[15] Reflecting from within the Indian religious milieu, George Soares-Prabhu also asserted that, since historical criticism is a method designed to obtain exact information, it is an ineffective and irrelevant method for interpreting the biblical text if its aim is personal transformation.[16] These assertions were heard as voices from the wilderness and made virtually no impact in the way biblical scholarship is conducted.

I hate to admit that the nature and purpose of theological education is not properly achieved using the current methods of Christian scholarship in theological schools around the world. It might not be too simplistic to argue that not only the area of biblical scholarship but also the whole Christian or theological or religious education in general has become defunct.

I spent about fifteen years in various teaching capacities in Scotland, Singapore and America, and during that time I never came across a single student who told me that she or he came to the school to learn how to achieve Christlikeness. Most students were ministry oriented or task oriented. Based on my exposure to Western theological education for two decades as a student and also as a professor, I wrote several articles to propose some ideas to renovate theological education. The main message that I hoped to convey through my essays was that we need to teach the Bible and other theological discourses to help students achieve personal transformation or spiritual formation first and then teach theological, vocational, ministerial, practical and missional formation as a next step.

I was often asked to explain the difference between Asian and Western theological discourses. I used to answer this way: Asian theology is to teach and learn theology for myself (to change myself), while Western theology is to teach and learn theology for others (to change others and the world). In this regard, I would suggest again that theological education needs reconfiguration to become self-transforming and missional (or mission oriented) while also utilizing the valued data, accumulated research and extensive

---

[15]Walter Wink, *The Bible in Human Transformation: Towards a New Paradigm in Biblical Study* (Philadelphia: Fortress, 1973).

[16]George Soares-Prabhu, "Towards an Indian Interpretation of the Bible," *Biblebashyam* 6 (March 1980): 154.

achievements of academic and critical scholarship. We need to reconfigure theological education to be *self-transforming*. We may have to design the curriculum of theological schools in a way that would orchestrate all classroom experiences to become self-transforming. Also we need to reconfigure theological education to be *missional*, or *mission oriented*. The authors of the New Testament books wrote them in the context of their missionary efforts to bring the gospel to the nations and to testify to the Gentiles concerning Jesus Christ. Not only mission-related courses but biblical studies, systematic theology and other areas of theology should be taught to enable students to share the gospel with non-Christians in the interest of teaching and inviting them to become disciples of Jesus Christ.

CONCLUSION

In conclusion, I would argue that the most urgent agenda for global Christianity today is to devise and implement ways to innovate or renovate Christianity before we try to articulate effective and culturally relevant strategies for evangelism. Now is the time to pay special attention to nurturing qualified Christian leaders who live Christianity by embodying and demonstrating Christlikeness in their everyday encounters with the world.

David Bosch used *Transforming Mission* as the title of his book. I strongly feel that it is time for us to transform the churches and the theological schools where Christian leaders are trained. In this sense, it will not be too provocative to say that the frontier of mission will have to be the churches and the theological schools. It is my prayer that SWM/SIS and Fuller Theological Seminary will implement a new set of initiatives (following in the footsteps of Donald McGavran) to reinvent, innovate and transform the current theological education to help future Christian leaders embody Christlikeness and re-envision the future of global Christianity.

7

What Does Rome Have to Do with Pasadena?

Connecting Roman Catholic Missiology with SWM/SIS Innovations

Stephen Bevans

INTRODUCTION

What does Rome have to do with Pasadena? This paraphrase of Tertullian's famous question[1] did not come immediately to mind when I first began thinking about writing this chapter, but the idea behind it did. I wasn't sure if there were indeed *any* connections between Roman Catholic missiological thinking and practice[2] and the many amazing innovations that have emerged out of Fuller's School of World Mission/ School of Intercultural Studies (SWM/SIS) in the last fifty years. Indeed, the difference between initiatives like Luis Bush's AD2000 and Beyond Movement and the Catholic Church's outreach in the Second Vatican Council's "Declaration on the Relation of the Church to Non-Christian Religions" (published exactly fifty years ago this fall)[3] seemed as great as

---

[1]Tertullian, *The Prescription Against Heretics* 7, in *Readings in the History of Christian Thought*, ed. Robert L. Ferm (New York: Holt, Rinehart and Winston, 1964), 4.

[2]In this essay I use the shorter term *missiology* to refer to both the theory (missiological thinking) and the practice of mission.

[3]See "AD2000 and Beyond Movement Overview," *AD2000 and Beyond: A Church for Every People and the Gospel for Every Person by AD 2000*, accessed February 9, 2016, www.ad2000 .org/ad2kbroc.htm; and "Declaration on the Relation of the Church to Non-Christian Religions, *Nostra Aetate*, Proclaimed by His Holiness Pope Paul VI on October 28, 1965," www.vatican .va/archive/hist_councils/ii_vatican_council/documents/vat-ii_decl_19651028_nostra-aetate_ en.html.

the gap between—at least in Tertullian's mind—Zeno's "painted porch" and "the Porch of Solomon."[4]

As I began to think seriously about what I was going to write, however, I was surprised, even astounded, at the connections I discovered. The SWM/SIS has actually had a direct impact on Catholic missiology in some cases, including innovations within it. In other cases there are interesting parallels between the two traditions. Some of SWM/SIS's innovations have no connection with Catholic missiology, however, and some Catholic missiological innovations have no connection with those developed at SWM/SIS and might even offer a friendly challenge to SWM/SIS.

These three relationships between Catholic missiology and Fuller's innovations suggest an outline for the development of this chapter. First, I would like to highlight several direct influences of Fuller's innovations on Catholic missiology—namely, Donald McGavran's influence on the Spiritan missionary to Tanzania, Vincent Donovan; Tom and Betty Sue Brewster's influence on the Society of the Divine Word missionary to Ghana, Jon P. Kirby; and Charles Van Engen's influence on my own ecclesiology. Second, I will note the parallels between Charles Kraft's work on contextual theology and that of the Catholic Magisterium and Catholic theologians; Luis Bush's AD2000 and Beyond Movement and the Catholic idea of the New Evangelization; and Fuller's Children at Risk emphasis and the Human Trafficking Initiative of Pope Francis, Archbishop of Canterbury Justin Welby and several Muslim leaders. Finally, I will reflect on three important Roman Catholic innovations that, at least to my mind, have little or no parallels in the missiology of SWM/SIS: the theology of liberation; the understanding of liturgy, prayer and contemplation as a constitutive element of mission; and the understanding and practice of mission as prophetic dialogue.

DIRECT INFLUENCES

Several of SWM/SIS's innovations—or, more precisely, innovative people—have had direct influence on practitioners of Roman Catholic missiology. Roman Catholic missionary Vincent Donovan found helpful ideas in his reading of Donald McGavran as he worked among the Maasai. Tom and

---

[4]*Encyclopedia of World History* (Oxford: Oxford University Press, 1998), 639, s.v. "Stoics"; Tertullian, *Prescription 7*.

Betty Sue Brewster had significant influence on Catholic anthropologist Jon Kirby, and my own approach to constructing a missionary ecclesiology has been influenced by the innovative ecclesiology of Charles Van Engen.

Donald McGavran's influence on Vincent Donovan. Vincent Donovan (1926–2000) was a member of the Catholic missionary Congregation of the Holy Spirit, and from 1955 until 1973 he worked as a missionary in Tanzania, East Africa, particularly among the Maasai people. His book *Christianity Rediscovered* was first published in 1978, reprinted in 1982, and issued in a twenty-fifth anniversary edition in 2003.[5] It is, to my mind, a modern mission classic. Responding to a question asked by *The Christian Century* about what one book he would recommend to a person starting out in pastoral ministry, Samuel Wells, vicar of St. Martin-in-the-Fields in London, wrote that it would be Donovan's book: "I return to this book more than almost any other because it reminds me why I'm a priest, what the church is, and how God is at work in places before I ever show up."[6]

Like Donald McGavran, whose thinking was stimulated by the frustration that his mission in India had spent large sums of money with very meager results in terms of Christian conversions,[7] Donovan was frustrated by the results of a century of missionary work in East Africa, especially among the Maasai. Missionary activity in East Africa had begun with the ransoming and Christianizing of slaves in Christian mission compounds, then continued with a network of schools that had been effectively taken over by newly independent governments in the 1960s. After independence and in the wake of the Second Vatican Council, missionaries were deeply involved in development work but were involved very little in direct evangelization.[8] In a letter "to a Bishop" that opens chapter two of his book, Donovan writes that despite a lot of very good work among the Maasai in an area called Loliondo, where he had been stationed for almost a year,

---

[5]Vincent J. Donovan, *Christianity Rediscovered*, anniversary ed. (1978; repr., 1982; Maryknoll, NY: Orbis Books, 2003).

[6]Samuel Wells, "Read This First," review of *Christianity Rediscovered*, by Vincent Donovan, *Christian Century*, April 14, 2014, www.christiancentury.org/reviews/2014-04/christianity-rediscovered -vincent-donovan.

[7]See C. Peter Wagner, "Church Growth Movement," in *Evangelical Dictionary of World Missions*, ed. A. Scott Moreau, Harold Netland and Charles Van Engen (Grand Rapids: Baker Books, 2000), 199.

[8]See Donovan, *Christianity Rediscovered*, 3-11.

the best way to describe realistically the state of this Christian mission is the number zero. As of this month, in the seventh year of this mission's existence, there are no adult Maasai practicing Christians from Loliondo mission. The only practicing Christians are the catechist and the hospital medical dresser, who have come here from other sections of Maasailand.[9]

In addition, even though children had been baptized, no one child had continued practicing her or his Christianity after leaving the school in the mission compound, all this after spending almost a quarter million Tanzanian shillings over the previous year.[10]

Because of such frustration, Donovan proposed to the bishop that he cut himself "off from the schools and the hospital, as far as these people are concerned—as well as the socializing with them—and just go and talk to them about God and the Christian message."[11] He knew it would be hard, particularly among the proud Maasai, but he wanted to try to bring what he eventually calls the "naked gospel"[12] to them—"unencumbered with the burden of selling them our school system, or begging for their children for our schools, or carrying their sick, or giving them medicine."[13]

The rest of the book tells the story of how this kind of "unencumbered" evangelization took place.[14] Of particular interest here is Donovan's use of McGavran's classic, *The Bridges of God*, in his approach to converting the Maasai people, not individually, but—in McGavran's phrase—according to the "homogeneous unit principle."[15] Because of the culture of the Maasai people, Donovan wrote, he could never have evangelized the Maasai as individuals. Rather, they had to be approached "on the level of a homogeneous group of people that considers itself a living, social organism distinct from other social groups."[16] As Donovan discovered as well, also with a reference to McGavran,

---

[9]Ibid., 13.

[10]Ibid.

[11]Ibid.

[12]Vincent J. Donovan, "The Naked Gospel: Stamping Out Ready-to-Wear Christianity" (interview), *U.S. Catholic* 46, no. 6 (1981): 24-31.

[13]Donovan, *Christianity Rediscovered*, 14.

[14]See my summary of the book in *Models of Contextual Theology* (Maryknoll, NY: Orbis Books, 2002), 66-67.

[15]Donald A. McGavran, *The Bridges of God: A Study in the Strategy of Missions* (1955; repr., Eugene, OR: Wipf & Stock, 2005); see Wagner, "Church Growth Movement," 200.

[16]Donovan, *Christianity Rediscovered*, 64. On the following page (65n2), Donovan references *Bridges of God*.

a community . . . will act as a unit, accepting you or rejecting you altogether. I found out that change, deep meaningful change, like the acceptance of a hopeful, expectant world vision, does not take place in one individual at a time. Groups adopt changes as groups, or they do not adopt them at all.[17]

An example of this approach to evangelization is found a few pages later in one of the most beautiful sections of the book. Donovan had come to a point where he thought that some of the people in one Maasai village were ready for baptism, so he proposed that they be baptized. A village elder, however, objected. He said that Donovan could not just baptize some of them and not others, even though not all of them were at the same point of faith. "We believe," he said. Maybe not everyone is at the same place, but the community would make sure that everyone would eventually arrive at full faith.[18] All would become disciples, to use McGavran's terminology, and would eventually be perfected.[19]

However, as John P. Bowen discovered on a trip to Tanzania, Donovan's work has not lasted the way he hoped that it would because of difficulties in ordaining Maasai leaders, the need for ongoing pastoral care, hierarchical opposition and the challenges of modernity to the Maasai way of life.[20] But for a shining moment, the vision of a Roman Catholic missionary was nourished by an innovation of an evangelical Christian, the first dean of Fuller Seminary's School of World Mission. Something worth notice indeed.

Tom and Betty Sue Brewster's influence on Jon Kirby. Jon P. Kirby is a member of the Society of the Divine Word (SVD)—my own missionary congregation—and spent some thirty years in Ghana, West Africa. It was in the Northern Ghanaian town of Tamale that, on completion of his doctoral studies in anthropology at the University of Cambridge, Kirby founded the Tamale Institute of Cross Cultural Studies (TICCS). In 1996 I spent three weeks at TICCS with several students from Chicago and experienced a shortened version of one of TICCS's courses on Ghanaian culture and language. The first week was a general introduction to Ghanaian culture in

---

[17]Donovan, *Christianity Rediscovered*, 66, referring to McGavran, *Bridges of God*, 12-13.

[18]Donovan, *Christianity Rediscovered*, 69-71.

[19]Wagner, "Church Growth Movement," 200.

[20]John P. Bowen, "'What Happened Next?' Vincent Donovan, Thirty-Five Years On," *International Bulletin of Missionary Research* 33, no. 2 (2009): 82, www.internationalbulletin.org/issues/2009-02/2009-02-079-bowen.html.

general and the local Northern Ghanaian culture in particular. The second and third weeks provided an introduction to the local Dagbani language, culminating in a three-day stay in a nearby village.

In the second and third weeks, Jon gave us an article by Tom and Betty Sue Brewster to read, their classic piece titled "Bonding and the Missionary Task: Establishing a Sense of Belonging."[21] Following the Brewsters' practice, even though we were going to be in the country only three weeks, we began learning Dagbanli, the language of the Dagbani people, who make up the majority of the population in that part of Ghana. In the beginning of the Brewsters' other classic text, *Language Learning IS Communication—IS Ministry!*, they credit Charles Kraft for the principle that if you spend two months in a culture as a missionary, you should spend two months learning the language. If the stint is six months, learn the language for six months, and so forth. Kraft insists: "Indeed, if we do no more than engage in the process of language learning we will have communicated more of the essentials of the Gospel than if we devote ourselves to any other task I can think of."[22]

The Brewsters insist on *language learning* rather than *language study*, insisting that "*normal language acquisition is a social activity, not an academic activity.*"[23] Kirby followed this method by having us learn—memorize, actually—several Dagbanli phrases and then go out and recite them to as many people as we could meet in an afternoon along the roads around TICCS. Ordinarily, in a full course at the institute, this learning would go on for several weeks, culminating in a longer stay in a village, where participants would speak with people, learn their language and bond with them. Kirby had clearly learned from this innovation by this couple closely associated with Fuller's SWM/SIS.

In an article of his own, published in 1995 in the journal *Missiology*, Kirby acknowledges his debt to the Brewsters' innovations, although he says that he had "always, rather instinctively" come to this conclusion on his own.[24]

---

[21]Published as E. Thomas Brewster and Elizabeth S. Brewster, *Bonding and the Missionary Task: Establishing a Sense of Belonging* (Pasadena, CA: Lingua House, 1984).

[22]Quoted in E. Thomas Brewster and Elizabeth S. Brewster, *Language Learning IS Communication—IS Ministry!* (Pasadena, CA: Lingua House, 1984), 1.

[23]Brewster and Brewster, *Language Learning*, 3; emphasis original.

[24]Jon P. Kirby, "Language and Culture Learning IS Conversion . . . IS Ministry," *Missiology: An International Review* 23, no. 2 (1995): 136.

Kirby suggests, however, that the notion of "communication" in the Brewsters' understanding needs some critique. To focus on communication as ministry itself, he says, is not enough, "because it points to the incarnational event, but is not in itself a reenactment of it."[25] To remedy this, Kirby offers the word *conversion* as a substitute for *communication*. He says,

> Language learning is, indeed, ministry but not just because it communicates the missioner's words or Christ's words, or even the missioner's whole "life-message"—though this is partially true. It is ministry primarily because it witnesses to a conversion process: the conversion of the missioners themselves. Missioners are really responsible for only one conversion, their own![26]

Kirby's critical appropriation of the Brewsters' insights is, to my mind, very well taken and evidences an important development of their innovative approach to language learning. Before I leave this section, however, I want to acknowledge the Brewsters' influence as well on several other of my SVD confreres. Mark Schramm, currently working as a pastor on the Caribbean island of Montserrat, studied with the Brewsters at Fuller in the late 1980s and returned to Ghana to direct a language-learning center in the town of Abetifi. Mark thus trained many other incoming missionaries to Ghana— Protestant and Catholic—in the Brewsters' innovative language-learning method. Roger Schroeder, my sometimes coauthor and good friend, studied the Brewster method for two summers at the Summer Institute of Linguistics in the late 1970s. Much of his work focuses as well on the Brewsters' insistence that the missionary be a "Learner, Servant, Story-Teller."[27] Finally, New Zealand–Papua New Guinea missionary Philip Gibbs has also profited much from their method in his own pastoral and scholarly work. In sum, Catholics have greatly profited from the work of Tom and Betty Sue Brewster, and Kirby, Schramm, Schroeder and Gibbs have influenced many students, missionaries and ministers in their teaching and writing.

Charles Van Engen's influence on my ecclesiology. A third direct influence of the SWM/SIS's innovations on Catholic missiology has been

---

[25]Ibid.

[26]Ibid., 137.

[27]See Brewster and Brewster, *Language Learning*, 13-15; see Roger P. Schroeder, "Entering Someone Else's Garden: Intercultural Mission/Ministry," in *Prophetic Dialogue: Reflections on Christian Mission Today*, ed. Stephen B. Bevans and Roger P. Schroeder (Maryknoll, NY: Orbis Books, 2011), 72-87.

Charles Van Engen's more dynamic and missionary understanding of the so-called four marks, dimensions or, using Van Engen's term, distinctives of the church. The idea appears in his book *God's Missionary People*, but he summarizes it concisely in his article "Church" in *The Evangelical Dictionary of World Missions*. The marks "call the church to be the unifying, sanctifying, reconciling, and proclaiming presence of Jesus Christ in the world, challenging local congregations to a transformed, purpose-driven life of mission in the world, locally and globally."[28]

In his dictionary article, Van Engen mentions that Darrell Guder has also taken this position. Guder, however, takes the idea one step further by reversing the order of the marks, thus making apostolicity foundational for all four and rooting them more firmly in mission. As Guder writes, "The fundamental and definitive characteristic of the church is its apostolicity, which is more than a genealogical term."[29]

It is with this variation on Van Engen's insight and a slight variation in order that I have developed in germ, and hope to develop more fully in the future, the treatment of the marks of the church in my own Catholic understanding of ecclesiology. The writing of this is a project I hope to begin seriously in the coming months, but it is a perspective on the marks of the church that I have been teaching for some years, ever since I read Van Engen's *God's Missionary People* in the 1990s. I have further modified the idea, however, to include a threefold identity of each mark. Thus the church *is* apostolic as a gift, the church is *called* to be apostolic in fidelity to its missionary nature and to let that apostolicity shape the church's entire thinking about itself, and the church is to *act* apostolically in mission in terms of its zeal and its fidelity to apostolic truth. Similarly, the church *is* catholic but *called* to be catholic in its appreciation of local identity and diversity in unity, and it is commissioned to *work* for the catholicity of the world by protecting and fostering diversity (in terms of culture, theology, gender and generational identity) in a constant dialogue for unity. Such unity *is* already a gift and yet *calls* the church to *work* for unity among Christians and to *work* as

---

[28]Charles Van Engen, "Church," in Moreau et al., *Evangelical Dictionary of World Missions*, 193; see also Charles Van Engen, *God's Missionary People* (Grand Rapids: Baker Academic, 1991), 59-71.

[29]Darrell L. Guder, "A Multicultural and Translational Approach to Mission," in *The Mission of the Church: Five Views in Conversation*, ed. Craig Ott (Grand Rapids: Baker Academic, 2016).

well for unity among all religions and peoples. Finally, the church *is* holy as God's special people and is therefore *called* to be holy as a sign of God's presence in the world. The church is called as well to *point out* the holiness beyond its boundaries and to invite people into the explicit relationship with God that it already enjoys.[30]

Obviously I have modified and developed the idea and incorporated it into a thoroughly Roman Catholic ecclesiology. And yet I owe the basic insight to Charles Van Engen's innovative and dynamic understanding of the church's four distinctives, or marks.

PARALLELS

One sign of the vitality of an idea or practice is that it appears among thinkers or practitioners from very different contexts. Such parallel ideas are seen in the innovative approach of Charles Kraft toward the contextualization of theology, developed at about the same time that Roman Catholics were beginning to talk about inculturation. Luis Bush's determination to evangelize the world through the AD2000 and Beyond Movement has a rough parallel in the Catholic Church's efforts of The New Evangelization, a movement that has subtly changed direction in the papacy of Pope Francis. A third striking parallel can be seen in Fuller's Children at Risk program and the commitment of Pope Francis, the Archbishop of Canterbury and the leaders of several other religions to work for the eradication of human trafficking.

Charles Kraft and inculturation. Rereading sections of Charles Kraft's 1979 *Christianity in Culture*, I came to a fresh realization of how innovative his work was at the time—and still is today. Kraft speaks of theology as "a disciplinary perspective on, or perception of, reality."[31] Historically in the church, he says, theology has been developed within the context of Western culture, resulting "in a large body of extremely insightful perceptions of the portion of reality revealed to people by God in and through the Christian Scriptures."[32] But this "body of perceptions" can never be an exhaustive expression of Christian truth.

---

[30]See Stephen Bevans, "Beyond the New Evangelization: Toward a Missionary Ecclesiology for the Twenty-First Century," in *A Church with Open Doors: Catholic Ecclesiology for the Third Millennium*, ed. Richard R. Gaillardetz and Edward P. Hahnenberg (Collegeville, MN: Liturgical Press, 2015), 18.

[31]Charles H. Kraft, *Christianity in Culture* (Maryknoll, NY: Orbis Books, 1979), 291.

[32]Ibid., 292.

In the first place, these perceptions have been generated primarily from within one particular culture. Second, they have been generated within disciplines within that culture. And, third, even within this cultural matrix they both differ and develop. Kraft's conclusion is that "*any monocultural perspective* on truth is no more complete than the single perspective of any given individual."[33] Theology, then, is essentially pluralistic, essentially a contextual endeavor. It is "*a dynamic discovery process engaged in by human beings according to human perceptions*. It is not simply the passive acceptance of a doctrinal product 'once and for all delivered.'"[34]

From the perspective of communication as well, Kraft insists that theology needs to be culturally and contextually aware of its relevance. It is the product of the perception of those who do theology, but it is useless if it is not perceived as relevant by those who hear it or read it. In his lapidary phrase, "theology perceived as irrelevant *is* irrelevant."[35] So theology needs to be developed that makes sense to Latin Americans, Asians and Africans and to women and men of various disciplines—psychologists, sociologists and chemists. It needs to be understood by people of various social locations: "by factory workers, by farmers, by engineers, by youth, by hippies, by blacks, by women's libbers, it must be translated into terms and concepts meaningful to every group."[36] I love the contextual rootedness of some of these words!

Kraft began teaching courses titled Christianity and Culture at SWM/SIS in 1971, and students in those classes, for example Darrell Whiteman, Kenneth Ross and Wayne Dye, have gone on to make their mark in missiology and contextual theology. It was in these years as well, in the wake of the Second Vatican Council's treatment of culture in its documents on the church in the modern world and on mission, that Catholic missiological thinking began to recognize the importance of a culturally and contextually sensitive reflection on and communication of the gospel. Referring to Pope John XXIII's memorable words at the opening of the council, the document on the church in the modern world declared that "theologians are invited to seek continually for more suitable ways of communicating doctrine to the

---

[33]Ibid.; emphasis original.
[34]Ibid., 294; emphasis original.
[35]Ibid., 296.
[36]Ibid., 297.

women and men of their times. For the deposit of faith or revealed truths
are one thing; the manner in which they are formulated without violence to
their meaning and significance is another."[37] In what is perhaps my favorite
passage in all the Vatican II documents, the document on mission calls missionaries (and I believe, a fortiori, theologians) to "learn by patient dialogue
what treasures a bountiful God has distributed among the nations of the
earth."[38] Ten years after the council, in 1975, Pope Paul VI spoke of the
importance of evangelizing the world's cultures, "not in a purely decorative
way, as it were, by applying a thin veneer, but in a vital way, in depth and
right to their very roots." This is because, as it has always been, "the split
between gospel and culture is . . . the drama of our time."[39] Pope John Paul
II as well often spoke of the need for such *inculturation*, as the term began
to be used among Catholics.[40] Most recently Pope Francis has also spoken
enthusiastically of the task of inculturation, exclaiming that "grace supposes
culture, and God's gift becomes flesh in the culture of those who receive it,"
and that "we would not do justice to the logic of the incarnation if we
thought of Christianity as monocultural and monotonous."[41] In words that
almost echo Charles Kraft's, Francis writes: "There are times when the
faithful, in listening to completely orthodox language, take away something
alien to the authentic Gospel of Jesus Christ, because that language is alien
to their own way of speaking to and understanding one another."[42] Theology perceived as irrelevant *is* irrelevant.

Christianity in Culture is to my mind a revolutionary book, and not only
among evangelicals. The book helped greatly in my own thinking, and I

---

[37]Paul VI, "Pastoral Constitution on the Church in the Modern World, *Gaudium et Spes* [GS], Promulgated by His Holiness, Pope Paul VI, on December 7, 1965," par. 62, www.vatican.va/archive/
hist_councils/ii_vatican_council/documents/vat-ii_const_19651207_gaudium-et-spes_en.html.
[38]"Decree *Ad Gentes* [AG] on the Mission Activity of the Church," par. 11, www.vatican.va/archive/
hist_councils/ii_vatican_council/documents/vat-ii_decree_19651207_ad-gentes_en.html.
[39]Paul VI, "*Evangelii Nuntiandi* [EN], Apostolic Exhortation of His Holiness Pope Paul VI to the
Episcopate, to the Clergy and to All the Faithful of the Entire World," par. 20, w2.vatican.va/content/
paul-vi/en/apost_exhortations/documents/hf_p-vi_exh_19751208_evangelii-nuntiandi.html.
[40]See Bevans, *Models of Contextual Theology*, 49-53.
[41]Francis, "Apostolic Exhortation *Evangelii Gaudium* [EG] of the Holy Father Francis to the
Bishops, Clergy, Consecrated Persons and the Lay Faithful on the Proclamation of the Gospel
in Today's World," St. Peter's, Rome, November 24, 2013, pars. 115, 117, w2.vatican.va/content/
francesco/en/apost_exhortations/documents/papa-francesco_esortazione-ap_20131124_
evangelii-gaudium.html.
[42]Ibid., par. 41.

featured Kraft's approach in my own book on models of contextual theology.[43] I know that the book had an influence on Robert Schreiter's book
on contextual theology as well,[44] and I am sure that investigation would
reveal its influence on many other Catholic theologians who have written or
tried to construct theologies in their own context. Charles Kraft's innovations are an amazing parallel to innovations in Roman Catholic missiology
and Roman Catholic papal teaching.

AD2000 and Beyond and the New Evangelization. The AD2000 and
Beyond Movement emerged to some prominence at the Lausanne II Conference in Manila in 1989 and was directed by Fuller PhD graduate Luis
Bush from 1989 until 2001. Ralph Winter, long associated with SWM/SIS,
spoke of the movement as "the largest, most pervasive global evangelical
network ever to exist." Bush himself coined the phrase "The 10/40 Window,"
a portion of the world between 10 and 40 degrees north of the equator where
"the world's least-evangelized poor are found." While the leaders of AD2000
and Beyond never imagined that the world would indeed be evangelized by
the turn of the millennium, from the start they challenged the church "to
face realistically its commission to make disciples of all peoples and to
pursue that priority with greater zeal and unity than ever before."[45]

Somewhat parallel to this urgent call for greater zeal and unity is the call
by Popes John Paul II and Benedict XVI for a "new evangelization" on the
part of the Roman Catholic Church. John Paul II's first use of the term occurred during his historic visit to Poland in 1979, although it was a phrase
used quite incidentally without a clue that it would become one of the
hallmarks of his papal teaching.[46] He used it again in a much more deliberate way in 1983 in an address to Latin American and Caribbean bishops
in Haiti, and again in the opening address at the Latin American Bishops'
Conference in Santo Domingo in 1992. In both talks he emphasized that
what was needed in Latin America was an evangelization that was "new in

---

[43]Bevans, *Models of Contextual Theology*, 38–39.

[44]Robert J. Schreiter, *Constructing Local Theologies* (Maryknoll, NY: Orbis Books, 1985).

[45]The quote from Ralph Winter and the other quotations in this paragraph are from "AD2000 and
Beyond Movement Overview," AD2000 and Beyond, June 30, 1999, www.ad2000.org/ad2kbroc.htm.

[46]See John Paul II, "Holy Mass at the Shrine of the Holy Cross: Homily of His Holiness John Paul II"
(Mogila, Poland, June 9, 1979), 1; *L'Osservatore Romano: Weekly Edition in English*, July 16, 1979,
11; *Acta Apostolicae Sedis* 71 (1979): 865, w2.vatican.va/content/john-paul-ii/en/homilies/1979/
documents/hf_jp-ii_hom_19790609_polonia-mogila-nowa-huta.html.

its ardour, methods and expression."[47] The term was used also in John Paul's 1990 mission encyclical *Redemptoris Missio*, and here it was applied not just to Latin America but to the entire church. Mission is to be carried out in ordinary pastoral work, in the first evangelization efforts of mission *ad gentes* and in "an intermediate situation, particularly in countries with ancient Christian roots. . . . In this case what is needed is a 'new evangelization' or a 're-evangelization.'"[48] John Paul also used the phrase "new evangelization" in his official messages (called Apostolic Exhortations) after the various regional Synods of Bishops that were held in preparation for the new millennium.[49] Although there was no direct connection between these synods and AD2000 and Beyond, the coincidence is notable: they are both calls for the church to "gear up" in preparation for the new millennium with a greater effort for world evangelization or, as it was increasingly being emphasized, for the "re-evangelization" of those areas of the world (e.g., Europe, North America, Australasia) that were becoming more and more secularized and nonreligious.

In 2005 Joseph Ratzinger was elected pope and quite deliberately took the name Benedict in reference to Benedict of Norsia, "one of the patron saints of Europe who . . . had exercised an enormous influence on Europe's Christian heritage."[50] As cardinal, Ratzinger had repeatedly expressed his concern for Europe's loss of faith and had called the church to witness more clearly to a truth that was not the result of mere experience but based in God's revelation.[51] As pope, he committed himself to saving Europe from postmodern relativism and unbelief, prompting him to create the Pontifical Council for Promoting the New Evangelization in September of 2010. In the official letter establishing the council, Benedict wrote of the need for "traditionally

---

[47]John Paul II, "Discourse to the XIX Assembly of CELAM" (March 9, 1983), 3: *L'Osservatore Romano: Weekly Edition in English*, April 18, 1983, 9; *Acta Apostolicae Sedis* 75 (1983): 778.

[48]John Paul II, "*Redemptoris Missio* [*RM*]: On the Permanent Validity of the Church's Missionary Mandate," par. 37, w2.vatican.va/content/john-paul-ii/en/encyclicals/documents/hf_jp-ii_enc_07121990_redemptoris-missio.html.

[49]For references to these documents, see Stephen Bevans, "New Evangelization or Missionary Church? *Evangelii Gaudium* and the Call for Missionary Discipleship," *Verbum* 55, no. 2-3 (2014): 163.

[50]Lieven Boeve, "Europe in Crisis: A Question of Belief or Unbelief? Perspectives from the Vatican," *Modern Theology* 23, no. 2 (2007): 209.

[51]Ibid., 208.

Christian territories" to develop a "renewed missionary impulse."[52] Shortly afterwards Benedict announced that the theme for the 2012 Synod of Bishops in Rome would be "The New Evangelization for the Transmission of the Faith."[53] What seemed to be emphasized in the threefold program of new evangelization that John Paul had outlined was that of a new ardor or zeal, rather than new methods or content. If we would only try harder, if we would only make the message clearer, we would succeed in our evangelization and, especially, our re-evangelization.

Interestingly, however, the synod did not go exactly as Benedict may have planned. Rather than focus on the renewed zeal of re-evangelizing the West, the synod seemed to call for a new emphasis on the entire church as missionary, in every situation in which it finds itself.[54] When, in November 2013, the newly elected Pope Francis issued his statement on the synod, he took the same tack. In fact, in calling for all Christians to be "missionary disciples,"[55] he seemed to emphasize the "new methods" and "new content" of the new evangelization much more than a call to "try harder." He called Christians to radiate joy, not to look like they had just come back from a funeral or were living life like Lent without Easter.[56] The church must evangelize primarily by "attraction," like a "Mother with an open heart," like the house of the father of the prodigal son, as a place where mercy is "freely given."[57] Francis, in fact, does not use the phrase "new evangelization" very much in the document—only about twelve times in the entire lengthy document. And yet, what he says is truly new and represents a fresh way to think about the church and its evangelizing mission.

In many ways the great, organized effort of the AD2000 and Beyond Movement and Pope Francis's efforts to evangelize by making the church more attractive and joyful are very different. And yet they represent important

---

[52]Benedict XVI, "Apostolic Letter in the Form of *Motu Proprio, Ubicumque et Semper*, of the Supreme Pontiff Benedict XVI Establishing the Pontifical Council for Promoting the New Evangelization," www.vatican.va/holy_father/benedict_xvi/apost_letters/documents/hf_ben-xvi_apl_20100921_ubicumque-et-semper_en.html.

[53]Benedict XVI, "Homily at the Conclusion for the Special Assembly for the Middle East of the Synod of Bishops," *L'Osservatore Romano: Weekly Edition in English* 27 (October 2010): 4.

[54]See Bevans, "Beyond the New Evangelization," 8-10.

[55]Francis, *EG*, par. 24.

[56]*EG*, pars. 10, 6.

[57]*EG*, pars. 14, 46, 114.

innovations—two parallel realizations that the church must indeed commit itself in our day to a renewed and deliberate task of evangelizing the world. **Children at Risk and the human trafficking initiative.**

> A young girl is orphaned when her parents die of AIDS . . . a boy barely nine years old is forced to become a child soldier . . . an innocent daughter is sold into human trafficking and sexually exploited. An alarming number of children struggle in unjust situations that put them in crisis. The church has a mandate to care for them—but how? Could a seminary play a role in bringing the kingdom of God to these situations?[58]

These were the questions the SWM/SIS was asking in 2002, when it made efforts to recruit David Scott for its new emphasis in Children at Risk. Now the SWM/SIS offers five master's degrees with an emphasis in Children at Risk—a truly important innovation in today's world, which has become keenly aware of situations of abuse and human trafficking in every part of the globe.

While it is not exactly a parallel, Catholic leaders have seen the importance of working to end all human trafficking, a great portion of which involves the trafficking of innocent children. In March 2014, the Vatican, together with the Archbishop of Canterbury and a number of Muslim leaders, inaugurated the Global Freedom Network (GFN) with the hope of eliminating human trafficking by 2020.[59] I myself heard a talk by the Archbishop of Canterbury's representative at the Vatican, former New Zealand archbishop David Moxom, speak in October 2014 of the initiative with extremely high hopes and deep conviction. On December 2, 2014, Pope Francis, Archbishop Justin Welby and several other world religious leaders signed a Declaration Against Slavery, and in his remarks at the ceremony Pope Francis spoke of slavery today as a crime against humanity.[60] As Francis put it eloquently—if also chillingly—

---

[58]David H. Scott, "Opening up Seminary's Arms to Children at Risk: The Conception and Birth of the 'Children at Risk' Emphasis at Fuller," *Our Mission Legacy* (blog), Fuller Theological Seminary, June 18, 2015, http://fuller.edu/blogs/global-reflections/posts/opening-up-seminary-s-arms-to-children-at-risk/.

[59]Andrea Gagliarducci, "Vatican Bails on Questionable Anti-Human Trafficking Initiative (Updated)," July 31, 2015, Catholic News Agency, www.catholicnewsagency.com/news/vatican-bails-on-questionable-anti-human-trafficking-initiative-11353/.

[60]Francis, "Ceremony for the Signing of the Faith Leaders' Universal Declaration Against Slavery, Address of His Holiness Pope Francis," December 2, 2014, w2.vatican.va/content/francesco/en/speeches/2014/december/documents/papa-francesco_20141202_dichiarazione-schiavitu.html.

I ask the Lord to grant us today the grace to convert ourselves in the proximity of every person, without exception, offering active and constant help to those we encounter on our path—whether it be an elderly person who has been abandoned by everyone, a worker unjustly enslaved or unappreciated, a refugee caught in the snares of the underworld, a young man or woman who walks the streets of the world, as a victim of the sex trade, a man or a woman driven to prostitution by the deception of people who have no fear of God, a boy or a girl mutilated for their organs—and who call to our conscience, echoing the voice of the Lord: I say to you whatever you do to the least of my brothers, you do to me.[61]

Unfortunately, however, in the last several months, it seems that the Vatican has left the board of the GFN because of issues with some questionable financial strategies of the Australian billionaire Andrew Forrest, who has been the principal funder of the initiative, but that does not mean that the Vatican has lessened its commitment to the fight against human trafficking.[62] Human trafficking in all its forms is something that Pope Francis, even while serving as Archbishop of Buenos Aires, had been openly opposed to, and he has come out strongly in this regard many times since becoming pope. It remains to be seen what will happen with the lack of connection between the Vatican (and most likely other religious leaders) and the GFN, but it is hard to imagine that it will lessen its calls to avoid buying cheap consumer goods, often the products of modern-day slaves, and to fully ethical business practices. There is no question that the Catholic Church is in full support of Fuller's innovation regarding Children at Risk, and of every initiative that stands on the side of the most exploited of humankind.

ROMAN CATHOLIC INNOVATIONS

To conclude this chapter, I would like briefly to outline three important innovations in Roman Catholic missiological thinking in the last fifty years. I may be mistaken in this regard, but I do not believe that there are any parallels to these innovations in the history of SWM/SIS. They are, however, extremely significant in Catholic missiology, and so I offer them here to complete the picture of Catholic practice and thinking regarding mission in

---

[61]Ibid.
[62]Gagliarducci, "Vatican Bails."

the last fifty years. Although Fuller has not neglected reflections and commitments to development issues and social justice, it has not focused particularly on liberation theology. While Fuller certainly sees the connection
between missionary activity and prayer, it has not made liturgy, prayer and
contemplation constitutive elements of missionary thinking or practice. Although the concept has been well received at SWM/SIS, the program has
not been at the forefront of developing an understanding of mission as the
practice of prophetic dialogue.

   Liberation theology. One of the great Roman Catholic innovations of the
last fifty years has been the emergence of liberation theology, with its roots
in Latin America in the late 1960s and early 1970s but with reverberations
in many other areas of theological thinking and practice from black theology in the United States and South Africa to Asian theologies of liberation
to feminist, postcolonial and queer theologies throughout the world.

   Liberation theology has its roots ultimately in the Catholic conviction of
the "analogy of being" and the potential sacramentality of all creation,[63] but
more immediately in the development of the great body of Catholic social
teaching, stretching back to Pope Leo XIII's encyclical *Rerum Novarum* in
1891.[64] It took concrete shape, however, at the 1968 conference of Latin
American bishops in Medellín, Colombia. As Roberto Oliveros summarizes
it, "the central themes at Medellín were the poor and justice; love for our
brothers and sisters, and peace in a situation of institutionalized violence; and
the oneness of history and the political dimension of faith."[65] In the wake of
Medellín, Gustavo Gutiérrez published his landmark volume, *A Theology of
Liberation*, in which he described this emerging theology as "critical reflection in the light of the Word."[66] As he went on to say, "Theology *follows*;
it is the second step. What Hegel used to say about philosophy can likewise

---

[63]See Stephen Bevans, "Catholic Method," in *An Introduction to Theology in Global Perspective*
(Maryknoll, NY: Orbis Books, 2009), esp. 189-92.

[64]See Pontifical Council for Justice and Peace, *Compendium of the Social Doctrine of the Church, to
His Holiness Pope John Paul II, Master of Social Doctrine and Evangelical Witness to Justice and Peace*
(2004; repr., Rome: Libreria Editrice Vaticana, 2005), www.vatican.va/roman_curia/pontifical_
councils/justpeace/documents/rc_pc_justpeace_doc_20060526_compendio-dott-soc_en.html.

[65]Roberto Oliveros, "History of the Theology of Liberation," in *Mysterium Liberationis: Fundamental Concepts of Liberation Theology*, ed. Ignacio Ellacuría and Jon Sobrino (Maryknoll, NY:
Orbis Books, 1993), 15.

[66]See Gustavo Gutiérrez, *A Theology of Liberation*, trans. Caridad Inda and John Eagleson
(Maryknoll, NY: Orbis Books, 1973), 11.

be applied to theology: it rises only at sundown. The pastoral activity of the Church does not flow as a conclusion from theological premises. Theology does not produce pastoral activity; rather it reflects upon it."[67] The innovative aspect of this understanding of theology was not that it offers a new *theme* for theologizing—although starting with the experience of the poor and oppressed was essential—but that it offered a new *way* of doing theology, a new method.[68] It was because of this methodological innovation that liberation theology was to influence so many aspects of theology in the succeeding decades, including the theological practice of evangelicals. Almost certainly, the emphasis on justice as part of evangelization that appears in the Lausanne Covenant—on the strong insistence of Latin American evangelicals like René Padilla and Samuel Escobar—and that has blossomed into a full-blown commitment in The Cape Town Commitment would not have been developed.[69]

Liberation theology fell on some hard times in the 1980s and 1990s in the pontificates of John Paul II and Benedict XVI. In 1984 especially, a very strong and quite negative appraisal of the movement was issued by the Congregation of the Doctrine of the Faith.[70] Nevertheless, in 1986 the Brazilian bishops met with John Paul II, who, after the meeting, addressed them in a letter that included this statement: "Liberation theology is not only expedient, but useful, and necessary."[71] The movement seems to have taken on new life with the pontificate of Pope Francis, a Latin American pope who has repeatedly called for "a Church which is poor and for the poor."[72] In many ways liberation theology is much different today from its origins in the years after Vatican II, but it nevertheless remains an important innovation in Roman Catholicism that has had a major impact on theology and missiology throughout the world.

---

[67]Ibid.

[68]Ibid., 15.

[69]Commission on World Mission and Evangelism, "Together Towards Life: Mission and Evangelism in Changing Landscapes," World Council of Churches, September 5, 2012, www.oikoumene .org/en/resources/documents/commissions/mission-and-evangelism/together-towards-life -mission-and-evangelism-in-changing-landscapes; and The Lausanne Movement, *The Cape Town Commitment* (Peabody, MA: Hendrickson, 2011).

[70]Congregation for the Doctrine of the Faith, "Instruction on Certain Aspects of the 'Theology of Liberation,'" August 6, 1984, www.vatican.va/roman_curia/congregations/cfaith/documents /rc_con_cfaith_doc_19840806_theology-liberation_en.html.

[71]See Oliveros, "History of the Theology of Liberation," 27.

[72]*EG*, par. 198.

Mission as liturgy, prayer and contemplation. An important document issued by the Vatican in 1984, named "liturgical life, prayer, and contemplation" as one of several "principal elements of mission," a designation that was repeated several years later in the document "Dialogue and Proclamation."[73] In many ways, this was a strange inclusion; we don't often think about our communal or personal prayer as participation in mission. And yet, upon further reflection, speaking of liturgy, prayer and contemplation as missionary acts in themselves makes a lot of sense. Liturgy, especially the Eucharist, is always a missionary act. As theologian Gregory Augustine Pierce writes, the most important moment of the Eucharistic celebration is not the pronunciation of the words of institution, or the homily or sermon, or even the communion. It is the moment of dismissal, when the congregation is charged to "go and announce the gospel of the Lord" or "go in peace, glorifying the Lord by your lives," as the new *Roman Missal*'s dismissal rites put it.[74] Orthodox Christians speak of Christians' daily life of witness as the "liturgy after the liturgy," or, as my colleague Richard Fragomeni has put it, we celebrate liturgy in church so we can worship God by our lives in the world.[75]

The importance for prayer as an act of mission was accented by the Catholic Church when in 1927 Francis Xavier, the great missionary to India and Japan, and Thérèse of Lisieux, a cloistered Carmelite nun, were declared patrons of the missions by Pope Pius XI. The title seemed appropriate for Francis Xavier, but why Thérèse? At fifteen years old she entered

---

[73]Secretariat for Non-Christians, "The Attitude of the Church Towards the Followers of Other Religions: Reflections and Orientations on Dialogue and Mission" (DM), *Acta Apostolicae Sedis* 75 (1984): 816-28; Pontifical Council for Interreligious Dialogue, "Dialogue and Proclamation— Reflection and Orientations on Interreligious Dialogue and the Proclamation of the Gospel of Jesus Christ (1)," Rome, May 19, 1991, par. 2, www.vatican.va/roman_curia/pontifical_councils/ interelg/documents/rc_pc_interelg_doc_19051991_dialogue-and-proclamation_en.html.

[74]Gregory Augustine Pierce, *The Mass Is Never Ended: Rediscovering Our Mission to Transform the World* (Notre Dame, IN: Ave Maria Press, 2007), 37-62; *The Roman Missal*, English trans. according to the Third Typical Edition (London: Catholic Truth Society, 2011), 708; see Andrew Budzinski, "New Roman Missal Part 4—Concluding Rites and Dismissal," *Lower Your Nets* (blog), November 20, 2011, http://loweryournets.blogspot.com/2011/11/new-roman-missal-part-4-concluding.html.

[75]See James J. Stamoolis, "Orthodox Theology of Mission," in Moreau et al., *Evangelical Dictionary of World Missions*, 715. Fragomeni expressed his idea in a keynote address at the National Catholic Mission Congress in 2000 in Chicago. See further development of these ideas in an ecumenical context in Stephen B. Bevans and Roger P. Schroeder, *Constants in Context: A Theology of Mission for Today* (Maryknoll, NY: Orbis Books, 2004), 362-66.

the Carmelite convent at Lisieux and never left. But when her memoirs were published several years after her death in 1897, it was revealed how passionate she was about missionary work and how intense were her prayers for the conversion of the world. Prayer, then, is a missionary act. It aligns a believer with God's purposes in the world; it opens us up so that God's will might be done in us and in God's creation; it transforms us into more available partners with God's work of mission.[76]

The attitude of contemplation also is an act of mission. If we are to be partners in God's work, we need to pay attention to the people among whom we live and the world in which we minister. Contemplation is the grace and acquired skill of seeing the world with God's eyes. Robert Schreiter recommends the practice of contemplative prayer especially for those involved in the ministry of reconciliation because it "allows one at once to acknowledge one's own wounds . . . and to learn to wait, watch, and listen."[77]

I believe that thinking missionally about liturgy, prayer and contemplation is one of the cutting-edge areas of missiology today. It is an innovation in Catholic missiology and one shared by other traditions as well.[78]

Mission as prophetic dialogue. To speak of mission as prophetic dialogue is not an innovation of the official Catholic Church but one developed by the religious missionary congregation to which I belong, the Society of the Divine Word, and developed in a particular way by Roger Schroeder and me in several publications in the last decade or so.[79] Although it has been recognized as an important innovation by a wider circle of missiologists than Catholics, the both/and nature of prophetic dialogue marks it with a particularly Catholic character. The listening, open aspect of the practice is important in mission, as is the clear, courageous, even countercultural aspect of prophecy.

---

[76]See the development of "Prayer and Contemplation" in Bevans and Schroeder, *Constants in Context*, 366-68.

[77]Robert J. Schreiter, "Mission for the Twenty-First Century: A Catholic Perspective," in *Mission for the Twenty-First Century*, ed. Stephen Bevans and Roger Schroeder (Chicago: CCGM, 2001), 35.

[78]See, e.g., Ruth A. Meyers, *Missional Worship, Worshipful Mission: Gather as God's People, Going Out in God's Name* (Grand Rapids: Eerdmans, 2014).

[79]See Bevans and Schroeder, *Constants in Context*; Stephen B. Bevans and Roger P. Schroeder, *Prophetic Dialogue: Reflections on Christian Mission Today* (Maryknoll, NY: Orbis Books, 2011); Cathy Ross and Stephen Bevans, eds., *Mission on the Road to Emmaus* (Maryknoll, NY: Orbis Books, 2015); Stephen Bevans, "Mission as Prophetic Dialogue: A Roman Catholic Approach," in Ott, *Five Views of Mission*.

On the one hand, mission is dialogue—for Catholics today, even funda-mentally so. The 1984 document on "Dialogue and Mission" cited previously puts it succinctly: "dialogue is . . . the norm and necessary manner of every form of Christian mission, as well as of every aspect of it."[80] In words bor-rowed from African American novelist Alice Walker, mission needs to be done with a heart "so open that the wind blows through it." Or, as my Pres-byterian colleague at Catholic Theological Union, Claude Marie Barbour, expresses it, one must engage in "mission in reverse."[81] Rather than coming into a ministry situation with ready-made answers or even ready-made questions, the attitude of dialogue calls for docility—that is, an ability to be taught by the people among whom one intends to minister. As Australian Catholic missiologist Noel Connolly writes, "most people listen more will-ingly to people who appreciate them and are learning along with them."[82]

But along with dialogue, mission is about prophecy. As I have dis-covered, however, prophecy is quite complex. One can be prophetic both in deed—in silent witness—and in spoken or written word. One can prophesy by offering a lifestyle or a word of hope in seemingly hopeless or very difficult situations, or prophecy can be expressed by an individual or a community that embodies the gospel message by the way that she or he or it lives. Prophecy can also be embodied in a countercultural lifestyle and by standing up to or speaking against any kind of injustice, oppression or moral evil.[83]

It has struck me in the last several years that doing mission as a practice of prophetic dialogue is very similar to doing theology contextually. The first task of doing contextual theology is to stop, listen, observe, contemplate and discern, in order to understand the situation in which one theologizes and in order to see what model or combination of models the context calls one

---

[80]DM, par. 29.

[81]Alice Walker, "A Wind Through the Heart: A Conversation with Alice Walker and Sharon Salzburg on Loving Kindness in a Painful World," *Shambala Sun*, January 1997, 1-5; and Claude Marie Barbour, "Seeking Justice and Shalom in the City," *International Review of Mission* 73 (1984): 303-9.

[82]Noel Connolly, "New Evangelisation in Australia," unpublished paper presented to the Sedos Sem-inar, April, 2013; this phrase, unfortunately, does not appear in the published (electronic) version.

[83]In these paragraphs I have been following rather closely Cathy Ross's and my introduction to *Mission on the Road to Emmaus*, xii-xviii.

to employ.[84] This is the same with doing mission as prophetic dialogue. What does a particular situation or context call for? Does it call us to simply listen, be open, be quiet, let go of our need to control? Or does it call for a clear proclamation of the gospel, a word of hope or a word of justice?

In the end, such discernment is spirituality, and perhaps this is the key to this innovation in missiology. Spirituality is not something separate from the actual doing of mission. It is part and parcel of it. But this should not be surprising. After all, mission is participation in God's work, God's mission, and God's work is always done in a rhythm of dialogue and prophecy, as a study of the Scriptures will easily attest. Prophetic dialogue is ultimately aligning oneself with the mission of God.

Conclusion

What does Rome have to do with Pasadena? I am persuaded that it has quite a lot to do with Pasadena. Many of the innovations of SWM/SIS over the years have had major influences on some key thinkers and practitioners of Catholic missiology. Others are very much in harmony with similar innovations in the Catholic Church. Still other Catholic innovations, while not directly connected with those of SWM/SIS, are perhaps challenges to it for further thought and action. As I conclude, my prayer is that SIS will continue in the great tradition of its history and continue to innovate in ways that connect with my own Catholic Church. In this way, God's reign will be continually witnessed to, and perhaps Jesus' prayer will one day be answered: "May they be one as We are one" (Jn 17:22 HCSB).

---

[84]See Bevans, *Models of Contextual Theology.*

PART 2

···

The Implications of Innovation

Back to the Future (Looking Forward)

8

Innovation at the Margins

Jayakumar Christian

INTRODUCTION

During a visit to a community in central India while working for World Vision India, I was invited into a home that was immersed in grief—a small hut with very little living space. The walls were blackened from soot. As the conversation progressed, the family shared its story of pain. The father was a daily wage earner in the local public works. He had contracted a strange infection, something entirely new to them (later to be identified as HIV/AIDS). The doctor who broke the news to him was not very sensitive to the emotional support he might need. So the father came home, promptly doused himself in kerosene and set himself on fire. This sad story explained the soot on the wall and the grief on their faces. The father was completely charred by the time the family returned. That morning (the day after the suicide) the mother, her brother and the children were debating "Who should be pulled out of school—the son or the daughter?"—"Who should be sent to work?"

Two thoughts came to my mind as I sat with them: first, the unfairness of the decision that had been thrust on this already vulnerable family and, second, the absence of the local church when the poor are grieving. Where is the church? Can the children of our nations face uncertain days because the God of the church lives?

The world is rushing to eliminate poverty. World leaders will gather to ratify the United Nations' Sustainable Development Goals for 2030, replacing the Millennium Development Goals 2015. A press release from the World Bank quotes the statement released by thirty religious leaders who contemplated the challenge of poverty in the world: "We have ample evidence from the World Bank

Group and others showing that we can now end extreme poverty within fifteen years." In 2015, our governments will be deciding on a new global sustainable-development agenda that has the potential to build on our shared values to finish the urgent task of ending extreme poverty. In the same press release, World Bank Group president Jim Yong Kim called on faith-based organizations to develop a moral imperative to frame the bank's goals to eliminate poverty. The faith leaders in their response stated: "We in the faith community embrace this moral imperative because we share the belief that the moral test of our society is how the weakest and most vulnerable are faring. Our sacred texts also call us to combat injustice and uplift the poorest in our midst." President Kim said:

> Faith leaders and the World Bank Group share a common goal—to realize a world free of extreme poverty in just 15 years. The moral imperative can help drive the movement to end poverty by 2030 by inspiring large communities to act now and to advocate for governments to do the same. These commitments from religious leaders come at just the right time—their actions can help hundreds of millions of people lift themselves out of poverty.[1]

The time has come for the church to rise up and respond with integrity.

A PROBLEM OF MISSIOLOGY

The absence of the church in the margins (where pain and grief abound) and the complacent church in the margins reflect the lack of a credible missiology relevant for the margins. We need a missiology that enables and encourages the local church in the margins to reach out with integrity. In this chapter I highlight five missiological themes that the church and the community of missiologists must grapple with (and resolve) for the local church to be relevant to the margins, without somehow feeling that they have compromised the mission of the church. These five themes also reflect the struggles of the grassroots practitioners. In his masterpiece on missiology, David Bosch reminded the church that "the poor are no longer miserly objects of mission; they have become its agents and bearers."[2] If they are agents

---

[1]World Bank Group, "Global Religious and Faith-Based Organization Leaders Issue Call and Commitment to End Extreme Poverty by 2030," press release, April 9, 2015, www.worldbank .org/en/news/press-release/2015/04/09/global-religious-faith-based-organization-leaders-issue -call-commitment-end-extreme-poverty-2030.

[2]David J. Bosch, *Transforming Mission: Paradigm Shifts in Theology of Mission* (Maryknoll, NY: Orbis Books, 1991), 436.

and bearers of mission, then the primary business of the community of missiologists ought to be to make the local churches credible and relevant to the margins.

The five themes requiring further missiological enquiry are:

1. a theology of *power* that makes sense for the margins

2. a theology of *identity* that heals

3. a theology of *anger* that provokes redemptive action

4. a theology of the *Holy Spirit* for prophetic presence in the margins

5. a theology of *truth* that confronts lies in the public domain

Before proceeding, it is appropriate to note that Fuller Seminary's School of Intercultural Studies (SIS)—earlier called School of World Missions—is credited with several missiological innovations. Among them are pioneering thoughts on church growth (Donald McGavran), theological education by extension (Ralph Winter), unreached people groups (with Lausanne; Ralph Winter), perspectives on the World Christian Movement (10/40 Window; AD2000 and Beyond; 4/14 Window: Luis Bush), Children at Risk and development missions (Bryant Myers) and many others. All of these are a reflection of the sensitivity of the school for grassroot realities. Fuller's SIS is known for its culture of "affirming mentorship." When I took on my doctoral study on "powerlessness of the poor," the faculty and my mentors in particular—Dr. Edgar Elliston, Dr. Paul Pierson, Dr. Charles Van Engen and Dr. Charles Kraft—contributed to rigor in study without tinkering with God's call in my life; for this I am grateful. How now might this legacy inspire further innovations in the area of mission and its intersections with poverty?

An Alternative Missiology for the Margins

The community of missiologists owes to the local church in the margins, and development practitioners specifically, an alternate reading of reality and solutions with credible biblical basis for issues that emerge in the margins. In our work with the poor, when we sincerely seek to serve the poor as an expression of our discipleship to our Lord and Savior Jesus Christ, we often grapple with several faith issues. Because of a legacy of fragmentation of our mission into priorities and hierarchies, work among the poor is always "accommodated," both in our strategies and in our worldview. Consequently, field-development practitioners are left with no other recourse except to look to the secular world and current development theories for frameworks and explanations. The theology of balance has not been helpful for the grassroot practitioners in the margin to live a life of credibility.

This chapter explores five themes from the margins that require missiological research and credible response—the way we think, act and organize mission at the margins.

A THEOLOGY OF POWER THAT MAKES SENSE FOR THE MARGINS

A significant aspect of any poverty situation is the issue of power and powerful people playing god in the lives of the poor; we need a theology of power that makes sense to the powerless margins.

The issue. Poverty and oppression are synonymous with powerlessness. Today's poverty is more about the growing gap between the rich and the poor than about absolute numbers. Poverty is about skewed and broken relationships. Poverty is about the powerlessness of many with power concentrated in the hands of a few. Further, this power-powerlessness relationship is founded on an interpretation of power—which includes interpretations of history, understandings of power, views of God and his expectations, valuations of persons and so on—devised by a handful of powerful people. It encompasses all of life—social, economic, political, bureaucratic and religious.

The perfect social harmony celebrated by the powerful is not without its cracks and flaws. Our understanding of poverty is determined by a minority, "less numerous, [which] perform[s] all political functions, monopolise[s] power and enjoy[s] the advantages that power brings."[3] These, the powerful, play god in the lives of the poor and form a "god-complex." These perceptions of power and powerlessness are often rooted in a people's worldview. The beliefs about power among the powerful are soon internalized by the powerless, who end up believing in the inevitability of their poverty.

The god-complexes (nonpoor people, structures and systems seeking to play god) in poverty situations seek to absolutize themselves. This

---

[3]Michael Curtis, ed., *The Great Political Theories* (New York: Avon Books, 1981), 2:332.

tendency to absolutize power, influence eternal tomorrows, overflow scope-specific influence, claim immutability or fear no power deflation are traits that are normally attributed to gods. The powerful seek to play this role in the lives of the poor.

Walter Wink's description of the "domination system"[4] parallels the description of the god-complexes in poverty relationships. Wink describes the domination system as a system that

1. demands that the world value power as an end in itself,

2. requires society to become more like itself,

3. acquires a sense of independence "beyond human control,"

4. assumes an identity of its own and

5. wounds the soul of its subjects.[5]

Such is the nature of the god-complex that holds the poor captive. These god-complexes operate through people, systems and structures.[6] Religious systems, mass media, law, government policies and people in powerful positions all serve to reinforce the god-complexes that keep the poor impoverished.

The missiological question. I would like to suggest that this "playing god" in the lives of the poor is an affront to the kingdom of God. Secular development theories suggest that a sustainable solution to poverty and powerlessness is about empowerment. It calls for a redistribution of the same power that in the first place created poverty and powerlessness—an operating model that recycles power.

We need a more radical solution than mere recycling of power. If we perceive poverty as the captivity of the poor within the god-complexes of the nonpoor and their structures and systems, then our response to poverty must involve the reversal of these god-complexes. We need to address these god-complexes—the persons, structures and systems, including their ideologies. If we perceive that this "playing god" is in direct contradiction to

---

[4]Walter Wink, *Unmasking the Powers: The Invisible Forces That Determine Human Existence* (Philadelphia: Fortress, 1986).

[5]Walter Wink, *Engaging the Powers: Discernment and Resistance in a World of Domination* (Philadelphia: Fortress, 1992), 40, 41, 54, 101.

[6]R. William Liddle, "The Politics of Development Policy," *World Development* 20, no. 6 (1992): 793-807.

the intents of the kingdom of God, then we need to consider an alternative that is consistent with the kingdom of God. The most radical alternative to these god-complexes is the establishment of the kingdom of God that does not coexist with other kingdoms and god-complexes. The kingdom of God, therefore, is not peripheral to the issue of responding to poverty but at the core. A model of transformation that confronts the god-complexes among the poor by proclaiming the kingdom of God and its understanding of power is more than simple development work. This is a ministry of a prophetic community that challenges the god-complexes.

The community of missiologists must rise to the occasion and enable the frontline development practitioners to live out their faith with an understanding of power that is consistent with the kingdom of God. We need an understanding of power that will grapple with harsh realities of the socio-economic-political nature of poverty without spiritualizing it—an understanding that power belongs to God (not to the people).

Can the church that worships a God who was crucified on the cross, marginalized and vulnerable redefine power? Are there clues at the cross for this radical redefinition? Or will the church simply buy into the world's understanding of power and feel permanently marginalized?

A Theology of Identity That Heals

Poverty and oppression are more than an issue of justice and dignity; they are the result of the marring of the identity of the oppressed. We need a missiology that applies the church's theology of *imago Dei* to heal the oppressed.

The issue. Most development theories of poverty and development, as well as religions, stop short in their analysis of poverty with merely enquiring into dignity and justice. Very often this inadequate analysis is a reflection of a lack of an adequate solution to the real issue of poverty and oppression. In our analysis of poverty, we are often confronted with the understanding that the poor are a significant cause for their own dismal state of affairs—their birth, antecedents, etc. This self-understanding of their identity wounds the soul and often breeds hopelessness. This wounding of the soul is not merely inherited; it is inflicted on the poor. By marring the identity, the powerful seek to inflict near-permanent damage to the poor. They do so in many ways.

First, flawed social norms and an accepted worldview of those in poverty are used to mar the identity of the poor. When traditions, fear of shame and marred identity combine, powerlessness is the product. The girl child has to drop out of school and become a laborer. Second, years of marginalization mar the identity of the poor. The fact that girls are born with a distinct social disadvantage leaves a negative imprint on their minds. This is more than stunting of the aspirations and awareness of the poor. The ability of the poor to critically reflect and analyze their situation has also been retarded. Years of exploitation have reduced the marginalized into dull, submissive living objects. Their perpetual exploitation freezes their minds. Consequently, self-image and identity are shaped by the hurt and pain that the poor carry in their minds. The dullness of the mind, along with the hurt and the pain, serves to perpetuate powerlessness among the poor. Third, economic systems see the poor as mere tools of production; their value to the system is their productivity and not their personhood. The powerful reduce the poor into mere objects. The poor become less than human in the process,[7] and their identity is defined by the mere-object status that is assigned to them. Fourth, the marring of the identity of the poor is a prelude to further exploitation. It seems natural that any exploitation and oppression must deal with the question of identity of the oppressed. Once the oppressor ascribes a low identity to the poor, then all the oppressor's consequent acts of exploitation are justified as legitimate. The low identity endorses all forms of oppression. The girl child will become unwanted before she is exploited by the oppressor. Through oppressive social norms, stunting of the mind, retarding of the reflective ability of the poor and reduction of the poor to mere objects, society mars the identity of the poor.

The missiological question. If marred identity is a significant cause for powerlessness and poverty, then mere acts of justice are not adequate to counter it. Can the church that believes all humans are made in the image of God offer assistance? Is there a possibility that the development industry and development practitioners can look to the church for sustainable solutions? We need a theology of identity that is rooted in the theology of *imago Dei*. We need a theology that goes beyond dignity and justice to healing the marred identity of the poor and the oppressed. Many world religions do not

---

[7]Paulo Freire, *Pedagogy of the Oppressed* (New York: Continuum, 1990).

believe all humans are made in the image of God. Christianity does. The church owes it to the nations to articulate its theology of *imago Dei* in terms of those whose identity is intentionally marred to keep them powerless.

A THEOLOGY OF ANGER THAT PROVOKES REDEMPTIVE ACTION

Poverty, oppression, injustice and abuse all tend to provoke anger in any society; anger provokes action. We need a theology that provides the local church in the margins an opportunity to grieve prophetically and pursue redemptive action.

The issue. Reflecting on his context in Psalm 39, David talks about wickedness (Ps 39:1) and vulnerability to the reproach of fools (Ps 39:8). He reflects on his state of mind with these words:

> "I will guard my ways
> > that I may not sin with my tongue;
> I will keep a muzzle on my mouth
> > as long as the wicked are in my presence."
> I was silent and still;
> > I held my peace to no avail;
> my distress grew worse,
> > my heart became hot within me.
> While I mused, the fire burned;
> > then I spoke with my tongue. (Ps 39:1-3)

Similarly, when Nehemiah considered the nobles who were exploiting their own people, he said, "I was very angry when I heard their outcry and these complaints. After thinking it over, I brought charges against the nobles and the officials" (Neh 5:6-7). Very often, working with the poor and the oppressed involves these emotions—emotions of anger. Nehemiah was angry too, reversed the system and put the nobles on the defensive.

Recently I was in a small railway station called Jarsidhi in East India, where I met a young girl of fifteen years who was cheerfully selling small handmade fans. I discovered that she was in the tenth grade; she wakes up early in the morning, at 4:00 a.m., to study and after school works in the railway station until 10:00 p.m. before she returns home. Her mother works for a meager income, and her father is too ill to work. I wondered when India would stop employing its children and their nimble fingers to solve India's poverty. I was angry.

The challenge we face today is not merely the huge numbers of the poor but a growing gap between the poor and the rich. The poor are marginalized. The prophet Amos talking about the exploitation of the poor as sin mentions they "trample on the needy, and bring to ruin the poor of the land" (Amos 8:4)—such an apt description of what the nations do to their poor, even today.

Recently the world was shocked at the images of three-year-old Aylan al-Kurdi, who fled with his family from the Syrian civil war but died on a Turkish beach. I am sure the parents of Aylan would have, in their own way, prayed: "Thy kingdom come." How would the church respond to that prayer from the margins?

The missiological question. The popular teaching about anger within Christian faith is one of restraint. "Do not let the sun go down on your anger" (Eph 4:26). Unfortunately, without being disturbed, there will be no concerted corrective action. Perhaps a lack of a theology of anger causes our churches that are present among the poor to remain complacent. We are probably too holy to get angry. We need a theology that will allow our bones to burn and cause us to get angry.

We need a missiology that will allow us to reread reality from a different perspective, not necessarily from the perspective of the powerful or the complacent. This rereading of our historical reality must affirm that God is active in the margins and interested in the history of the poor. This is a very liberating alternative. This rereading of history and seeing God's action in history opens up the possibility of the powerless "imagining" the future anew. The future need not be a mere extension of their distorted version of history anymore. The new future need not be out of bounds for the poor. The marginalized that are constantly denied this history-making role and are tools in the hands of the history makers of the world have a new opportunity to imagine a future characterized by hope.

This imagining of a new future (by peoples whose histories have been reread and identities clarified) is, to use Walter Brueggemann's words, a ministry of "prophetic imagination." This prophetic imagination must precede any concrete response.[8] In this task of imagining a new future, the "prophet of God" provides the leadership. Brueggemann goes on to say that the *vocation*

---

[8]Walter Brueggemann, *The Prophetic Imagination* (Philadelphia: Fortress, 1978).

of the prophet is to keep alive the ministry of imagination and hope and to provide a liberating alternative to what has been for generations the accepted reading of history and reality, that of the powerful. It is important that the church rediscover the Jesus who did not hesitate to take the whip.

A THEOLOGY OF THE HOLY SPIRIT FOR A PROPHETIC PRESENCE IN THE MARGINS

Even as we battle with "principalities" and "powers" (Eph 6:12 KJV) and invest life among the oppressed, we need to understand fully the power of the Holy Spirit in grappling with the realities of the margins.

The issue. In addition to the aspects of poverty already cited, a major cause for poverty is the role of the principalities and powers. Poverty is not only rooted in the fall of humans but is also a result of the present working of the Evil One. Missiologists and grassroots practitioners affirm that "behind all poverty is the devil, . . . [and] the ultimate cause of poverty is the devil himself."[9] Therefore, authentic and sustainable involvement among the poor will involve confrontation with the powers of the Evil One. For "the Son of God was revealed for this purpose, to destroy the works of the devil" (1 Jn 3:8). There are several ways in which the devil and his forces influence persons in any situation. Let me confine myself to the role of the principalities and powers in poverty situations.

First, the powers reinforce the various deceptions that have roots in a people's belief system. They blind the mind (see 2 Cor 4:4). The devil and his forces are great deceivers (see 2 Tim 2:26; Gal 4:3; Eph 2:12). Second, the principalities and powers have the ability to attack the body through disease (see Mt 9:32-33; Lk 13:16; 2 Cor 12:7). People in poverty also become dependent on the village priests and witchcraft, and this becomes another drain on their already meager financial resources. Third, the role of the principalities and powers in influencing people (especially among the poor) through compulsive dependence on certain habits is also well known. These habits then result in the perpetual socioeconomic captivity of the households. Fourth, the devil attacks the very relationships that were meant to serve as positive agents in our journey toward becoming what God wants

---

[9]Michael Duncan, *A Journey in Development*, Bridges 3 (Melbourne: World Vision, 1990), 9.

us to be. He reinforces all divisive forces and creates new ones. He sows seeds of enmity between people and keeps the poor who are already on the fringe of society divided. Marred relationships are a mark of abiding in death, while unity and brotherhood are a sign of life.

Fifth, the devil also exploits the curses that people cast on each other. "A curse is the invocation of the power of Satan or of God to affect negatively the person or thing at which the curse is directed."[10] Sixth, the cosmic principalities and powers seek to go beyond controlling people's minds to controlling their wills. Consequently, hopelessness and powerlessness set in. Seventh, the devil and his forces seek to mar the identity of persons involved in poverty relationships. It exploits the marred identity, the hurt from broken relationships and the pain of captivity to a harsh religious belief system in order to further mar the identity of the poor and reinforce their powerlessness. Therefore, the principalities and powers play a crucial role in intensifying the powerlessness imposed by society on the poor, by reinforcing the oppression, by manipulating the will and by marring the identity of the poor.

The missiological question. These challenges demand that development practitioners rediscover the power of the Holy Spirit in the context of development work. First, the work of the Holy Spirit in the life of the agent of transformation is critical. Transformation of life always involves investment of life. The lives of staff and their relationships matter. The spirituality of the staff is key to transformation. We need to enable the agents of transformation to fully understand the import of Luke 4:16-19, where Jesus announced that his Nazareth manifesto is a derivative of the "Spirit of the Lord . . . has anointed me."

Next, the context of poverty involves battle with principalities and powers. Transformational initiatives must essentially be an effort to unmask the principalities and powers. We need to confront the devil and his forces in the context of poverty relationships. Prayer and fasting, the protection of the whole armor of God and the gifts of the Spirit are key instruments required for this battle.

We need to develop a missiology for the margins that will necessarily involve the whole armor of God, the work of the Holy Spirit to transform the agent of transformation and the gifts of the Spirit for work relevant to the margins.

---

[10]Charles Kraft, *Defeating the Dark Angels* (Ann Arbor, MI: Servant, 1992).

A THEOLOGY OF TRUTH THAT CONFRONTS LIES IN
THE PUBLIC DOMAIN

If poverty and oppression are about captivity in a web of lies, then response to the margins is about proclamation of truth; we need a theology of truth that challenges these lies.

The issue. Many of the issues outlined above are rooted in issues of truth, perception, beliefs and worldview. The god-complexes that I referred to earlier are rooted in ideologies that Walter Wink refers to as spiritual interiority, an inner reality that governs and holds together structures, systems and people. This inner reality provides the logic for the structures and systems and interpretations for the ultimate values of life and events. This is the ideological center that shapes structures, systems and people. Since these ideological centers deal with ultimate values in life, I refer to them as "inner spirituality." These "spiritual interiorities" of the god-complexes are inextricably related to structures and systems. They form the spirituality of the various economic, social, political, bureaucratic and religious structures and systems. These inner spiritualities become the system above the systems. They provide that underlying "spiritual dimension in the victimization of the poor and the power-accruing activity of the systems."[11]

Another common element in various poverty relationships is the distortion of truth. The god-complexes, the distortion of history, the marring of identity, the fragmentation of relationships, the role of the principalities and powers, and inadequacies in the worldview of all cultures' themes are all undergirded by lies. Flawed assumptions and interpretations that are rooted in the religious systems, the worldview of a people, and the work of the principalities and powers sustain oppressive relationships. The poor are captive in a web of flawed assumptions and false interpretations. Both the poor and the nonpoor believe these lies and thus ensure the perpetuation of the powerlessness of the poor.

The missiological question. A critical issue that we are confronted with as we seek to respond to poverty and marginalization is lies. If poverty is the captivity of the poor in the web of lies under the monopoly of these spiritual interiorities that seek to maintain the oppression of the poor, then the most

---

[11]Robert C. Linthicum, *Empowering the Poor* (Monrovia, CA: MARC Publications, 1991), 19.

appropriate response of the church will involve proclaiming the truth. Transformational initiatives must proclaim truth in public places, truth about the identity of the poor (that they are made in the image of God), truth about power, truth to the cosmic powers and the Truth that sets us free. This ministry of proclaiming truth within poverty situations is the task of a prophetic community. Transformation must seek to establish truth and righteousness in poverty situations. We need a missiological frame to understand the church's presence among the poor as a prophetic presence—proclaiming truth.

CONCLUSION

The conversation in that little hut in India was painful. The mother and the uncle debated all possible options, with the little children watching the pain on their faces. I sat there in anger wondering what the Lord's Prayer could mean for this family: "Your will be done, on earth [in this home] as it is in heaven" (Mt 6:10). If one of those little children should face uncertain days, the church must prove its relevance in the margins.

The church needs a theology that will make sense to the margins. We need a theology that will bring healing to the wounded soul and marred identities. We need a theology that will allow the bones of the local church to burn and be angry, provoking redemptive and prophetic presence. We need a theology that will be dependent on the Holy Spirit and his work and presence among us. We need to equip the local church to be prophetic, proclaiming the truth in the public domain, in the margins.

As for the development practitioners, these contributions from the community of missiologists will mean protecting their integrity and witness through life in the margins. The work of mission in the margins will then serve as a credible and radical alternative to the secularists who are fast taking over the humanitarian industry.

These issues from the margins, if addressed diligently and with rigor, have the potential to transform missions as a whole, to create a deep sense of restlessness and trigger movements. For, after all, the history of Christian missions and the church is about movements (so I learned from SIS). The question before us should be, are we willing to allow our missiology to be shaped by issues from the margins, or will it continue to maintain the status quo?

9

Mission Trajectories in the Twenty-First Century

Interfaith Roads Best Traveled

Terry C. Muck

INTRODUCTION

With regard to the Christian mission endeavor to reach people belonging to other religions, we are at a crossroads. Three roads enter the intersection. The three roads might be called Contestation Street, Consilience Freeway and Confession Driveway. All three roads come from somewhere located in the two thousand years of Christian history, and, presumably, all three have reasonably discernible futures as we exit this particular time and place. At least we like to think we can discern their futures, the directions Contestation Street, Consilience Freeway and Confession Driveway might take as they exit this particular intersection we call "now." But can we? Do we even try?

In one sense, the challenge to our mission to people of other religions is as plain as day—it always has been. People belonging to the world religions called Hinduism, Buddhism, Confucianism/Taoism and Islam need to hear the message of Jesus Christ, and they have been the subject of intense Christian mission efforts for two or three centuries now. Yet very little mission fruit, relatively speaking, has been harvested as a result of this work. Although we have contested their belief systems effectively, loved and aided their people groups with admirable Christian compassion, and modeled Christian living and being as well as can be expected given our fallenness and fallibility, the results have not matched the efforts. It is as if we are stuck in a huge traffic jam of religions.[1]

Todd Johnson and Kenneth Ross estimated that 34.8 percent of the world's population was Christian in 1910. Their estimate for 2010 dropped to 33.2 percent.[2] One hundred years of mission effort, in what was heralded to be the "Christian century," left us no better off than when we started.[3] During that same period, Hinduism, Confucianism/Taoism and Islam had all increased their percentages of believers among the world's population.[4] Islam in particular grew from 12.6 percent to 22.4 percent. Even allowing for the fact that much of the growth of these other religious groups was more strongly tied to birthrate growth than to conversion growth, it is a record that should concern us.[5]

It is time to ask how we should exit the religious congestion of our time. We need to do it now because others are asking the same question and offering their own answers. The so-called new atheists have an answer: marginalize religious faith, particularly Christianity, or attempt to do away with it altogether.[6] The Islamic State has another answer—simply blow up the congested intersection, leaving their radical and heterodox version of Islam as the only religion left standing.[7] We may have a similar goal (of dominating

---

[1] See chapters on "Buddhism" in *Handbook of Religion: A Christian Engagement with Traditions, Teachings, and Practices*, ed. Terry Muck, Harold Netland and Gerald McDermott (Grand Rapids: Baker Academic, 2014).

[2] Todd Johnson and Kenneth Ross, eds., *Atlas of Global Christianity 1910–2010* (Edinburgh, UK: Edinburgh University Press, 2009), 7.

[3] At the beginning of the twentieth century, some expected to witness the dominance of Christianity worldwide. It was to be the "Christian century." One writer, John R. Mott (sometimes called the "father of the ecumenical movement") coined a phrase, "the evangelization of the world in one generation," that captured this missional optimism.

[4] Indeed, it was the failure of mission to the great world religions, Hinduism, Buddhism, Confucianism/Taoism and Islam, that left us worse off after a hundred years of mission work. This is all the more significant when compared with the great successes we had among the indigenous religious groupings in Africa and Oceania. In 1910, 9.4 percent of Africa was Christian; by 2010, 47.9 percent was Christian. In Oceania, by 2010 an astounding 78.6 percent of the population was Christian.

[5] Johnson and Ross, *Atlas*, 7.

[6] For a sampling of some new atheist work, see Richard Dawkins, *The God Delusion* (New York: Bantam, 2006); Daniel Dennett, *Breaking the Spell: Religion as a Natural Phenomenon* (New York: Penguin, 2007); Sam Harris, *The End of Faith* (New York: Norton, 2005); and Christopher Hitchens, *God Is Not Great* (New York: Twelve, 2007).

[7] Also called the Islamic State of Iraq and the Levant (ISIL), the Islamic State of Iraq and Syria (ISIS), the Islamic State of ash-Sham and Daesh. All are controversial names, even the shortened and most commonly used Islamic State. Most Muslims around the world object to the use of the word *Islamic* in the titles, not wanting to be identified with their barbarity. They judge the group

the field of religion), but we have radically different means to suggest. Yet the means we have been using are not working. Let me suggest that the time has come to reassess our mission efforts to people of other world religions.

Let's start by analyzing how we got into this congested intersection in the first place. Let's travel back along Contestation Street, Consilience Freeway and Confession Driveway, tracing their histories and the rationales that built the roads. Let's look at the places we've been; examine the results, positive and negative, that each path has produced; and focus especially on how these three roads look today.

CONTESTATION STREET

Contestation means framing the Christian mission effort as a contest with non-Christian religions and secular ideologies, what Paul called the "principalities" and "powers" (Eph 6:12 KJV).[8] It means challenging false teachers whenever they present counterfeit versions of the gospel or, like the "sorcerers" in Acts, attempt to sell the power of the gospel of Jesus Christ as a means of making profit for themselves.[9] There is no more graphic representation of missional contestation in Scripture than Elijah leading the prophets of Yahweh against the prophets of Baal on Mount Carmel, a story related in 1 Kings 18:16-46. At stake in all these contests, even the Old Testament ones, are the vindication of Jesus' life and teaching, the validation of gospel truth, and the victory of the church.

It is tempting to think that the roots of missional contestation, conflict and confrontation lie in disagreements over competing religious truths. Such is probably not the case, however. If the sociobiologist nonpareil E. O. Wilson is even close to being right, the human drive to confront is genetic in origin. In answer to the question as to whether human beings are innately aggressive toward one another, Wilson answers yes: "Innateness refers to the measurable

---

to be unrepresentative of true Islam. The issue points up the difficulty in applying a religious studies principle that is—letting religious groups identify and name themselves.

[8]See Ephesians 6:12 NRSV: "For our struggle is not against enemies of blood and flesh, but against the rulers, against the authorities, against the cosmic powers of this present darkness, against the spiritual forces of evil in the heavenly places."

[9]See, for example, Romans 16:17-18: "I urge you, brothers and sisters, to keep an eye on those who cause dissensions and offenses, in opposition to the teaching that you have learned; avoid them. For such people do not serve our Lord Christ, but their own appetites, and by smooth talk and flattery they deceive the hearts of the simple-minded"; Acts 8:9-24, the story of Simon the Sorcerer.

probability that a trait will develop in a specified set of environments, not to the certainty that the trait will develop in all environments. By this criterion human beings have a marked hereditary predisposition to aggressive behavior."[10]

Religion, according to Wilson, is "one of the universals of social behavior" and "in all probability an ineradicable part of human nature."[11] As such, it regularly gets attached to any one of the

> seven different aggressive behaviors that are hardwired into our nervous systems: defense and conquest of territory, assertion of dominance within well-organized groups, sexual aggression, acts of hostility by which weaning is terminated, aggression against prey, defensive counterattacks against predators, and moralistic and disciplinary aggression used to enforce the rules of society.[12]

In other words, the theological demand to defend the gospel finds ready and willing support in the biological makeup of human beings.

Support for human contestation comes from other sectors of the human community as well. If Emmanuel Levinas is right, we become human persons only after we see ourselves over against other human persons. The first moments of real consciousness, the development of self and the consummation of our creative purpose become real as we confront the difference that other human beings present to us.[13] William James noted that religious persons can have any one of four different existential approaches to religious being, although James did not come close to anticipating the nature and complexity of hybrid personal identity (including religious identity) that our postmodern brothers and sisters are calling to our attention.[14] Contestation with other human beings and comparison to different human beings make us what we are—what we are intended to be.[15]

And, yes, philosophical contestation is a feature of our religious lives. Religions, especially the world religions, have teachings and doctrines and beliefs and philosophies. It is normal (that is to say, human) for us to compare our Christian teachings, doctrines, beliefs and philosophies with those of

---

[10]E. O. Wilson, *On Human Nature* (Cambridge, MA: Harvard University Press, 1978), 101.
[11]Ibid., 169.
[12]Ibid., 102.
[13]Emmanuel Levinas, *Totality and Infinity* (Cedar Rapids, IA: Duquesne University Press, 1969).
[14]William James, *The Varieties of Religious Experience* (New York: Longmans, Green, 1902).
[15]Homi Bhabha, *The Location of Culture* (1994; repr., London: Routledge, 2004).

other religions. Even a cursory examination of how basic Christian dogmas developed in early church councils makes clear that specific doctrines most often were articulated after being challenged by another religion's teaching.

Contestation Street has been heavily traveled by Christian missionaries through the ages. Christian uber-missionary Paul was a contester of sophisticated skill. He cajoled, debated, confronted and preached, making no bones about the fact that he was willing at any time and place to give witness to the hope that was within him.[16] The early church, once Constantine converted, used Roman military might to aid the conversion of pagan Europe. In other parts of the world, the crusaders crusaded, the inquisitors inquisited and the colonialists colonized, taking full advantage of their cultural dominance to spread the gospel. To attempt a reading of Christian mission history by excising the embarrassingly frequent incidences of conflict would probably reduce Kenneth Scott Latourette's seven volumes and 3,493 pages of the *History of the Expansion of Christianity* to a ten-thousand-word essay.[17]

In just these few paragraphs, you may have noticed an important feature of the way I have been describing Contestation Street. It may seem to you as if I have indiscriminately lumped together the good, the bad and the ugly of Christian mission contestation. Contestation can include the good—comparative conversations with one's neighbor, sermons extolling the value of Christian faith over against other alternatives and the simple desire to see local churches grow—all contestation-based means that most of us would endorse. But contestation can also manifest a dark side—religious war, violence against individuals in the name of one's religion, and political and economic favoritism to Christians—all mission means that have at some times and places been used to champion the gospel and with which most of us feel uncomfortable.

I plead guilty to this observation, and let me say here that all three roads we are going to examine are the same—all have good, bad and ugly manifestations. It is up to us to choose which is which. Which manifestations are good: faithful

---

[16] 1 Peter 3:15: "Always be ready to make your defense to anyone who demands from you an accounting for the hope that is in you." In Acts 9:26-30 Paul cajoled Barnabas in Jerusalem; in Acts 14:15-17 he preached at Lystra; in Acts 17:16-34 he debated with unbelievers at Athens; and in Galatians 2:11-14 he confronted Peter at Antioch. These are only examples of the many other places where Paul contested for his faith.

[17] Kenneth Scott Latourette, *A History of the Expansion of Christianity*, 7 vols. (New York: Harper & Brothers, 1937–1945).

to Scripture, productive of human flourishing, capable of bringing glory to God? Which manifestations are bad: methods that in their emphasis on manipulation and violence work against the loving, gracious message of the gospel? And which manifestations are ugly—that is, ineffective means of reaching people for Christ?

In order to find biblical acknowledgment that contestation can be either good or bad, we need look no further than the story of Jesus' arrest in the Garden of Gethsemane. One of Jesus' followers, in an attempt to defend Jesus from a mob sent by the chief priests, drew a sword and cut off an ear of one of the attackers. Jesus stridently rejected this "mission method." Too much contestation? But then a few verses later he rebukes Peter for not showing enough gumption when he denies Jesus three times to those questioning him. Too little contestation? (See Mt 26:47-56, 69-75; Mk 14:43-52, 66-72.) How do we find the right balance?

We need to begin with a set of theological principles. When we begin to look for those principles, we find an irony. As ubiquitous as contestation has been in the *practices* of Christian mission, it is telling that it appears far less frequently in mission *theologies*. It is difficult, in fact, to envision a theology of mission that is based purely on contestation. Even the most radical of exclusivistic and separatistic theologies are constrained to find a place for God's grace, an acknowledgment that modifies the contest aspect of mission, seasoning it with what we are going to call in the next section the consilience of mission.

One of the best examples of a mission theology that presents a positive spin on and a central place for contestation comes from Jewish theology, the post-Holocaust survival theology of Emil Fackenheim (1916–2003). Fackenheim was a Jewish philosopher and Reform rabbi who argued that we needed a new post-Holocaust theology, a theology built on an imperative requiring Jews to carry on Jewish existence. It is a theology of survival. He frequently compared the theology he was recommending to the 613 laws or *mitzvot* given to Jews in the Torah: "In order to deny Hitler a posthumous victory we advocate a 614th *mitzvot*: continue Jewish existence and life."[18]

Fackenheim summarized the most important features of this survival theology in his primary work, *To Mend the World*:

---

[18]Emil Fackenheim, *To Mend the World: Foundations of Post-Holocaust Jewish Thought* (Bloomington: Indiana University Press, 1982), xx.

We are, first, commanded to survive as Jews, lest the Jewish people perish. We are commanded, secondly, to remember in our very guts and bones the martyrs of the Holocaust, lest their memory perish. We are forbidden, thirdly, to deny or despair of God, however much we may have to contend with him or with belief in him, lest Judaism perish. We are forbidden, finally, to despair of the world as the place which is to become the kingdom of God, lest we help make it a meaningless place in which God is dead or irrelevant and everything is permitted. To abandon any of these imperatives, in response to Hitler's victory at Auschwitz, would be to hand him yet other, posthumous victories.[19]

Clearly, a religious tradition and its people can be pushed to the brink of extinction, and in the face of this threat, what is left but contestation? And Fackenheim would surely say that the command to contest for one's religious existence is the responsibility not only of the members of that tradition but of all good people everywhere. It is the responsibility of Jews, he would say, but also the responsibility of us as Christians.[20] In the grand scheme of life, it is clear that religions do compete and will always compete—but there is a contest that runs deeper than that, the contestation against evil.

Finally, how common is contestation in mission to people of other religions today? Here is what Franklin Graham, head of the Christian relief and development organization Samaritan's Purse, has to say about Islam: "We are under attack by Muslims at home and abroad. We should stop all immigration of Muslims to the United States until this threat with Islam has been settled. Every Muslim who comes into this country has the potential to be radicalized—and they do their killing to honor their religion and Muhammad."[21] Clearly, contestation—good, bad and ugly—is a primary feature of Christian mission past, Christian mission present and, as we will shortly recommend, Christian mission future.

CONSILIENCE FREEWAY

Consilience has been as ubiquitous a framing device for Christian mission as contestation. In many ways it is a feature of Christian mission that emphasizes the unique aspects of Christian teaching in ways that contestation

---

[19]Ibid., 310.
[20]Ibid., 278-89.
[21]Franklin Graham, Facebook post, July 23, 2015.

does not. As the reader will intuitively know, there is nothing at all unique about the contest of the religions. All religions play the same game, even to the point of borrowing strategic initiatives from one another, especially the ones that are bearing fruit. Nothing spreads faster in the global religious communities than an effective mission innovation. The same cannot be said to be true of consilience.

What is consilience? Near the beginning of the last section on contestation, we shared some biological observations from E. O. Wilson, so let's do the same in this section on consilience. Wilson says that consilience is a way of linking the great branches of learning, including linking science and the humanities. In its most precise definition, consilience refers to the confluence of research results across several disciplines. For example, if a biologist, a psychologist, a sociologist and a philosopher all announce research results that agree with one another, then that overall result is much stronger than if just one discipline unearthed a finding.

Wilson jumps immediately from this specific definition of consilience, something we might even call commonsensical, to the broader implications of this, the unity of knowledge: "Consilience is the key to unification. . . . The ongoing fragmentation of knowledge and resulting chaos in philosophy are not reflections of the real world but artifacts of scholarship."[22] As might be expected, Wilson argues from what he calls the Ionian Enchantment, a belief of scientists going back to Thales in the sixth century BCE and forward to Albert Einstein in the twentieth century that the world is a unity, operating in all fields from a common set of laws and principles. Wilson quotes Einstein: "It is a wonderful feeling to recognize the unity of a complex of phenomena that to direct observation appear to be quite separate things."[23]

Christian mission operates with a similar sense of wonder and anticipation. Paul in his letter to the Ephesians begins with a vision of a similar unity: "he has made known to us the mystery of his will, according to his good pleasure that he set forth in Christ, as a plan for the fullness of time, to gather up all things in him, things in heaven and things on earth" (Eph 1:9-10). The biblical conception of unity begins with creation: since God created everything there is, then it is a unified whole. Genesis says that "in

---

[22]E. O. Wilson, *Consilience: The Unity of Knowledge* (New York: Knopf, 1998), 8.
[23]Ibid., 5.

the beginning . . . God created the heavens and the earth" (Gen 1:1)—that is, everything. The psalmist is clear that all human governments and their rulers are subject to God's laws:

> [God] cuts off the spirit of princes,
>   [he] inspires fear in the kings of the earth. (Ps 76:12)

Paul, again in Romans, finds God's grand unity in human nature: "For what can be known about God is plain to them, because God has shown it to them. Ever since the creation of the world his eternal power and divine nature, invisible though they are, have been understood and seen through the things he has made" (Rom 1:19-20).

The mission urge provides the scriptural *locus classicus* for consilience. Matthew tells us to love our neighbors as ourselves (Mt 22:34-40) and goes on to include enemies in the list of neighbors (Mt 5:43-47; see also Rom 12:20). In the two-thousand-year history of Christianity, the specific definition of who is enemy to the Christian faith has changed frequently, but the command to love them unconditionally, just as we would love God and friends, has not. The Bible teaches that love of one's enemies is the ultimate test of completeness:

> You have heard that it was said, "You shall love your neighbor and hate your enemy." But I say to you, Love your enemies and pray for those who persecute you, so that you may be children of your Father in heaven; for he makes his sun rise on the evil and on the good, and sends rain on the righteous and the unrighteous. For if you love those who love you, what reward do you have? Do not even the tax collectors do the same? And if you greet only your brothers and sisters, what more are you doing than others? Do not even the Gentiles do the same? Be perfect, therefore, as your heavenly Father is perfect. (Mt 5:43-48)

At its best, Christian mission has stood for this kind of universal love and respect. Early Christians became known as the people who loved one another—not only one another but the poor, despised and forgotten of society around them. Tertullian tells us that it was the early Christians who would claim the unwanted dead and give them a decent burial.[24] This they

---

[24]Tertullian, *Apology* 39.

did when they were a struggling, persecuted minority in early Rome. Once they gained cultural power, Christian missions became an unbeatable combination of proclamation, education, medical care and justice. As sociologist Robert Woodberry has shown, the presence of Christian missionaries was (is?) a valid indicator of a flourishing society.[25]

Not to be left out of this search for consilience are the religions. There have always been missionaries who have considered missional consilience with other religions to be an indispensable part of their task. One thinks of James Legge among the Confucianists and Taoists in China, Karl Reichelt among Buddhists in Hong Kong, E. Stanley Jones among Hindus in India, and Samuel Zwemer among Muslims in the Middle East. Each of these missionaries showed remarkable openness to common truths that would emerge when Christianity's teachings were compared with the teachings of Hinduism, Buddhism, Confucianism/Taoism and Islam. Remember the point of consilience: if common truths emerged from different fields of studies, the results of those truths can be considered stronger than if they emerged from just one field. When other religions teach the same things that we as Christians teach, we should be overjoyed. Our case for Christ has been made even stronger.

Unfortunately, just as there were good, bad and ugly forms of contestation, there are good, bad and ugly forms of consilience. An overenthusiastic commitment to the Consilience Freeway can too quickly lead to universalism and ideological pluralism—and it has in the history of Christian mission. When the scandal of particularity of the Christian revelation—the belief that God appeared to humanity in a single person and place—is not used to balance the scriptural endorsement of consilience, we find words like perennial philosophy, unity of all religions, religious pluralism and the like intruding on orthodoxy. Sometimes these movements take institutional form. The Unitarian Universalist Association, a Christian denomination, seeks wisdom from six sources: personal experience, prophetic utterances, world religions, Jewish and Christian teachings, humanist teachings and spiritual teachings.[26]

---

[25]Robert Woodberry, "The Missionary Roots of Liberal Democracy," *American Political Science Review* 106, no. 2 (2012): 244-74.

[26]"Sources of Our Living Tradition," Unitarian Universalist Association, accessed January 31, 2016, www.uua.org/beliefs/what-we-believe/sources.

The irony of Christian approaches to consilience is this: it is only when we acknowledge the uniqueness of the Christian story and the various ways God has chosen to relate to his ultimate creation, human beings, as creator, redeemer and sustainer that we find a framework for the unity that Paul speaks of in Ephesians. Without that framework we are left with a rather amorphous, Kantian version of the Golden Rule. Of course, since different people groups think in radically different ways about how they would ideally like to be treated, it becomes clear that the Golden Rule provides little in the way of specific ethical guidance at all.

Consilience today? Recently, for another project, I did a detailed study of the ways we read the parable of the good Samaritan—when I say "we" I mean not just those of us who are evangelical Christians, but the ways our culture at large understands the parable of the good Samaritan. The Western cultural zeitgeist is to see it as a general recommendation and universal obligation to treat everyone with the compassion of a good Samaritan.[27] Hospitals that no longer have anything to do with their religious roots are named after the good Samaritan. Anyone who makes the evening news for doing almost any act of human kindness is called a good Samaritan. The meme of the good Samaritan has become a culturally acceptable way to present Christianity to skeptics.

But is this meme really the point of the parable of the good Samaritan? Perhaps it is as a derivative implication of the story. The main point of the story, however, was to answer the rich young ruler's question about what he had to do to be saved. And Jesus's answer to that question made clear that in Jesus' mind salvation came from what the Good Samaritan (that is, Jesus) did for all of us lying in the ditch. Our lives should be lived in imitation of Jesus' paradigmatic act of grace. The parable is not about an Enlightenment concept of universal ethical obligation. It is Christian soteriology based on Christian christology actualized in Christian ethics as the fruits of the Spirit of Christ living in us.[28]

Consilience still is a valuable, even indispensable framework for Christian mission, but it may be the most misunderstood (i.e., the most "ugly") of our three frameworks.

---

[27]See Terry C. Muck, "Missio-logoi, Interreligious Dialogue, and the Parable of the Good Sa-maritan," *Missiology* 44 (January 2016): 5-19.

[28]I have been strongly influenced in this reading of the parable of the good Samaritan by Charles Taylor, *A Secular Age* (Cambridge, MA: Harvard University Press, 2007), 738-39.

CONFESSION DRIVEWAY

There is an important third way we frame Christian mission these days: confession. We call it confession, but it could be called credo, witness or testimony. Confession is not just a Christian thing. All people in religious mode seem to have an urge to talk about what they believe in a winsome way so that other people will listen. Such speaking has power. Phenomenologist of religion Gerardus van der Leeuw uses the term *testimony* to describe and explain the nature of such power:

> Whoever speaks, therefore, not only employs an expressive symbol but goes forth out of himself, and the word that he lets fall decides the matter. Even if I merely say "Good Morning," to someone I must emerge from my isolation, place myself before him and allow some proposition of my potency to pass over into his life, for good or evil. . . . Whoever asserts anything "poses" and thus exerts some influence; but he also "exposes" himself.[29]

For van der Leeuw, confession (testimony) is thus an unavoidable consequence of being in religious mode and, especially, of speaking of one's religion, even when the intention may have nothing to do with influencing other people. This type of confession "pertains to every living religion."[30] But for some religions confession becomes intentional. When it does, it changes character, van der Leeuw says, and becomes "a fully conscious propaganda of doctrine and worship."[31] Christians call this mission, Muslims *dawah* and Buddhists *dharmadhatu*.[32] These are the great mission religions.

Perhaps the biblical text that captures the essence of mission in this sense of being a confession is the parable of the talents (Mt 25:14-30). For Christians, you see, confession is neither a personal, therapeutic exercise nor an attempt to impose one's faith on others. It is more an obligation to engage others in faith talk, and the first step toward that end is to expose oneself. It is that exposure of one's beliefs that leads to engagement with the

---

[29]Gerardus van der Leeuw, *Religion in Essence and Manifestation* (New York: Harper & Row, 1963), 403-4.

[30]Ibid., 612.

[31]Ibid.

[32]See Larry Poston, *Muslim Dawah in the West* (London: Oxford University Press, 1992); and Mahinda Deegalle, *Popularizing Buddhism: Preaching as Performance in Sri Lanka* (New York: State University of New York Press, 2007).

religious other. As the parable of the talents teaches, that kind of exposure is risky. But we are to take the risk rather than bury our beliefs in the sand out of fear of losing them.

The root issue in all religion discussions is the primacy of personal experience, of individual faith. In the realm of religious studies, the person who brought this to our attention was Wilfred Cantwell Smith, who, in *The Meaning and End of Religion*, argued that the operative unit of religion is not the big religions but the individual faith of each human being.[33] In Christian theology, H. Richard Niebuhr brought it to our attention in *The Meaning of Religion*, where he argued that revelation occurs within a tradition as individuals in communities apprehend what God is doing.[34] In Christian mission theology Frances S. Adeney brings this to our attention in several of her works where she explains the hermeneutical circle, which describes in some detail what happens when each of us is confronted with new religious ways of thinking.[35]

The most fundamental biblical instance of confession is what many consider the first and simplest of the creeds of Christianity: "Jesus is Lord."[36] Paul made this simple confession the cornerstone of his theology. In his letter to the Romans, he states, "because if you confess with your lips that Jesus is Lord and believe in your heart that God raised him from the dead, you will be saved. For one believes with the heart and so is justified, and one confesses with the mouth and so is saved" (Rom 10:9-10).[37] For Paul, confession begins with a personal quest—the quest to believe and then express that belief.

But this personal quest for salvation quickly, seamlessly, becomes missional. His argument for this missional framing of confession consists of four parallel questions that build on one another:

---

[33] Wilfred Cantwell Smith, *The Meaning and End of Religion* (Minneapolis: Fortress, 1991).

[34] H. Richard Niebuhr, *The Responsible Self* (Louisville, KY: Westminster John Knox, 1999).

[35] Frances S. Adeney, *Graceful Evangelism* (Grand Rapids: Baker Academic, 2010). See also chapters 16 and 17 in Terry Muck and Frances S. Adeney, *Christianity Encountering World Religions* (Grand Rapids: Baker Academic, 2009), 221-41.

[36] "Jesus is Lord" is the shortest creedal affirmation in the New Testament. That these are the direct words of Scripture and that the statement is very short have made it the poster-child creed of Christianity. Three other creeds are considered authoritative to some degree by almost all Christians: the Apostles' Creed, the Nicene Creed and the Athanasian Creed.

[37] See also Acts 10:36 and 1 Corinthians 12:3. A variant of the creed appears in Philippians 2:11: "Jesus Christ is Lord."

- But how are they to call on one in whom they have not believed?

- And how are they to believe in one of whom they have never heard?

- And how are they to hear without someone to proclaim him?

- And how are they to proclaim him unless they are sent? (Rom 10:14-15)

The confession "Jesus is Lord" is not part of a contest, a one-upmanship designed to put other people down, nor is it an expression of unity. It is a statement of intention, a way of saying, "Here is where I am coming from. In order to understand what I am giving witness to and how I think it is important to you, you need to understand what I am all about."

As it was with contestation and consilience, there have been good, bad and ugly confessions of "Jesus is Lord" throughout mission history. Part of the reason for this is that faith is a very personal thing, and the form faith takes in each individual can vary dramatically depending on time, place and personality. For examples of this, consider one of the most tangible forms of missional confession—the written form of confession, such as Augustine's classic *Confessions* or the confession written by Russian novelist extraordinaire Leo Tolstoy in *A Confession*.[38] Both are classic expressions of the genre, but they are very different.

But the missional framings of confession, even allowing for individual religious differences, can also be bad. At times in our Christian mission history, confession has been used not as a baseline missional foundation but as a litmus test for orthodoxy. The most pronounced example of this was the Inquisition, in which the orthodoxy of one's confession became, literally, a matter of life and death. This may seem an extreme example, and it surely is at one end of the good-bad spectrum of the ways of using missional confession. But how often do we find ourselves using it that way—as a way of determining inclusion or exclusion?

As a frame for mission, confession is not used to determine either the inclusion or the exclusion of the missionary himself or herself, nor as a bar to jump over or a hoop to jump through for the ones receiving our confession of faith. Rather, confession is the foundation on which one's mission is built. It is the precursor to doing mission. It is a *preparatio evangelica*, a preparation

---

[38]Augustine, *Confessions* (New York: Penguin Classics, 1961); and Leo Tolstoy, *A Confession* (1882; repr., New York: Penguin, 2008).

for doing mission to nonadherents of Christianity. Put another way, it is like a key that unlocks the meaning of mission for people of other world religions. How, indeed, can we call on the one we have not believed in—or expect others to?

We used an important word in that last sentence: *believed*. For the Christian, a creed is to be believed. That is our mode of acceptance of our creed. Such is not the case for all religions vis-à-vis their "creeds." Muslims, for example, have a creed called the shahadah. The shahadah is as follows: "There is one god, Allah, and Muhammad is Allah's prophet."[39] Muslims are to embrace this creed by *reciting* it. Anyone who can recite it is considered a Muslim. Jews, for another example, have what might be called a creed, the *Shema*: "Hear, O Israel: The LORD our God, the LORD is one" (Deut 6:4 NIV). For Jews, the mode of embrace of the Shema is to *hear* it. Perhaps the most unusual, to our way of thinking, of a religion's embrace of its creed is how Sikhs honor their creed, the Five Ks (*panj kakar*)—they are to *wear* the five words beginning with *K* that declare to the world that they are Sikh: long hair (*kesh*), a wooden comb (*kangha*), a metal bracelet (*kara*), a short pair of undergarment pants (*kachera*) and a short curved sword or knife (*kirpan*).[40]

The confessional way of framing Christian mission is alive and well in our existential age, although it sometimes seems that the only truly important things about religious faith these days are what I believe, how I feel and where I do mission when in religious mode.

THREE OPTIONS, THREE FUNCTIONS

It is tempting to see these three roads of Christian mission as optional ways of framing the Christian mission effort. In one way of looking at Christian history, they are three different options. It depends on how we define the word *option*. By *option* do we mean equally valid ways from which we can choose one—and feel comfortable with other Christians choosing one of the others? Or by *option* do we mean three mutually exclusive paths with one

---

[39]The shahadah is made up of two parts, both of which appear in several places in the Qur'an, but not together. Islamic tradition has put them together in what is considered the first and most important of the Five Pillars of Islam.
[40]See Harjinder Singh, *The Sikh Code of Conduct* (Walsall, UK: Akaal, 2009).

right one—and we choose the right path, even if it is the road less taken? Especially the road less taken?

As seen from the preceding discussion, contestation, consilience and confession are all part of our mission heritage. They all have biblical warrants, traditional church support and many clear examples of their use in mission history, and they probably all resonate with your experience of mission these days. Nothing I have said in the preceding paragraphs would be a surprise to any of you sitting here today, especially a group of Christians so expert in understanding the Christian mission effort down through the years. You may have even begun to do in your minds what I am about to attempt now— propose a way of stitching the three mission roads together in a mission theology whole.

Let's begin by considering three ways of approaching this task. Our first option would be to choose one—contestation, consilience or confession—as the right way to frame the Christian mission task. A second option would be to rank them one, two, three, with the first being the most important frame but the other two adding support to that most important one. And the third option would be to say all three are important parts of the mission whole, and we must seek a way of framing the Christian mission effort that accommodates all three. Let's spend a moment unpacking further each of the three options.

The choose-the-right-one option. It may be that as I went through my descriptions of the three frames—contestation, consilience and confession— you found yourself especially warm to one of the three. It may also be the case that you found yourself especially negative about one or the other of the three. If this is the case, it may be that you would like to use one as the frame and raise objections about the other two. I would be most interested in your defense of this position, but it is not one I take. I believe that all three have clear warrants from Scripture, tradition and social science findings.

The rank-them option. Or it may be that you like one of the frames especially well but also see strengths in the other two. You do not want to jettison the other two altogether, but you want to reserve a special place, as a governing frame, so to speak, for the one frame you find the most convincing. I think that this is also a defensible position, one that stakes out a middle ground between the choose-the-right-one option and the all-three-are-valid option. But, again, I lean toward the all-three-are-valid option. So let's take a closer look at that one.

The all-three-are-valid option. When I described the three frames, I took pains to show that the beliefs that support each frame and the actions that are manifested in mission according to each frame take good, bad and ugly forms. And I hope you agree that when I described some of those beliefs and some of those actions, it was not particularly difficult to distinguish the good from the bad. That is, it is fairly easy to make the judgment that religious terrorism is bad contestation and street preaching is good contestation. Or that seeking unity in the name of Christ is good consilience and a total relativism regarding religious difference is bad consilience. Or that confession used as witness is good while confession used as manipulation of a particular circumstance for personal gain is bad.

The really challenging thing about the all-three-are-valid option, however, is that if you put them all on an equal footing, another frame needs to be created in order to determine which frame is most useful in any given circumstance. As you may have already intuited, that frame is what is usually called contextualization these days. The context determines whether the contestation frame, the consilience frame or the confession frame is the right one to use as a theoretical base from which to determine practical mission steps. In some contexts it may be that a contest among the religions is taking place, in some the best way to view the mission task is to see ourselves as partners with other well-intentioned religious, and in still others all that is called for is a frank, personal sharing of religious stories. But which is which?

The key to understanding how the three framings of Christian mission work together lies in the realization that the three framings have different functions. Consilience functions as the goal of mission, contestation as the everyday dynamic of mission that moves us toward the goal and confession as the existential motivation that urges us to move along. All three functions are necessary for successful mission to take place. The way I identified the three frames in the initial illustration of three roads entering an intersection was intended to point out the difference in the functions.

I identified consilience as the Consilience Freeway since one takes a freeway to get from here to there, point A to point B. When on a freeway, we pay little attention to scenery; we avoid the distraction of small towns. The freeway is all there is, and everything is measured by the speed it gets us to our destination. Our eyes are on the destination, and missional consilience is the same. Unity of all in Christ is the destination, and we measure everything we do by its appropriateness to arriving at that destination.

Contestation, on the other hand, is more like a city street—Contestation Street—that moves us through different neighborhoods. Every block or two we may be faced with a different driving challenge, and we have to change our driving technique based on the driving conditions we encounter. When on a freeway, we can set the accelerator on seventy and steer. But on Contestation Street we must stop and go, detour around construction sites, change lanes frequently, pay attention to state-mandated driving restrictions and the like. Mission in the neighborhoods is indeed a contest, and we best view it as such.

And confession? I called it Confession Driveway because confession is what gets us from our home to the street where the action really is, and from there to the freeway if conditions call for it. Each of our driveways is a little different. Driveways are very personal, but without the initial driveway we cannot even enter into the game. We are committed to mission because of our experience of Christ and the gospel. Nothing happens until that commitment is a factor—until we not only acknowledge our commitment but embrace it and then testify to it in whatever context we find ourselves.

All three of these mission functions are necessary, and how they fit together in any given situation is the whole point of contextualization. Importantly, the three are different functions and cannot be conflated but must be complementary to one another. The challenge of mission, especially among people of different religions, is how to use them in a complementary way. Since no two situations are the same, the ways they fit together are endlessly complex. Let me end this section, however, with three overall comments, which I will put in question form:

- Regarding Confession Driveway, the primary question is, how do we confess without too quickly jumping to either contestation or consilience?

- Regarding Contestation Street, how do we contest the other religions without making our confession a thinly disguised cover for triumphalism or a threat to the goal of unity in Christ?

- Regarding Consilience Freeway, how do we acknowledge consilience as
  our ultimate goal without weakening the will to contest when necessary
  or without reducing confession to a romantic exercise in feel-goodism?

To summarize, we are the inheritors of three different ways of framing
the Christian mission task to people of other world religions. All three—
contestation, consilience and confession—have strong scriptural warrants
and have, in the main, produced faithful and effective mission and missions.
One of the keys to effective missions is to know which mission frame will
be most effective in any particular mission situation. The choice of frame is
greatly aided by the recognition that each frame has a different function—
consilience as goal, contestation as dynamic and confession as existential
validator—and the most effective mission will take place when function
matches context. Mission to people of other world religions is a constant
negotiation of mission frame and, within each frame, among appropriate
and inappropriate methods.

10

Mission in the Islamic World

Making Theological and Missiological
Sense of Muhammad

John A. Azumah

INTRODUCTION

In its Scriptures, Islam, which came seven hundred years after Christianity,
claims to share in the same prophetic tradition with Judaism and Christianity.

> And dispute ye not with the People of the Book, except with means better
> (than mere disputation), unless it be with those of them who inflict wrong
> (and injury): but say, "We believe in the revelation which has come down to
> us and in that which came down to you; Our Allah and your Allah is one; and
> it is to Him we bow (in Islam)."[1]

Muhammad called on Jews and Christians as witnesses against his pagan
Meccan adversaries, apparently before personally encountering Jewish and
Christian communities. Upon encountering Jewish communities in Medina
in 622, a violent falling out took place with a resultant hardening of position
toward Jews. The Qur'an continued to espouse positive views about Christians as "nearest among them in love" to Muslims in contradistinction to
Jews and pagans, who are "strongest among men in enmity to the believers"
(Q 5:82). Jesus allegedly prophesied the coming of Muhammad by name (Q
61:6) with qur'anic recitations seeking to defend Jesus against what was perceived as Jewish polemic and boastfulness:

---

[1] Q 29:46. Unless otherwise stated, all qur'anic citations are from Abdullah Yusuf Ali, *The Holy
Qur'an: Translation and Commentary* (Karachi, Pakistan: Khalil Al-Rawaf, 1946).

That they [the Jews] said (in boast), "We killed Christ Jesus the son of Mary, the Messenger of Allah";—but they killed him not, nor crucified him, but so it was made to appear to them, and those who differ therein are full of doubts, with no (certain) knowledge, but only conjecture to follow, for of a surety they killed him not:—Nay, Allah raised him up unto Himself; and Allah is Exalted in power, Wise. (Q Nisa' 4:157-158)

This situation was to change after meeting with real Christians. Muslim tradition reports Muhammad, before and at the outset of his prophetic career, meeting Christian figures like Bahira and Waraqa Ibn Nawfal, who predicted and confirmed his prophetic vocation, respectively. The only recorded account of Muhammad's encounter with a Christian community, however, took place in 632, a few months before his death. A delegation of Melkite Christians from Najran (South Yemen), including a bishop, visited Muhammad in Medina, ostensibly in response to the edict for all tribes to surrender. The two parties engaged in doctrinal disputation, with significant differences regarding the person and mission of Jesus. From this time, the defense of Jesus against the Jews is extended to Christians.[2] Islam is now the only religion accepted by God (Q 5:3). Believers are no longer permitted to befriend Christians (Q 5:51). Christians, like the Jews, should be fought into submission by the Muslim community (Q Tawbah 9:29).

J. M. Gaudeul concludes from Muhammad's encounters with Jews and Christians as follows: "Islam owes its existence as a separate religion to the fact that its message and its founder were rejected first by the pagans of Mecca, then by the Jews and finally by the Christians. One would say: Islam exists because dialogue failed."[3] Kenneth Cragg observes: "This is the inward tragedy, from the Christian angle, of the rise of Islam, the genesis and dissemination of a new belief which claimed to displace what it had never effectively known."[4]

Whatever we make of the early encounters, the critical fact is that Muslims have a set of teaching in the Qur'an and traditions about Jews and Christians and their respective beliefs that they uphold as revealed truth. Islam has also

---

[2] A. Guillaume, *The Life of Muhammad: A Translation of Ibn Ishaq's Sirat Rasul Allah* (Oxford: Oxford University Press, 1955), 270-77.
[3] J. M. Gaudeul, *Encounters and Clashes: Islam and Christianity in History* (Rome: Pontifical Institute for Arabic and Islamic Studies, 2000), 1:17-18.
[4] Kenneth Cragg, *The Call of the Minaret*, 3rd ed. (Maryknoll, NY: Orbis Books, 1985), 219.

developed its own distinct set of truth claims about its prophet, and whether these are historically verifiable or not, it is the witness Christians have to engage with and make sense of. Christians (and Jews) have, since the inception of Islam, been doing just that. How Christians in their mission to Islam over the centuries have tried to make theological and missiological sense of the prophet of Islam is the subject of this essay. And we will examine this first of all by outlining the Islamic witness or portraits of Muhammad as Muslims present it.

ISLAMIC PORTRAIT(S) OF MUHAMMAD

Muhammad is believed to have been born in 570 CE. His father, Abdullah, died before he was born, and his mother, Amina, passed away when he was only six. An uncle, Abu Talib, took care of him. A rich widow, Khadija, employed Muhammad to take care of her trading business. When he was twenty-five and she was forty, the two got married. Muhammad is believed to have had his call to prophethood in 610 CE while meditating in a cave outside Mecca.

Muhammad then started his public preaching of the worship of one God to the polytheistic society of Mecca in 613 CE and met with opposition but was shielded by his clan ties, which included an influential uncle and a wealthy wife. These two, however, passed away in 619, leaving him in a vulnerable position in Mecca. Some merchants from Medina invited him to migrate to their town, and in 622 he accepted the invitation and escaped to Medina, hotly pursued by his Meccan enemies.

The move from Mecca to Medina is known as the *Hijra* and is very significant in Islam, for it is the year of Muhammad's "migration," rather than of his birth, call or death, that marks the beginning of the Muslim calendar. This year also marks a division between two phases of his prophetic career. During the twelve-year period in Mecca (610–622 CE), Muhammad's mission was a preparatory one in which he preached, warned and used peaceful persuasion. But the fulfillment of his mission came during the ten-year period in Medina (622–632 CE), when he established a theocracy in which his religious beliefs were integrated in a political, judicial and military framework.

In Medina, Muhammad and his followers resorted to the traditional Arab nomadic practice of raiding other groups. The raids provoked a series of battles with the people of Mecca. Muhammad and his followers won the first major battle, the battle of Badr in 624, but the next year they were defeated at the battle of Uhud. When a third battle loomed in 627, they successfully protected Medina by digging a trench around it, with the result that this battle is known as the Battle of the Trench. In the wake of this battle, orders were issued for the assassination of a number of Muhammad's opponents. Between six hundred and nine hundred Jewish men were massacred in Medina while the Jewish women and children were taken as slaves.

In 630, Muhammad marched on Mecca with ten thousand men and captured the city. He executed a few of his leading opponents and granted a general amnesty to the rest. Two years later, he ordered all idol worshipers in Mecca to surrender and convert to Islam within the next four months, or face attack. Later that same year (632), Muhammad died in the bosom of his beloved wife, Ayisha, leaving the task of consolidation to four of his close associates and successors (caliphs), who are known as the Rightly Guided Caliphs.

Montgomery Watt's *Muhammad: Prophet and Statesman*[5] sums up the two portraits of Muhammad's prophetic career: (1) a prophet, warner in Mecca who for twelve years preached the worship of the one God, Allah, promised paradise (*janna*) to those who would heed his message and warned of an eternal punishment in hell (*jahanna*) to those who would reject him and (2) a statesman, or head of state, lawgiver and commander-in-chief, who ruled over a community in Medina, and for ten years led them in conquests. He transitioned from a preacher leaving judgment in the hands of God to becoming the vehicle through which God exacts punishment on enemies.[6] Islamic mysticism, jurisprudence, theology, politics, theory of war, family and personal laws are all drawn from Muhammad's prophetic career in Mecca and Medina.

Muhammad's Significance

The Islamic shahadah or *kalima* (creed)—"There is no god but Allah, and Muhammad is the Messenger of Allah"—is the first of Five Pillars of Islam.

---

[5]W. Montgomery Watt, *Muhammad: Prophet and Statesman* (Oxford: Oxford University Press, 1961).

[6]D. Marshall, *God, Muhammad and the Unbelievers: A Qur'anic Study* (Surrey, UK: Curzon Press, 1999).

The shahadah calls for the submission to God's will (as contained in the Qur'an) and to Muhammad as prophet and statesman. In Islam, God is always coupled with Muhammad. To obey, disobey, deny, fight or separate oneself from one of them is to do the same to the other. One must desire, fear, love and be more devoted to them both than to one's family. A Muslim is therefore a person who has surrendered to God's will and decrees in the Qur'an and to the prophetic authority or rule of Muhammad. Hence, "to become a Muslim [is] to become a subject,"[7] and to convert from Islam is to commit treason.

The qur'anic portrait of Muhammad is that of a messenger of God whose mission is in line with the biblical tradition represented by Abraham, Moses, Noah and Jesus. He is fully human and mortal:

> Muhammad is no more than a messenger: many were the messengers that passed away before him. If he died or were slain, will ye then turn back on your heels? If any did turn back on his heels, not the least harm will he do to Allah; but Allah (on the other hand) will swiftly reward those who (serve Him) with gratitude. (Q 'Imran 3:144)

The Qur'an proclaims Muhammad as the last prophet and the "Seal of the Prophets" (Q 33:40). He it is who brought the long line of prophethood from Adam through Abraham, Noah and Moses to Jesus (124,000 in total, according to tradition) to an end, and there will be no prophet after him. By the leave of Allah, all prophets are endowed with powers to perform miracles as signs confirming their prophethood. Muhammad's miracle is the "matchless Qur'an" (Q 10:37-38). Since no one could produce anything that could match the poetic beauty of the Qur'an, the argument goes, the Qur'an itself is a miracle. Its production was also a miracle because it refers to Muhammad as *ummi*, which Muslims interpret as meaning that he was illiterate (although many Western scholars dispute this claim). As an illiterate, Muhammad could not have composed the Qur'an, thus confirming the miraculous status of Islam's Scripture.

Even though, as a human being, Muhammad is called on to seek forgiveness for his own sins (Q 40:55; Muhammad 47:19), nevertheless, his life serves as an eternal model for Muslims: "Ye have indeed in the Messenger

---

[7]Cragg, *Call of the Minaret*, 142.

of Allah a beautiful pattern (of conduct) for any one whose hope is in Allah and the Final Day, and who engages much in the Praise of Allah" (Q 33:21). Believed to be the perfect embodiment of the will of God (in the Qur'an), Muhammad's example, the Sunna, is the second most important source for Islamic faith and practice.

Islamic traditions and Muslim devotion paint a completely different portrait of Muhammad from that of the Qur'an. While the Qur'an insists that Muhammad is fully human and that worship is due only to God, that his only miracle is the Qur'an itself, Muslim devotion and traditions have made extravagant claims on his behalf. In Islamic traditions, Muhammad is surrounded by miracles: a gazelle spoke to him; a palm tree trunk sighed when he no longer leaned against it while preaching; a poisoned sheep warned him not to eat it; a handkerchief with which he had wiped his mouth and hands would not burn in a furnace. Traditions also report his splitting the moon in two; trees, doors and windows bowing down to him; his healing broken limbs with the touch of his hand; his casting out demons and multiplying food through prayer to feed his followers.[8]

Whether in West Africa, Turkey or Indonesia, stories about Muhammad's life have permeated popular Muslim thought and poetry, which is full of descriptions of his marvelous attributes and actions. Every detail of his life is attributed to divine permission or command. He is the most favored intercessor on the day of judgment and the best and greatest of the prophets. He is regarded as sinless and is referred to as "the perfect human being." His name is never uttered or written without an invocation of blessing (*tasliya*—"May the blessings and peace of Allah be upon him"). As one leading scholar on the subject puts it, "The *tasliya* has become an essential, sometimes it would seem, the essential of the life of salvation and devotion" to Muslim believers.[9]

Muhammad has a total of two hundred and one titles (as compared with ninety-nine for God) and also shares most of the attributes given to God. He is called the preexistent Light of God (*Nur Muhammadi*) from which God created other souls in his image. He is reported to have said, "Whoever has

---

[8]See *First Encyclopaedia of Islam: 1913–1936*, ed. H. A. R. Gibb et al. (Leiden: Brill, 1993), s.v. "Muhammad."

[9]Constance E. Padwick, *Muslim Devotions: A Study of Prayer-Manuals in Common Use* (Oxford: Oneworld, 2003), 154.

seen me, has seen Allah."[10] As with God, any representation of Muhammad in the form of drawing or photograph is strictly prohibited. Muhammad Iqbal, a leading twentieth-century Pakistani Muslim mystic and scholar, stressed the importance of the prophet of Islam in his daring statement: "You can deny God, but you cannot deny the Prophet."[11]

So in effect, we have three portraits of Muhammad in the Islamic witness: prophet, statesman and mediator. In their religious expression and orientation, different Muslim groups have drawn from the different portraits of Muhammad. The mystics draw from his withdrawals and meditations; theologians draw from his preaching; jurists explicate the shari'a from his legal edicts and rulings in the Qur'an and Sunna; political theorists draw from his career as statesman in Medina; and activists and militants draw on his military exploits in the Sira. So there is a sense in which we can talk of "Muhammads" in Islam: Muhammad of the shari'a espoused from Qur'an and Sunna (legalism); Muhammad of the Sira with his military exploits (jihad); and Muhammad of the mystical tradition with his intercessory role (popular devotion). Having thus given an account of the Muslim witness about their prophet, we now proceed to look at some representative Christian attempts at making theological and missiological sense of Muhammad.

MUHAMMAD AND THE CHRISTIAN

The earliest well-known Christian articulation of Muhammad and Islam can be traced back to John of Damascus (675–753) of the Greek Orthodox tradition. John, like his father and grandfather before him, worked in the "ministry of finance" of the caliphate until his resignation around 724, when he became a monk and moved into a monastery outside of Jerusalem. Writing about Islam under the title *Heresies in Epitome: How They Began and Whence They Drew Their Origin*, John describes Islam (and other Christian movements), as "the forerunner of the anti-Christ" and "a false prophet" named "Mameth": who, "having casually been exposed to the Old and the New Testament and supposedly encountered an Arian monk, formed a heresy of his own."[12]

---

[10]Annemarie Schimmel, *And Muhammad Is His Messenger: The Veneration of the Prophet in Islamic Piety* (Chapel Hill: University of North Carolina Press, 1985), 125.

[11]Michael Nazir Ali, *Frontiers in Muslim-Christian Encounter* (Oxford: Regnum Books, 1987), 135.

[12]Daniel J. Sahas, *John of Damascus on Islam: The "Heresy" of the Ishmaelites* (Leiden: Brill, 1972), 133.

The evidence John produced against Muhammad's prophethood included dreams, lack of witnesses, lack of scriptural support and lack of integrity in a man who prophesies in his own interest. John was writing from the safety of his monastery for a Christian audience, and his approach was clearly negative and polemical. Although he concluded that Muhammad was a false prophet, he saw Islam as a heresy and Muhammad as misguided by an Arian Christian monk. In other words, John did not think Muhammad was inspired by the devil. He never resorted to insults or cursing Muhammad. More importantly, John showed a rare accurate knowledge of Islam and engaged with the teaching as Muslims presented it. He did not try to get around the Islamic witness or use Christian criteria to evaluate Muhammad's claims.

Catholicos Timothy I (728–823), a Nestorian patriarch and a contemporary of John of Damascus, is another key early Christian leader who attempted to make theological sense of Muhammad. In a fascinating dialogue with Caliph al-Mahdi (775–785) in 781, Timothy respectfully but firmly denied the Muslim claim that Jesus prophesied the coming of Muhammad in the Gospels. "So far as Muhammad is concerned I have not received a single testimony either from Jesus Christ or from the Gospel which would refer to his name or to his works," was Timothy's reply.[13] He further refuted the claim that the promise of the Paraclete in the Gospel of John refers to Muhammad. Unrelenting, al-Mahdi, as if acknowledging that Jesus said nothing about Muhammad, pressed Timothy: "What do you say about Muhammad?" To which Timothy replied:

> Muhammad is worthy of all praise, by all reasonable people, O my Sovereign. He walked in the path of the prophets, and trod in the track of the lovers of God. All the prophets taught the doctrine of one God, and since Muhammad taught the doctrine of the unity of God, he walked, therefore, in the path of the prophets. Further, all the prophets drove men away from bad works, and brought them nearer to the good works, and since Muhammad drove his people away from bad works and brought them nearer to good ones, he walked in the path of the prophets. . . . Finally Muhammad taught about God, His Word and His Spirit. Muhammad walked, therefore, in the path of all the prophets. Who will not praise, honour and exalt the one who not only fought for God in words, but showed also his zeal for Him in the sword?[14]

---

[13]Gaudeul, *Encounters and Clashes*, 2:249.
[14]Ibid., 2:251.

Mistaking Timothy's reply for an admission of Muhammad's prophethood, the caliph interjected: "You should, therefore, accept the words of the Prophet . . . that God is one and that there is no other one besides him." In other words, if you believe all that you've said about Muhammad, you should accept his teaching and convert to Islam. To this Timothy replied: "This belief in one God, O my Sovereign, I have learned from the Torah, from the Prophets and from the Gospel. I stand by it and shall die in it."[15] The rather enigmatic response of "he walked in the path of the prophets" aside, it is clear that in contrast to John of Damascus, Timothy was respectful of Muhammad and courteous to his Muslim overlord without conceding any theological ground. John adopted the polemical approach while Timothy opted for the apologetics path.

A key figure whose views on Muhammad had significant influence in the Western (Latin) churches is Peter the Venerable (1094–1156), also known as Peter of Cluny. Committed early to monastic life, Peter rose to become the abbot of the Benedictine Abbey of Cluny, France, in 1122. Peter commissioned Robert of Ketton to undertake the first translation of the Qur'an into Latin with the help of a Muslim named only as "Muhammad," ostensibly to ensure that the translation was done "with the fullest fidelity, without anything left out by deceit."[16] "Concerning Mahumeth," Peter writes, he "cannot be called or considered a prophet." He proceeds to describe the prophet of Islam as "a swindler," "a murderer," "a traitor," "an abominable adulterer" who contradicts himself in the Qur'an and performed no miracles and who in light of the gospel "could not be a prophet."[17] Against the backdrop of militant crusades, and hoping his work would be translated into Arabic for Muslims to read, he wrote: "I do not attack you—Muslims—as our people often do, by arms; but by words; not by force, but by reason; not in hatred, but in love."[18] Really?

Peter's views were clearly influenced by the crusading fervor and popular animosity toward Muslims and Islam at the time. Nevertheless, his motivation for the translation of the Qur'an and other works on Islam into Latin was to inform Christians in the West about Islam for the

---

[15]Ibid., 2:252.
[16]Ibid., 1:144.
[17]Ibid., 2:253-54.
[18]Ibid., 1:145.

purpose of evangelizing Muslims. In his approach Peter opted for the war of words or polemics rather than the open warfare of the crusaders of his time. In that sense, Peter's approach was a major departure from prevailing hostile Christian attitudes to Muslims. Yet, he demonized and vilified Muhammad. Commenting on Peter's influence, J. M. Gaudeul notes: "By reason of his intellectual approach and his missionary zeal, Peter of Cluny can be said to have opened new perspectives heralding the developments that took place in the Western Church's approach to Muslims in the 13th and 14th centuries."[19] The polemical approach very much dominated medieval and premodern Christian discourse on Muhammad, from the public denunciations of the martyrs of Cordoba of the ninth century and persisting into the sixteenth century during the Protestant Reformation.

The reformers, especially Martin Luther and John Calvin, had their own views about Islam and Muhammad at a time when Western Europe was under the threat of being overrun by the Ottoman Turks and Caliph Suleiman the Magnificent (1494–1566). Vienna was under siege in 1529, and the fear of Muslim Turks entering Western Europe was real. In Luther's words, the Turk is a "destroyer, enemy and blasphemer of our Lord Jesus Christ, a man who instead of the gospel and faith sets up his shameful Mohammed and all kinds of lies, ruins all temporal government and home life or marriage, and his warfare, which is nothing but murder and bloodshed, is a tool of the devil himself." There was no question in Luther's mind that Muhammad was a false prophet "because he himself openly admits that he does not embrace the teaching of the prophets and apostles." The emperor, not the church, is called to fight the Turks but purely and simply to protect and defend his subjects, not to defend the gospel or the faith. If the emperor's task were really "to destroy unbelievers and non-Christians, he would have to begin with the pope, bishops, and clergy, and perhaps not spare us or himself!"[20]

John Calvin (1509–1564), unlike Martin Luther, had a generic and rather superficial knowledge of Islam. He never read the Qur'an, for instance. Attacking the Turks, the Jews and the "Papists" in equal measure, Calvin

---

[19]Ibid., 1:147.
[20]Sarah Henrich and James L. Boyce, "Martin Luther—Translations of Two Prefaces on Islam: Preface to the *Libellus de ritu et moribus Turcorum* (1530), and Preface to Bibliander's Edition of the Qur'ān (1543)," *Word & World* 16, no. 2 (1996): 262-64.

claims "the Turks adore/worship a devil under the name of God" and describes Muhammad as "a deceiver," "an apostate" and "the companion of the Pope who has done his very best to seduce those poor people." Muhammad and the pope together represent "the two horns of the Anti-Christ" in the book of Daniel.[21] Like Luther, Calvin disapproves of the church's promulgation of war against the Turks and insists that war is permissible only in the name of the emperor. It has to be emphasized, nevertheless, that the views of Luther and Calvin were clearly shaped by the imminent threat of war and that they employed Islam and Muhammad as a foil against the Roman Church and the pope.

The negative and polemical appraisals of Muhammad largely held sway within Protestant mission circles during the eighteenth- and nineteenth-century missionary movement. Karl G. Pfander spoke for many Protestant missionaries of his time when he concluded in his *Mizan ul-Haqq* ("Balance of Truth"), published in the mid-nineteenth century: "On the whole, then we conclude that Muhammad's claim to the prophetic office was not substantiated by any miracles, as the Qur'an distinctly proves; the miracles mentioned in the Tradition being in themselves too absurd, too contrary, in some instances, to the Qur'an, and too ill-corroborated to be accepted as having really occurred."[22]

MUHAMMAD RECONSIDERED

From the nineteenth through to the mid-twentieth centuries, nuanced and positive works on Muhammad by leading Christian Islamicists and theologians started to appear, challenging the entrenched negative attitudes. These perspectives ranged from acknowledging Muhammad's sincerity to accepting his prophethood in some limited sense to more recent calls for unqualified recognition of Muhammad as prophet. These attempts have emerged, partly in response to persistent Muslim demands for a Christian recognition of Muhammad's prophethood, for the sake of dialogue. Mahmud Aydin, a Turkish Muslim academic writes: "It is very difficult for a sensible

---

[21]Jan Slomp, "Calvin and the Turks," in *Christian-Muslim Encounters*, ed. Yvonne Yazbeck Haddad and Wadi Zaidan Haddad (Gainesville: University Press of Florida, 1995), 130-32.

[22]C. G. Pfander, *The Mizan ul-Haqq* (1st ed., 1835; enl. W. St. Clair Tisdall, 1910; repr., Villach, Austria: Light of Life, 1986), 326.

Christian not to use the title 'Prophet' for Muhammad. . . . Christians who refuse to use the title 'Prophet' for Muhammad offend Muslims and make it difficult to establish better relations with them."[23]

The French Catholic Islamicist Jacques Jomier cautioned against Christians using the title *prophet* for Muhammad on the grounds that it means different things to Muslims and Christians. He suggests that it is important, however, for Christians "to recognize the truths that the Muslim message contains . . . and to see Muhammad as a religious and political genius."[24] Christian Troll, another key Roman Catholic Islamicist, while maintaining a clear stance against the negative attitudes toward Muhammad, takes a cautious positive view:

> In a theological sense, Christians cannot recognize Muhammad as a prophet without denying their own faith. In an attitude of critical openness, however, they certainly can and should give serious consideration to the witness of Muhammad's life and teaching and the challenges these pose to them. To do so is indeed to bear witness with both confidence and humility to the universal and all-embracing lordship of Jesus, "the heir of all things, through whom [God] also created the worlds" (Hebrews 1.2).[25]

In the assessment of Montgomery Watt, a leading Scottish authority on Muhammad, Christians should accept Muhammad "as a religious leader through whom God has worked, and that is tantamount to holding that he is in some sense a prophet."[26] Kenneth Cragg, a hugely influential voice when it comes to Christian theological engagement with Islam in the recent past, talks about the "prophetic" in relation to Muhammad in ways that can and indeed have been (mis)interpreted as a recognition of Muhammad's prophetic status. Cragg refers to Muhammad as "prophet of the Qur'an" and consistently uses the title *prophet* to refer to him.[27] There is however, "no point at which Cragg unequivocally affirms that Christians can or should

---

[23]Mahmut Aydin, "Contemporary Christian Evaluations of the Prophethood of Muhammad," *Encounters: Journal of Inter-Cultural Perspectives* 6, no. 1 (2000): 42.

[24]Kate Zebiri, *Muslims and Christians Face to Face* (Oxford: Oneworld, 1997), 200.

[25]Christian Troll, "Changing Catholic Views of Islam," in *Islam and Christianity: Mutual Perceptions Since the Mid-20th Century*, ed. Jacques Waardenburg (Leuven: Peeters, 1998), 19–77.

[26]William Montgomery Watt, *Christian-Muslim Encounters: Perceptions and Misperceptions* (New York: Routledge, 1991), 148.

[27]Kenneth Cragg, *Muhammad and the Christian: A Question of Response* (London: Longman & Todd, 1984).

regard Muhammad as a prophet."[28] On the contrary, Cragg sees Muhammad's resort to temporal and military power, the *hijra*, in contrast to Gethsemane, as an irreducible difference between Islam and Christianity.

Norman Daniel, who undertook an important survey of medieval and modern Christian views of Islam and Muhammad, appears to reject any hesitation or qualifications Christians express toward Muhammad's prophethood. He asserts that "it is essential for Christians to see Muhammad as a holy figure; to see him, that is, as Muslims see him. . . . If they do not do so, they must cut themselves off from comprehension of Islam, by cutting themselves off from Muslims."[29] The problem, though, is that a prophet is more than a holy figure. Another leading Christian Islamicist, Hans Küng, is even more forthright in his criticism of Christian reluctance in recognizing Muhammad as a prophet:

> Anyone who puts the Bible and the Qur'an side by side and reads them will recognize that the three revelatory religions of Semitic origin—Judaism, Christianity and Islam—and especially the Hebrew Bible and the Qur'an all have the same basis. One and the same God speaks clearly in both. "Thus says the Lord" in the Hebrew Bible corresponds to the "Say" (qul: 332 times) of the Qur'an; the biblical "Go and proclaim!" corresponds to the Qur'anic "Arise and warn!" . . . So isn't it perhaps simply a dogmatic prejudice for Christians to recognize Amos and Hosea, Isaiah and Jeremiah and the extremely violent Elijah as prophets, but not Muhammad?[30]

The positive and even radical views of these individual scholars do not represent or reflect official ecclesiastical positions. Vatican II in its landmark statement, *Nostra Aetate*, declares: "The Church regards with esteem also the Moslems. They adore the one God, living and subsisting in Himself; merciful and all-powerful, the Creator of heaven and earth, who has spoken to men; they take pains to submit wholeheartedly to even His inscrutable decrees."[31] Yet, Muhammad is never mentioned by name in the document,

---

[28]David Marshall, "Muhammad in Contemporary Christian Theological Reflection," *Islam and Christian-Muslim Relations* 24, no. 2 (2013): 7.

[29]Norman Daniel, *Islam and the West: The Making of an Image* (Oxford: Oneworld, 1993), 336.

[30]Hans Küng, *Islam: Past, Present & Future* (Oxford: Oneworld, 2007), 123.

[31]"Declaration on the Relation of the Church to Non-Christian Religions, *Nostra Aetate*, Proclaimed by His Holiness Pope Paul VI on October 28, 1965," par. 3, www.vatican.va/archive/hist_councils/ii_vatican_council/documents/vat-ii_decl_19651028_nostra-aetate_en.html.

which is a clear indication of the theological difficulty Muhammad's prophethood continues to pose to the church. For its part, the World Council of Churches, in its *Guidelines for Inter-Religious Dialogue* issued in 1979, states: "As a religion which began after the time of Christ, and therefore after the New Testament had been completed, Islam has always presented a theological challenge to Christians especially in relation to Muhammad's status as Prophet and the Qur'an's status as Revelation." The challenge is simply stated and left as a challenge. No attempt is made to address it.

The first semiofficial church statement ever offering a clear, positive assessment of the prophetic status of Muhammad comes from a consultation organized by the Islam in Europe Committee of the Conference of European Churches in 1984. The statement reads:

> Christians must always remember Christ's injunction: "Judge not that ye be not judged" (Matt. 7:1). The Muslims revere a succession of holy prophets from Adam to Muhammad who were entrusted with an infallible message. On the other hand Christians respect Old Testament prophets as fallible yet inspired messengers of repentance in the service of the One God. The New Testament writers continue this tradition, speaking of "the spirit of prophecy, which God shall pour upon all flesh" (Acts 2:17). *It is therefore possible for Christians to recognize Muhammad as a prophet*, but only in the context of this tradition. We must nevertheless ensure that our Muslim friends understand the subtle differences between the two perspectives, for Christians believe that revelation comes from one who is greater than all the prophets (Heb. 1:3).[32]

In other words, Christians can recognize Muhammad as a prophet but not as infallible, as Islam teaches, and Muslims should be reminded that Jesus is greater than all the prophets, including Muhammad. It is noted toward the end of the statement that "there was a long and controversial discussion following the reading of the report," which means some at the consultation thought the statement went too far. Yet Muslims would reject the statement outright as demeaning to their prophet.

Nevertheless, the question of Muhammad's prophetic status is not merely a theological or philosophical question. It is a political and existential one. The

---

[32]Jan Slomp, "Debates on Jesus and Muhammad in Europe, India and Pakistan," in *World Christianity in Muslim Encounter: Essays in Memory of David A. Kerr*, ed. Stephen R. Goodwin (London: Continuum, 2009), 2:314; emphasis original.

evidence can be seen in the blasphemy laws in many Muslim countries, the worldwide violence prompted by the Danish cartoons in 2005, the controversial YouTube video titled the *Innocence of Muslims* in America in 2012 and, most recently, the *Charlie Hebdo* cartoons that prompted the ensuing massacre of twelve journalists in Paris in January 2015. Silence on the question of Muhammad is therefore no longer an option; neither are simplistic answers.

It should be noted that all the different irenical Christian theological reflections about Muhammad outlined in the preceding paragraphs had two main purposes. First, these are, in the main, internal Christian theological reflections about Muhammad. Second, these were conscious attempts to move away from centuries-long negative representations of Muhammad with the view of enhancing better relations with Muslims. In recent decades Protestant missionary attitudes have moved away from calling Muhammad an impostor or the anti-Christ to appreciating his positive and admirable qualities and sincerity as a religious figure. The Protestant missionary view, however, remains overwhelmingly opposed to recognizing Muhammad as a prophet.[33] That is, until now!

During the last quarter of the twentieth century, proponents and advocates of the missiological approach variously referred to as an "insider movement" or "Muslim followers of Jesus" have joined in a discourse about the prophetic status of Muhammad. This new discourse is primarily an attempt at making theological space for Muhammad for the sake of Muslim followers of Jesus—that is, Muslims who accept Jesus as their Lord and Savior but choose to remain socially and legally Muslim, to attend worship in the mosque and to confess the shahadah. It is not my intention to go into the debate of the missiology of the insider movement; however, I will briefly highlight a recent instructive article by Harley Talman titled "Is Muhammad Also Among the Prophets?"[34] This article is an example of Protestant missionary attempts at making theological space for Muhammad.

Talman begins by raising serious doubts about the credibility of traditional Islamic accounts of Muhammad. He states that "the most widely accepted version of Muhammad, based upon Islalmic traditions, is dubious."[35]

---

[33]Zebiri, *Muslims and Christians Face to Face*, 108-15.
[34]Harley Talman, "Is Muhammad Also Among the Prophets?," *International Journal of Frontier Missiology* 31, no. 4 (2014): 169-90.
[35]Ibid., 171.

After discrediting the mainstream Muslim witness of their prophet, Talman cites early Syrian Christian and Jewish sources to make the point that Muhammad and Islam have not always been viewed negatively by Christians. Rather, Islam was viewed as a form of Christianity, albeit a heretical form, and Muhammad was accepted as a prophet. As evidence, Talman cites early Christian figures like Catholicos Timothy I and some leading contemporary Christian scholars of Islam who call for the recognition of Muhammad as a prophet. The writer goes on to insist that there is biblical and historical evidence that prophecy has not ceased; therefore, Muhammad's prophetic claims should be positively considered by Christians. "Like a number of Christian scholars of Islam," he argues,

> I believe there is biblical warrant for considering the possibility of some kind of positive prophetic status for Muhammad. I have shown that biblical and mission theology can allow for this. However, it does entail seeking to interpret the Qur'an exegetically and with regard to its biblical subtext, rather than primarily through the lens of later Islamic tradition.[36]

In what is clearly a very thoughtful and carefully considered article, Talman offers the following answers to the question, Is Muhammad also among the prophets? Christians "may be able to more readily support his being a prophet of the common kind—not the canonical kind (like the prophetic and apostolic writers of the Holy Bible)." And "we could allow the possibility that Muhammad is a prophet in the biblical sense." He concludes: "This paper has provided theological, missiological, and historical sanction for expanding constricted categories of prophethood to allow Christians to entertain the possibility of Muhammad being other than a false prophet. He may be seen as fulfilling a prophetic role."[37] These tentative answers are all in keeping with the spirit of humility Talman calls for in his article.

It appears to me, however, that in order to accord Muhammad the status of a prophet of sorts, Talman has to first of all Christianize or convert Muhammad into an anonymous Christian. Mainstream Muslim sources about Muhammad are rejected while marginal Christian sources are drawn on to arrive at his conclusions. In fact, what Talman does with Muhammad is exactly what

---

[36]Ibid., 182.
[37]Ibid., 181-85.

Muslims have done with Jesus. In order for Jesus to be a prophet in Islam, he is portrayed in Islamic garb. In effect, Talman succeeds in creating a Muhammad that many Christians will find difficult to accept and no Muslim will recognize. While I agree that any serious scholarship of Islam should treat the Qur'an and the Hadith with critical openness, a truly academic research has to endeavor to engage the internal logic of Islamic witness itself.

And if one is to take the Islamic witness seriously, there are only two possible outcomes. Become a Muslim (not muslim) or stay out of Islam. For, as rightly observed by Troll, "from the Muslim perspective, Christians who say that Muhammad is a prophet but do not become Muslims either do not know their own (Christian) faith or are merely playing games."[38] The truth of prophetic revelation is not just truth to be asserted by mere intellectual assent; it is truth that calls for recognition and *participation*. Prophets did not come to make fans. They came to gather followers, people who will heed their message and change their ways of thinking and life in conformity with their prophetic teaching. In the final analysis, Muhammad is not a prophet merely because the Qur'an says he is. He is a prophet because a community of believers confess him as such. There can be no prophet (or savior) without a body of believers. In other words, the offices of prophet and savior are conferred and validated by the ummah in Islam and the church in Christianity.

It is one thing to make theological sense of Muhammad and a completely different thing to make theological space for him. The latter easily ends up renouncing, revising or downplaying orthodox doctrines on both sides. Hans Küng's and Talman's approaches are in some major ways guilty of this. A more helpful approach is to take the Islamic witness seriously, debate and evaluate it rigorously and fairly as is, and draw conclusions that the mainstream on both sides can recognize. It is about respecting and preserving the internal logic and integrity of the traditions. Kenneth Cragg and Daniel Madigan are Christian scholars who have reflected on the critical importance of understanding and respecting the integrity of the truth claims of Islam and Christianity. Madigan emphasizes that for Muslims Muhammad is not the Word made flesh but the bearer of the Word (as Mary is for Christians). Revelation may be important in Islam, but incarnation is the mode God chose

---

[38]Christian W. Troll, *Dialogue and Difference: Clarity in Christian-Muslim Relations* (Maryknoll, NY: Orbis Books, 2009), 120.

for revealing himself in Christianity (Heb 1:1-2). Madigan believes that a firm grasp of this will prevent Christian responses to Muhammad from making the fundamental category mistake of assuming that Muhammad "is being proposed as a replacement [or supplementary] savior."[39]

As a Christian from the Global South, I can understand and appreciate Western Christian attempts at moving away from the long tradition of negative appraisals of Muhammad. But what I find difficult to understand is when Western Christians make assertions on behalf of Christians the world over such as "Christians should/can recognize Muhammad as a prophet." Moreover, the question is always posed and answered as if Christians have the power to make and unmake prophets. But as a Christian with Muslim relatives, I see the issue slightly differently. It is like asking me, a Ghanaian, whether Robert Mugabe is a president or not. Of course, Mugabe is a president, *of Zimbabwe*! Similarly, the answer to the question of whether Muhammad is a prophet is of course, he is a prophet, *of Islam*. Muhammad's family life, devotional and spiritual experiences, and public life (in all their complexities and contradictions) have shaped the collective memories, identities and the trajectory of the religious orientations of multitudes over the centuries. I accept and respect Muhammad as the *Prophet of Islam* for the sake of the over a billion and half Muslims around the world, some of whom are fellow citizens, neighbors, friends and family relations that I honor. In return I expect my Muslim friends and relatives to accept and respect Jesus as the Lord and Savior of over two billion Christians in the world, even if they can't accept and confess him as such.

---

[39]Daniel Madigan, "Jesus and Muhammad: The Sufficiency of Prophecy," in *Bearing the Word: Prophecy in Biblical and Qur'ānic Perspectives*, ed. Michael Ipgrave (London: Church House, 2005), 90-99.

11

Emergence of New Paths

The Future of Mission in Roman Catholicism

Mary Motte

INTRODUCTION: A BEGINNING POINT—"THE END IS WHERE WE START FROM"

All endings are new beginnings, and since this chapter is about the future of mission in Roman Catholicism, it seems appropriate to begin with an ending.[1] Six years ago, on May 30, Ewert Cousins, Professor of Religious Studies at Fordham University, died at age eighty-one. A quiet, persistent scholar, Cousins was acknowledged for his insight into Saint Bonaventure's vision that God's love continually interacts with creation.[2] He was known also for his grasp of the vision of Teilhard de Chardin's understanding of the cosmic dimensions of Christ in relation to evolution and recognized for his insight into the sacred as the basis for Native American religious belief.[3] Cousins understood the emerging urgency that everywhere in the world people are undergoing the most radical, far-reaching and challenging transformation in history.

---

[1] This section's subhead comes from T. S. Eliot, "Little Gidding," in *Four Quartets* (1943; repr., New York: Harcourt, 1971), 59.

[2] Ewert Cousins, "Bonaventure's Christology: A Resource for the Third Millennium," in *That Others May Know: Essays in Honor of Zachary Hayes, OFM*, ed. Michael F. Cusato and F. Edward Coughlin (St. Bonaventure, NY: Franciscan Institute, 1997), 212-13.

[3] There are several references in his writing where Teilhard refers to the Cosmic Christ—e.g., *Catholicism and Science* (1946), *Cosmic Life* (1916), *Reflections on Original Sin* (1947) and *The Divine Milieu* (1926–1927). See also Ewert Cousins, "The Nature of Faith in Inter-Religious Dialogue," *The Way* 78 (1993): 32-41; and idem, "Francis of Assisi and Interreligious Dialogue," *Dialogue and Alliance* 5:2 (1991): 20-33. And see Rich Heffern, "Ewart Cousins, Editor of the Classics of Western Spirituality, Dies," *NCR Today* (blog), *National Catholic Reporter*, June 3, 2009, http://ncronline.org/blogs/ncr-today/ewart-cousins-editor-classics-western-spirituality-dies.

He noted that the very survival of life on our planet is situated between chaos and destruction on one hand and creative transformation and the birth of a new consciousness on the other. Shortly before his death he wrote,

> Forces, which have been at work for centuries have in our day reached a crescendo that has the power to draw the human race into a global network and the religions of the world into a global spiritual community.[4]

As we confront the terrible suffering and losses of children, women and men in their excruciating experiences of migration, natural disasters, hunger, illness and death, a sharp awareness of the global leads us beyond boundaries to growing consciousness about human suffering. We ponder its relation to scientific discovery and theological discernment that God's work in creation continues to unfold before us. For those of us who share the Christian vision, this interaction between suffering, discovery and discernment offers a new way of insight into the mystery of God through our contemplation of the Trinity, creating, loving and transforming. Raimundo Panikkar has left us the richness of his theological consideration of the Trinity.[5] Denis Edwards tells us that the foundation for a theology that takes evolution seriously is found in a trinitarian vision of God as a God of mutual relations, a God who is communion in love, a God who is friendship beyond all comprehension.[6]

In this chapter I will attempt to illustrate the significance of our historical moment beginning with the Second Vatican Council of 1962–1965, and to examine the intensive search to grasp the significance of mission that has been taking place among Roman Catholics since the council. I will focus on the new paths that emerged from the council that have provoked new ways of thinking, seeing and engaging in mission. This work is carried out with deep awareness and gratitude for the related developments taking place through the missiological insights of conciliar and evangelical Christians. Their contributions continue to enrich the conversation with the insights of Lausanne and Geneva, as together we seek to discern the meaning of mission

---

[4]Ewert Cousins, "Religions of the World: Teilhard and the Second Axial Turning," *Interreligious Insight* 4, no. 4 (2006): 9, http://interreligiousinsight.org/October2006/Cousins10-06.pdf.
[5]Raimundo Panikkar, *The Silence of God: The Answer of the Buddha* (Maryknoll, NY: Orbis Books, 1989), 141, 166, 169.
[6]Denis Edwards, *The God of Evolution* (Mahwah, NJ: Paulist, 1999), 15.

for this time.[7] Perhaps it is not fantastic to imagine the coincidence of grace in these two jubilees that now bring together in a space of gratitude the evangelical tradition of the SWM/SIS here at Fuller and the anniversary of the conclusion of the Second Vatican Council with its impact on mission for Roman Catholics. The Spirit of God has gifted us with a deepening collaboration and spirituality in our discernment of a new vision of mission. The words of T. S. Eliot in "Little Gidding" capture something of how this vision, rooted in the mystery of the incarnation, might be experienced, when he refers to our ongoing exploration that at the end brings us to the point from which we started, when we will know it for the first time.[8]

SOURCES OF A NEW VISION EMERGING IN THE WORK OF VATICAN II: A "MESS" GIVING BIRTH TO TRANSFORMATION

Jorge Mario Bergoglio became Pope Francis, the bishop of Rome, on March 13, 2013. A few months after his election, Francis went to the World Youth Day in Brazil. There he shared his expectation:

> What is it that I expect as a consequence of World Youth Day? I want a mess. We knew that in Rio there would be great disorder, but I want trouble in the dioceses! . . . I want to see the Church get closer to the people. I want to get rid of clericalism, the mundane, this closing ourselves off within ourselves, in our parishes, schools or structures. Because these need to get out![9]

During his visit to Paraguay in July 2015, Pope Francis repeated his image of a mess in his talk with young people: "Make a mess, but then also help to tidy it up: a mess which gives us a free heart, a mess which gives us solidarity, a mess which gives us hope."[10]

It would seem that for Francis the image of mess describes the situation through which the church draws closer to the lives of people: a church rid of clericalism, a church not turned in on itself. A mess gives one a free heart;

---

[7]For example, the Association of Professors of Mission, the American Society of Missiology, the Gospel and Our Culture Network, the Overseas Ministries Study Center, the *International Bulletin of Missionary Research* and the Commission on World Mission and Evangelism.

[8]Eliot, "Little Gidding," sec. 5.

[9]Raymond Arroyo, "The 'Messy,' Alluring Grace of Pope Francis," Commentary, *National Catholic Register*, August 1, 2013, www.ncregister.com/daily-news/the-messy-alluring-grace -of-pope-francis.

[10]Elish O'Gara, "Pope Francis Urges Young People to 'Make a Mess,'" *Newsweek* (European edition), July 14, 2015.

a mess makes solidarity and hope possible. These images of a mess suggest something good, positive, something of God. They seem to propose that the Holy Spirit is actively involved in the inner dynamics of a mess. If we can look at a mess and perceive the interactive energy of the Holy Spirit, then we are able to see in a new way.[11]

Many of us who are members of Roman Catholic missionary congregations and who lived through the aftermath of Vatican II in our communities can recall our experiences of messiness. I do not believe many of us recognized the interactive energies of the Holy Spirit in those messes we encountered. Struggles were experienced during the council through opposing views. The historic structures of Roman Catholicism, especially since the time of the Reformation, made it difficult to perceive anything good in the opposite point of view. However, often in the encounter between two points of view, in the messiness of arguments, the Holy Spirit stirs up something new. The new is ultimately what appears in the documents of Vatican II. The work of the Holy Spirit emerges in new insights after long and difficult labors and offers signposts for the mission of the church in its journey into the future. With Pope Francis theologizing the concept of mess, we can reread our earlier experiences and recognize the mysterious, strange wisdom of the Holy Spirit at work in the heart of conflict as we struggled with the vision of Vatican II. We can see the newness into which God is calling us: "Behold, I make all things new" (Rev 21:5 KJV).

We are nearing the end of the fiftieth anniversary of Vatican II this year, and much has been written to celebrate the tremendous insights from the council. Here I will simply try to note the principal orientations that deeply disturbed constructs of mission held by Roman Catholics, eventually opening them to new possibilities. At the opening of the Second Vatican Council on October 11, 1962, John XXIII, while assuring the continuity with the earlier councils of Trent and Vatican I, states the need for

---

[11]Cf. *Evangelii Gaudium* or *The Joy of the Gospel*, the first major document of Pope Francis. It offers his vision of the church. See Francis, "Apostolic Exhortation *Evangelii Gaudium* [*EG*] of the Holy Father Francis to the Bishops, Clergy, Consecrated Persons and the Lay Faithful on the Proclamation of the Gospel in Today's World," St. Peter's, Rome, November 24, 2013, w2.vatican .va/content/francesco/en/apost_exhortations/documents/papa-francesco_esortazione-ap_20131124_evangelii-gaudium.html. His vision of a poor church for the poor is also often repeated through his gestures, his meetings and his talks.

a new approach, leading "toward a doctrinal penetration and formation of consciences . . . and perfect conformity to the authentic doctrine." Insisting that "the deposit of faith," must be preserved in its substance, he also insisted that "the way in which it is presented is another." He carefully differentiates between the substance of the deposit of faith—that is, the Magisterium—and the way in which it is presented.[12]

In this way, at the beginning of the council, Pope John XXIII indicated that the principal orientation of the council would be pastoral. Joseph Chinnici notes that John XXIII broke with a mentality and practice shaped by both the juridical-social-customary arrangements of the Constantinian era and the apologetic doctrinal postures associated with the Counter-Reformation.[13] The pope spoke of a new moment in history as one leading to a new order of human relations.[14] The important influences set forth in documents from Vatican II are too many to review in detail in this chapter.[15] But to affirm that indeed the signposts for the future are embedded in the Second Vatican Council, some of those signposts are noted that have already set in motion a profound shift toward transformation into missionary disciples. Such disciples witness growing awareness of the humility of God bending low and washing feet in the incarnation through solidarity with the poor. The text that served as a powerful inspiration for many Catholic missionaries was that of Luke 4:16-30.

Gaillardetz and Clifford describe the significance of Vatican II through their consideration of the principal ideas that wove through the work of the council.[16] Drawing on material of John O'Malley, an expert on the council, they analyze the pastoral nature of the documents through the kind of language that is used. The harsh language of condemnations and penalties used by previous councils is replaced by horizontal terms like *brothers and sisters*,

---

[12]See John XXIII, "Opening Speech for Council of Vatican II," October 11, 1962, www.ourladys warriors.org/teach/v2open.htm; and Joseph P. Chinnici, "Reception of Vatican II in the United States," *Theological Studies* 64 (2003): 461-94.

[13]Chinnici, "Reception of Vatican II."

[14]John XXIII convoked The Second Vatican Council, opened it on October 11, 1962, and closed the first session in December 1962. He died on June 3, 1963. Paul VI succeeded him and carried forward the work of Vatican II to the conclusion of the fourth session in December 1965.

[15]Austin Flannery, *Vatican Council II: The Conciliar and Post-Conciliar Documents* (Collegeville, MN: Liturgical Press, 1984).

[16]Richard R. Gaillardetz and Catherine E. Clifford, *Keys to the Council: Unlocking the Teaching of Vatican II* (Collegeville, MN: Liturgical Press, 2012), xvii.

people of God, the priesthood of all believers, and *collegiality.* The council uses words of reciprocity like *cooperation, partnership* and *collaboration;* terms of humility in words like *pilgrim* and *servant;* and words of interiority such as *charism, conscience, joy* and *hope, grief* and *anguish.* This attention to language reflects the council members' intention to attract those who would read the documents in order to emulate an ideal.[17]

Two documents, the Constitution on the Sacred Liturgy, *Sacrosanctum Conclium (SC),* and the Constitution on Divine Revelation, *Dei Verbum (DV),* provide critical insights expressing ways of seeing that are essential for the church in order to penetrate the renewal of the liturgy in Vatican II and its approach to divine revelation.[18] The centrality of the paschal mystery in the life and prayer of the church can be seen in

> the council's reflection on the sacraments, the life of holiness, the vocation of humanity, and the mission of the church in the world. For Catholics who lived through the period during and immediately following the Second Vatican Council, the changes brought about in the liturgy—the prayer of the church— were perhaps the most visible and immediate expression of the reforms the council effected.[19]

The Constitution on Divine Revelation represents a shift from a propositional view of revelation to one that centers on the living Word incarnate as Jesus of Nazareth, which makes it possible to direct both Scripture and tradition as distinct but interrelated mediations of the same living Word.[20] This approach to Scripture indicates the council's conviction that God shares his very self with us, willing that we become sharers in the divine nature.[21] The key text of this constitution is this statement:

> The tradition which comes from the apostles makes progress in the church, with the help of the Holy Spirit. There is a growth in insight into the realities and words that are being passed on.[22]

---

[17]Ibid.
[18]Ibid., 1-38.
[19]Ibid., 1.
[20]Ibid., 40-41.
[21]Paul VI, "Dogmatic Constitution on Divine Revelation, *Dei Verbum,* Solemnly Promulgated by His Holiness Pope Paul VI on November 18, 1965," par. 2, www.vatican.va/archive/hist_ councils/ii_vatican_council/documents/vat-ii_const_19651118_dei-verbum_en.html.
[22]Gaillardetz and Clifford, *Keys to the Council,* 41; *Dei Verbum,* par. 8.

The Constitution on the Sacred Liturgy and the Dogmatic Constitution on the Church, *Lumen Gentium* (*LG*), confirm that every baptized person is incorporated into the life and mission of Jesus, into the paschal mystery of Christ, and therefore is a missionary.[23] Being a missionary is no longer the prerogative of a member of a missionary congregation, as was generally the case among Roman Catholics.

At the time of the council, the great stumbling block for the Roman Catholic Church remained the experience of the Reformation. However, an ecumenical vision emerged bearing fruit before the council began.

> The origin of the Pontifical Council for Promoting Christian Unity is closely linked with the Second Vatican Council. It was Pope John XXIII's desire that the involvement of the Catholic Church in the contemporary ecumenical movement be one of the Council's chief concerns. Thus, on 5 June 1960, he established a "Secretariat for Promoting Christian Unity" as one of the preparatory commissions for the Council, and appointed Cardinal Augustin Bea as its first President. This was the first time that the Holy See had set up an office to deal uniquely with ecumenical affairs.[24]

This openness to the ecumenical movement included a representation from various Christian traditions at the council and acceptance through the Pontifical Council for Christian Unity to participate in the World Mission Conference in Mexico City in 1963.[25] The Decree on Ecumenism, *Unitatis Redintegratio* (*UR*), has led to a series of collaborative experiences deepening our understandings of Scripture, worship and prayer. A Joint Working Group Between the World Council of Churches and the Roman Catholic Church has just celebrated its fiftieth anniversary.[26] Through collaboration,

---

[23]Paul VI, "Constitution on the Sacred Liturgy, *Sacrosanctum Concilium*, Solemnly Promulgated by His Holiness Pope Paul VI on December 4, 1963," par. 6, www.vatican.va/archive/hist_councils /ii_vatican_council/documents/vat-ii_const_19631204_sacrosanctum-concilium_en.html; and Paul VI, "Dogmatic Constitution on the Church, *Lumen Gentium*, Solemnly Promulgated by His Holiness Pope Paul VI on November 21, 1964," par. 11, www.vatican.va/archive/hist_councils /ii_vatican_council/documents/vat-ii_const_19641121_lumen-gentium_en.html.

[24]"History," The Pontifical Council for Promoting Christian Unity, www.vatican.va/roman_curia /pontifical_councils/chrstuni/documents/rc_pc_chrstuni_pro_20051996_chrstuni_pro_en.html.

[25]Thomas F. Stransky, "From Mexico City to San Antonio," *International Review of Mission* 79, no. 313 (1990): 40-53.

[26]"Documents of the Joint Working Group Between the Roman Catholic Church and the WCC," World Council of Churches, www.oikoumene.org/en/resources/documents/commissions/jwg-rcc -wcc/documents-of-the-joint-working-group-between-the-roman-catholic-church-and-the-wcc;

the fundamental importance of common witness and ecumenical prayer for unity has been recognized and developed. There are likewise multiple instances of Christians working together on behalf of justice; peace and integrity of creation; and being with the poor, migrants and refugees, as well as in collaborative research and study of mission. The enormous significance of praying and working together and of avoiding proselytism continue to be sources of energy inspired by the Holy Spirit.

The decree concerning the Roman Catholic Church's relations with followers of other religions, *Nostra Aetate* (*NA*), poses the greatest challenge to those trying to discern paths of mission into the future. The importance of human relations and the development of inductive approaches in dialogue are slowly and painfully reshaping the search for a way forward. I recall an experience during a session on interfaith dialogue at a World Council of Churches meeting to which persons of faith traditions other than Christian had been invited. During a pause in the discussion, I was sitting on a bench in the hallway outside our meeting room. Raj, a young Hindu man from the Caribbean, came over and sat down. As we chatted, he asked me, "Do you know how it feels to be always called 'The Other'?" His question pierced through all my thinking of interreligious dialogue. I thought how isolated I had made him feel. I asked myself then, and continue to do so now: This person is certainly one who is deeply loved by God. How has God communicated that to him? Would the love of God leave some persons without any insight into God's love, holiness, graciousness?

Jacques Dupuis notes that *Ad Gentes* (*AG*), the decree on missionary activity from the council, speaks of seeds of the Word and elements of truth and grace; *Nostra Aetate* speaks of a ray of that truth that enlightens all men and women. While the council's insight into the significance of religious traditions other than Judeo-Christian was limited, Dupuis indicates the importance of some actions that occurred following the council:

> prophetic gestures and often remarkably open words of Pope John Paul II which encourage new steps forward to be taken toward a broader theological opening and more courageous concrete stances. . . . Like all councils in the

---

Theodore A. Gill, "Joint Working Group: 50 Years of Mutual Commitment," World Council of Churches, June 22, 2015, www.oikoumene.org/en/press-centre/news/joint-working-group-50-years -of-mutual-commitment.

life of the Church, Vatican II does not represent a last word, but rather a first word; it points in the direction in which to walk in order to reach a broader understanding of God's design for humankind, which will always remain beyond our complete comprehension.[27]

Nostra Aetate has led to profound study, excavations of new ways of seeing and profound suffering. With the irony of truth, Joseph Ratzinger, later Pope Benedict XVI, is quoted at the beginning of one of Jacques Dupuis's books:

> What the Church needs today, as always, are not adulators to extol the status quo, but men whose humility and obedience are no less than their passion for truth: . . . who brave every misunderstanding and attack as they bear witness; . . . who, in a word, love the Church more than ease and the unruffled course of their personal destiny.[28]

The concept of "dialogue of life" has evolved many places in Asia. Religious women, particularly, choose to live in situations among neighbors of other faiths, meeting the women in their daily tasks and conversations. Prayer has been shared as appropriate. Franciscan Missionaries of Mary observe Ramadan with their Muslim neighbors in North Africa. These neighbors initiated a deeper understanding of mission for the sisters when they begged them to remain in the midst of a dangerous situation, offering to protect them. From this experience came the concept of fidelity to the people to whom one is sent, a basic orientation in mission. This orientation shines a light on how mission is evolving to a more dynamic understanding of being a missionary disciple, of communicating the good news of Jesus Christ by walking in solidarity together.

Three decrees—namely, those on the Missionary Activity of the Church, *Ad Gentes*; on Religious Liberty, *Dignitatis Humanae*; and on the Church in the Modern World, *Gaudium et Spes*—led missionary congregations to examine their mission theology and practice.[29] The importance of the search for truth, and each person's responsibility in conscience to adhere to the

---

[27]Jacques Dupuis, *Christianity and the Religions: From Confrontation to Dialogue* (Maryknoll, NY: Orbis Books, 2002), 259.

[28]Ibid., vii.

[29]The Superiors General of the Men's Missionary Congregations, who were present at Vatican II, set up the foundations for SEDOS, *Servizio e Documentazione e Studie*. SEDOS in a short time opened membership to women's missionary congregations, which were not represented at the council. SEDOS continues this function of research and study into mission today.

truth once discovered by personal assent, indicated the need for more profound understanding of how the gospel is communicated and received.[30]
The obligation to communicate the gospel and the requirement that we take
into account the joys and hope and the grief and anguish of the people to
whom we are sent brought missionary congregations into long, agonizing
searches for how to realize these calls from the council—a search that continues to evolve in an unfolding dynamic.

The decree on Religious Life, *Perfectae Caritatis* (*PC*), called congregations of religious women and men to return to their sources and identify
their founding charism in the writings and practice of their founders. After
the council, the congregations were asked to convoke a Special General
Chapter. The signposts from Vatican II, together with the clarity of the
founding charism, enabled them to question much in their spirituality, life
and practice of mission and to recognize how much of their vision and
practice had become entangled with ideas and practices alien to their
founding charism. Clarity about the founding charism of each congregation
opened members to see in a new way, identifying the creative challenges
before them as they embraced the vision of Vatican II and of their founders
and foundresses. The "mess" was not absent, but from the arguments, the
deep experience of God's Spirit kept emerging, and prayer brought oppositions together in a new way.

These are some of the signposts from Vatican II that have pointed ahead
to something still to be realized more fully. The inspirational vision of the
council finds its source in the apostolic faith expressed in the gospel and in
the first Christian communities. Missionaries, well practiced in the art of
waiting for the outcome of their labors, expected, however, that Vatican II
would bring about a swift transformation in mission. I recall hearing, with
some degree of deep discouragement, that it would take fifty years for
Vatican II to be fully received. That was forty years ago. Of course, many
changes have occurred in the life of the church and of missionary congregations. Now, fifty years after Vatican II, we are experiencing an always greater
depth of renewal and new ways of seeing.

---

[30]"Decree *Ad Gentes* on the Mission Activity of the Church," par. 2, www.vatican.va/archive/
hist_councils/ii_vatican_council/documents/vat-ii_decree_19651207_ad-gentes_en.html.

Toward a New Creation: Bending Low and Washing the Feet of Another

When Pope Francis created new cardinals in February 2015, he reminded them that

> Jesus was more interested in embracing lepers and every kind of outcast than observing the ritual purity and prudent deliberations of the doctors of the law.
>
> "I desire mercy and not sacrifice. . . . What matters for Jesus is, above all, reaching out to save those far off, healing the wounds of the sick and restoring everyone to God's family!" the pope said. "And this is scandalous to some people!" . . .
>
> "I urge you to serve the church in such a way that Christians—edified by our witness—will not be tempted to turn to Jesus without turning to the outcast, to become a closed caste with nothing authentically ecclesial about it," he said. . . .
>
> "Truly, dear brothers, the gospel of the marginalized is where our credibility is at stake, is discovered and is revealed!"[31]

Francis offers an incisive image of church, well rooted in apostolic experience and directed toward a profound transformation of present practice. He told the cardinals to reach out to those on the margins, even those who have lost their faith, or have turned away from the faith, or say they are atheists. He urged them to imitate his patron saint, Francis of Assisi, by embracing the leper and accepting all the different types of outcasts.[32]

This chapter is about the future of mission in Roman Catholicism. The religious orders of missionaries of both women and men have been making profound efforts at renewal in line Vatican II. These efforts are evidenced in their commitment to the way of life and mission to the people to whom they are sent. In 1946, John Considine of Maryknoll had published *Call for Forty Thousand*, three years after the bishops of Central America had asked for help in renewing the church. In 1961 John XXIII asked North American religious to pledge 10 percent of their members to Latin America.[33] Many of

---

[31]Robert Mickens, "Could Pope Francis Be Any Clearer About His Vision for the Church?," *Consistory 2015, A Roman Observer* (blog), *National Catholic Reporter*, February 16, 2015, http://ncronline.org/blogs/roman-observer/could-pope-be-any-clearer-about-his-vision-church.

[32]Ibid.

[33]Angelyn Dries, *The Missionary Movement in American Catholic History* (Maryknoll, NY: Orbis Books, 1998), 810-11.

the congregations not traditionally recognized as missionary sent their members. Engagements of this kind, as well as the increasing internationality of congregations, led to a new understanding of mission and identity of the missionary. As witnessed at the National Mission Congress held in Baltimore in 1983, the commitment to being a missionary was not limited to canonical identification of a congregation but was related profoundly to an engagement with the people, especially the poor.[34] As Anthony Gittins, a professor of missiology, once said, mission is just in front of your feet.[35] Mission has gradually been transformed into fidelity to the people and involves walking with them in solidarity, bearing witness to the gospel of Jesus. From the people, the missionaries always receive more than they give, often encountering a witness to truth and holiness from those who welcome them to a strange place. In 1991 the second part of a study by the US Catholic Mission Association was completed. *To Be Hope and Joy: Presence Bearing A Glimpse of God* considered the motivation of those who were engaged in cross-cultural mission in another country.[36] While not intended as a definitive word on mission at that time, the study tries to capture insight into mission as it was being lived by men and women, the majority of whom were members of religious congregations. In the words of the respondents there is beauty and energy that capture a snapshot of how the transformation to a new way of seeing was occurring through solidarity with the people who welcomed them.

After Vatican II, Catholic laity became increasingly engaged in mission; the numbers of Associations of the Faithful, of which many were members, grew significantly.[37] These are groups of laywomen and laymen, married or single, approved by the Holy See for the purpose of evangelization. They are sent in mission to proclaim the gospel, whether in their countries of origin or in other countries. Most of their missionary journeys are short term, but the commitment is generally for a lifetime, and they resume specific commitments in evangelization on a regular basis.

---

[34] Anthony Bellagamba, ed., *Baltimore '83: Experiences and Reflections on Mission: Mission Congress 1983* (Washington, DC: United States Catholic Mission Association, 1983).

[35] Session at Mission Resource Center, Franciscan Missionaries of Mary, Spring 1990.

[36] Mary Motte, *To Be Hope and Joy: Presence Bearing a Glimpse of God* (Washington, DC: United States Catholic Mission Association, 1991).

[37] *Directory*, International Associations of the Faithful, Pontifical Council for the Laity, www.vatican.va/roman_curia/pontifical_councils/laity/documents/rc_pc_laity_doc_20051114_associazioni_en.html.

Founded on the conviction that every person is loved by God, the desire to build respectful relationship with others continues to lead women and men into the journey of another people. A new way of seeing requires a starting point of being with the people in openness to discover how God is acting in their lives, then, together with them, discerning the truth and presence of God's love, moving forward from that space to encounter the future. From the Christian perspective, this way of seeing, this understanding of relationship and this solidarity on a journey require ongoing contemplation of the mystery of God's trinitarian love. Two images from different Christian traditions remain with me. One is of an evangelical missionary who went to a village where the people are Muslim. Convinced that he must witness to his Christian faith, he decided to approach a man sitting on a bench along the road. As the Christian missionary approached, the Muslim man invited him to sit down. The Christian, who later told me of his experience, said somehow he was inspired not to witness immediately but to ask the Muslim about his experience of God. This Muslim was a Sufi, and as he began to speak readily about his experience of God, the Christian man encountered a powerful experience of the holiness of God. Their conversation proceeded from that encounter. And as he spoke to me I thought of Francis of Assisi and his encounter with the Sultan of Egypt many centuries before, which resulted in a profound contemplative experience and witness of the infinite mystery and love of God for both.[38] Another image comes from three of my Franciscan Missionaries of Mary sisters in the mountains of North Africa, who tell us, "In our daily journeying with these Nomad Women in Algeria, the Lord is present, even when he seems to be absent; it is this certitude which enables us to continue."[39]

Everyone who is baptized is a missionary, and Pope Francis has affirmed that understanding once again in *Evangelii Gaudium*, saying that we are all missionary disciples.[40] While this universality of the missionary vocation

---

[38]Mary Motte, "The Image of the Crucified God," in *The Agitated Mind of God: The Theology of Kosuke Koyama*, ed. Dale T. Irvine and Akintunde E. Akinade (Maryknoll, NY: Orbis Books, 1996), 73-87; and Kathleen A. Warren and Jaysiri Hart, *The Footprints of Francis and the Sultan: A Model for Peacemaking* (Cincinnati: Franciscan Media, 2012), DVD.

[39]Rosanna Bigoni, "Walking Together—Algeria," Franciscan Missionaries of Mary, accessed April 22, 2016, www.fmm.org/pls/fmm/v3_s2ew_consultazione.mostra_pagina?id_pagina=2613.

[40]Francis, *Evangelii Gaudium*, pars. 119-21.

has been troubling to some, there are clear indicators that such a conviction, affirmed by the Second Vatican Council, is a vital component of the transformed living of mission.

Relationships understood as new ways of loving one another that lead to new ways of seeing, and new understandings of diversity, describe the meaning of a missionary disciple.[41] Marty Shea, a Maryknoll missioner in a Guatemalan Refugee Camp, describes mission in the camp:

> It's just being there
>   *with others*
> all the others in the crowd
> as we seek to help one another
>   *get close enough*
> to touch the hem of His garment.[42]

CONCLUSION: "ON RAZED LAND LIFE BREAKS THROUGH"

Gradually the signposts that came from the council pointing to a new way of being church are becoming steps of confirmation on the journey.[43] At this moment we seem to be at a critical juncture of something new. We experience the grace of living in a *kairos*[44] or unique moment. It would seem that Pope Francis has been called to lead the church into this new moment to a fuller realization of Vatican II. Much of what the world is experiencing in the witness of Pope Francis has come from his conversion experience earlier in his life. In a recent article in *America*, Diego Fares tells us that in 2006, while giving the Spiritual Exercises to bishops in Spain, Cardinal Bergoglio gave an opening talk on the Magnificat. He drew on the images of "feeling like stewards, not owners, and humble servants like our Lady [Mary, the

---

[41] Theresa Baldini and Madeline McHugh, "Prayer and Peace Presence in South Sudan," in John C. Sivalon, *God's Mission and Postmodern Culture: The Gift of Uncertainty* (Maryknoll, NY: Orbis Books, 2012), 94.

[42] Marty Shea, "What's Mission After Fifty Years?," in Sivalon, *God's Mission and Postmodern Culture*, 99.

[43] The section subtitle is taken from Francis, *Evangelii Gaudium*, par. 276.

[44] *Kairos* (καιρός) is an ancient Greek word meaning the right or opportune moment (the supreme moment). The ancient Greeks had two words for time, *chronos* and *kairos*. While the former refers to chronological or sequential time, the latter signifies a moment of indeterminate time in which something significant happens.

mother of Jesus], not princes."[45] Fares notes that this pastoral option is not just for bishops, but it applies to every missionary disciple, each one in her or his own condition. The call to be pastors not princes does not convey scorn but rather calls for a deeper insight into its meaning; it is part of a discernment about an epochal change, a time when "we will know the missionary joy of sharing life with God's faithful people as we strive to light a fire in the heart of the world."[46]

For more than two-and-a half years we have witnessed the actions and words of Pope Francis. His penetration of the Word of God through prayer and meditation is evident in his ability to convey the joy and compassion of the gospel. He is painfully aware of his sinfulness and need for forgiveness.[47] He relates to others with respectful humility, choosing to be a missionary disciple. We can now imagine the vision of the Second Vatican Council coming to fuller realization in a poor church for the poor. Our role as missionary disciples moves beyond barriers to embrace the challenging transformations of our history. Walter Kasper notes that the challenge of Francis's pontificate is far more radical than most suspect. He continues:

> It is a challenge of conservatives, who don't want to let themselves be surprised any more by God and who resist reforms, just as it is for progressives, who expect feasible, concrete solutions right here and now. The revolution of tenderness and love and the mysticism of open eyes could disappoint both groups and in the end, nevertheless, receive its due. For the joy of the gospel has a promise whose realization never completely comes to fulfillments in history.[48]

The paths of a missionary church have emerged in varying ways from the work of Vatican II. The women and men who have given form and substance to these paths need to continue discerning how God is leading. This discernment has experienced the richness of ecumenical challenge and collaboration, and the point reached through our discoveries calls us to

---

[45]Diego Fares, "'Pastors, Not Princes': The Role of the Bishop Under Pope Francis," *America*, July 6-13, 2015, http://americamagazine.org/issue/pastors-not-princes.

[46]Francis, *Encyclical Letter Laudato Si' of the Holy Father Francis on Care for Our Common Home* (Vatican City: Libreria Editrice Vaticana, 2015), n. 271; w2.vatican.va/content/francesco/en/encyclicals/documents/papa-francesco_20150524_enciclica-laudato-si.html.

[47]Antonio Spadara, "A Big Heart Open to God: The Exclusive Interview with Pope Francis," *America*, September 30, 2013, http://americamagazine.org/pope-interview.

[48]Walter Kasper, *Pope Francis' Revolution of Tenderness and Love: Theological and Pastoral Perspectives* (Mahwah, NJ: Paulist Press, 2015), 92.

continue. "The joy of the gospel fills the hearts and lives of all who encounter Jesus."[49] Everywhere in the world people are undergoing the most
radical, far-reaching and challenging transformation in history. At the beginning I quoted Ewert Cousins, who suggested that the very survival of
life on our planet is situated between chaos and destruction on the one
hand and creative transformation and the birth of a new consciousness on
the other.[50] This is the context energizing our *kairos* moment. As we attempt to envision how all this will shape the future of mission, the affirmation arises before us and within us that the return to the wellspring of
the gospel is the way into the future. It is a revolution of mercy.[51]

---

[49]*Evangelii Gaudium*, par. 1.
[50]Cousins, "Religions of the World," 9.
[51]See Kasper, *Pope Francis' Revolution of Tenderness and Love*, 93.

12

Revisiting Mission in, to and from
Europe Through Contemporary
Image Formation

Anne-Marie Kool

INTRODUCTION

Positioning Europe in the worldwide field of mission implies the construction and maintenance of images about Europe and European Christianity. Images then fuel specific types of missionary enterprise and play an important role in motivating funding. One of the most remarkable sources of such images is the *Atlas of Global Christianity*, which aims to present an "accurate, objective and incisive analysis of the worldwide presence of Christian faith."[1]

The introduction to the atlas states that its goal is to provide "as nuanced a picture as possible" of the history of Christianity over the last one hundred years, showing a general pattern that is "unmistakable," with Christianity experiencing a "severe recession on the European continent" while it has undergone "unprecedented growth and expansion" in other parts of the world.[2] "Authoritative statistics" are projected on maps to offer a "visual representation of the numerical strength or weakness of Christianity."[3]

---

[1]Todd M. Johnson and Kenneth R. Ross, eds., *Atlas of Global Christianity, 1910–2010* (Edinburgh: Edinburgh University Press, 2009), xi. All other references to the *Atlas* in this chapter will be assumed to be the work of the editors unless accompanied by contributor names and their article titles.

[2]Ibid.

[3]Ibid.

This general image or overview on the first pages of the atlas raises several questions. Why is reference made only to Europe as having experienced "a severe recession" and not to North America? The decline of 15.9 percent in Europe hardly differs from the 15.1 percent decline in North America.[4] What implicit assumptions lie behind the assessment of this image of Europe? The atlas was widely praised by reviewers for its "detail beyond belief"[5] as "impressive but improvable," with the amount of work needed to collect and estimate these data described as "mind-boggling."[6] However, some reviewers have expressed caution with regard to the accuracy of the figures,[7] suggesting that readers not engage in statistical analysis without "robustly" checking the data, "[because] they contain random error and probably some systematic error," even though these estimates are considered "extraordinarily valuable."[8]

These initial questions show the importance of entering into a conversation concerning the assumptions and the methodologies that impacted the construction of these images in the atlas in terms of their emergence, formation and dissemination. In this chapter, I will identify some of the most significant images used in the *Atlas of Global Christianity* concerning Europe and European Christianity. Exploring their formation, I focus on the "lenses" shaping the creation of these images. Can we uncover the implicit assumptions of the underlying missiological theory, the perceptions, and the related conceptual and methodological problems? To review their dissemination, I will look at why and how these images are used to promote a certain mission strategy and to motivate funding of the mission enterprise. Image-formation theory helps us to discover in what sense images are orchestrated a priori in an attempt to influence or direct people. It is important to understand what may be the hidden agendas behind this desire to influence mission strategy. The study of image formation deals with the nature of the lenses that may magnify, demagnify, distort or omit certain elements of reality. This chapter uses as its theoretical framework

---

[4]Ibid., 57.

[5]Peter Brierley, "World Religion Database: Detail Beyond Belief," *International Bulletin of Missionary Research* 34, no. 1 (2010): 18-19.

[6]Robert D. Woodberry, "World Religion Database: Impressive—but Improvable," *International Bulletin of Missionary Research* 34, no. 1 (2010): 21-22.

[7]Brierley, "World Religion Database"; Woodberry, "World Religion Database"; Jan A. B. Jongeneel, "Book Review: *Atlas of Global Christianity*," *Exchange* 40, no. 2 (2011): 211-14.

[8]Woodberry, "World Religion Database."

contemporary image-formation theory, used in, for example, Roma studies[9] and the survey of national stereotypes.

IMAGES USED IN THE *ATLAS OF GLOBAL CHRISTIANITY* TO DESCRIBE EUROPEAN CHRISTIANITY

The following six most significant images are used in the *Atlas of Global Christianity* to capture Europe and European Christianity: secularized Europe, the changing landscape in European Christianity, institutional erosion in historic churches, migration as a factor in revitalization, growth of independent churches at the periphery and a shift of European Christianity from the center to the margins.

Secularized Europe. In the atlas, the image of a secularized Europe occurs most frequently, with secularization "drastically" affecting every country of Europe, particularly Western Europe.[10] The authors make a variety of claims: that the "considerable loss of membership" is caused by the loss of relevance of institutionalized religion, that Mediterranean Europe copes with "a crisis of unprecedented proportions" in tackling a "pervasive wave of secularization" and that the most serious challenge in Eastern Europe is "the power of the ever-intensifying processes of secularization and globalization."[11]

This image of a secularized Europe is ambiguous. On one hand, maps of the continent show the percentage of "professing Christians" to be 80.2 percent.[12] On the other hand, there are other images portraying a continent in "severe recession."[13] The secularization of Europe is considered an undeniable fact by the atlas. José Casanova has suggested that instead we should talk of the "unchurching of the European population" and of "religious individualization." Many people have ceased to participate in religious practices but still

---

[9]Klaus-Michael Bogdal, *Europa erfindet die Zigeuner: Eine Geschichte von Faszination und Verachtung* (Berlin: Suhrkamp, 2011); cf. Klaus-Michael Bogdal, "Europe Invents the Gypsies: The Dark Side of Modernity," trans. Christopher Gilley, *Eurozine*, February 24, 2012, www.eurozine .com/articles/2012-02-24-bogdal-en.html.

[10]Johnson and Ross, *Atlas of Global Christianity*, 172.

[11]Huibert Van Beek and André Karamaga, "Protestants 1910–2010," in Johnson and Ross, *Atlas of Global Christianity*, 88; Johnson and Ross, *Atlas of Global Christianity*, 167; Vladimir Fedorov, "Christianity in Eastern Europe," in Johnson and Ross, *Atlas of Global Christianity*, 158.

[12]Johnson and Ross, *Atlas of Global Christianity*, 57.

[13]Ibid., passim.

maintain high levels of individual religious beliefs.[14] The complexity of this image is demonstrated not only by the phenomenon of "believing without belonging"[15] but also by the reverse of "belonging without believing,"[16] and even by "non-believing and non-belonging" as "'secular' and 'Christian' cultural identities are intertwined in complex and rarely verbalized modes among most Europeans."[17] This complexity is illustrated by a case study from the Czech Republic, considered to be one of the most secular and atheistic countries in the world. Pavel Cerny describes Czech atheism as "very particular." Czech society is more anticlerical than atheistic; Czech people refuse the Christian God but do not cease to believe in something. Cerny states: "There is no real secularism in our country. Various 'gods' are back. The Czech society is not secular in religious terms. Many seekers long to taste and experience something transcendental."[18]

The changing landscape in European Christianity. A second dominant image is that of a changing landscape in European Christianity. The atlas notes the rise of agnostics and atheists (soon about 22 percent of the population), portrayed as causing a large shift away from Christianity in Western Europe.[19] That in turn signals an intense transformation in Europe's religious demography. In the atlas, the decline of Christianity in Europe is seen as "defections," mainly folks leaving the established churches to become agnostics and atheists, and is considered "the evidence of secularization."[20] On the other hand, the atlas notes the growth in the number of "Independents" and the so-called Marginal Christians as rapidly growing traditions that, coupled with immigration, are impacting the growth of Christian communities in Europe.

---

[14]José Casanova, "Religion, European Secular Identities, and European Integration," *Transit* 27 (2004), www.eurozine.com/articles/2004-07-29-casanova-en.html.

[15]Grace Davie, *Europe, the Exceptional Case: Parameters of Faith in the Modern World*, Sarum Theological Lectures (London: Darton, Longman & Todd, 2002).

[16]Casanova, "Religion, European Secular Identities," quoting Danièle Hervieu-Léger.

[17]Detlef Pollack, Olaf Müller and Gert Pickel, "Church and Religion in the Enlarged Europe: Analysis of the Social Significance of Religion in East and West," in *The Social Significance of Religion in the Enlarged Europe: Secularization, Individualization, and Pluralization*, ed. Detlef Pollack, Olaf Müller and Gert Pickel (Burlington, VT: Ashgate, 2012), 6.

[18]Pavel Cerny, "Thinking About Mission and the Development of the Church Within the Secular Context of the Czech Environment" (lecture, "Die Zukunft der Kirche in Europa," International Symposium sponsored by the Institut zur Erforschung von Evangelisation und Gemeindeentwicklung [IEEG] of the Universität Greifswald, Greifswald, Germany, May 28-30, 2015).

[19]Johnson and Ross, *Atlas of Global Christianity*, 172.

[20]Ibid., 156.

It is remarkable that the atlas sets clear boundaries by offering two clear-cut images, one of a "professing Christian" and another of someone who has shifted away from Christianity to a stance of agnostic or atheist. The images from other sources, including the World Christian Database (WCD), from which the atlas derives its data,[21] show a more diffuse picture,[22] a large grey zone like that described by Cerny in the Czech Republic.

In comparison, the European Values Study (EVS) shows that Europe is not as secularized as it seems, with about half of all Europeans praying or meditating at least once a week. Atheists constitute a small minority in a kind of "cafeteria religion" or a "church-free spirituality." The EVS concludes: "Europeans remain religious, their approach is eclectic. . . . Meanwhile many institutionalized churches, especially in the West, are running empty."[23]

Institutional erosion in historic churches. A closely linked third image in the atlas is that of institutional erosion in the historic churches. The atlas reports that institutionalized religion is "certainly on the wane," especially Christianity. However, one can also observe that religion has not disappeared but has taken different forms.[24] Protestantism has proved more vulnerable to this "institutional erosion."[25] The atlas presents an "unmistakable, indeed gross 'decline'" in the outer expressions of church attendance and Christian belief virtually all over the European continent.[26] The Scandinavian churches are no exception, with 80 percent of children being baptized but less than 2 percent of the population regularly attending a church. In Sweden the decline has been most dramatic from 99 percent identifying as Christian in 1910 to 66 percent in 2010. As an "outside insider," Daniel Jeyaraj is more specific about the reasons, observing that people in the Western world are kept away from the church because of "ongoing denominational squabbles," conflicts among Christians, inconsistent Christian attitudes toward ethical issues, and

---

[21]Ibid., 342–43.

[22]Cf. Stefan Paas, "The Use of Social Data in the Evangelization of Europe: Methodological Issues," *International Bulletin of Missionary Research* 37, no. 1 (2013): 9.

[23]European Values Study, "Religion," accessed February 2, 2016, www.europeanvaluesstudy.eu/page/religion.html.

[24]Andre Droogers, "Christianity in Western Europe 1910–2010," in Johnson and Ross, *Atlas of Global Christianity*, 170.

[25]David Martin, "Christianity in Europe, 1910–2010," in Johnson and Ross, *Atlas of Global Christianity*, 155.

[26]Martin Conway, "Christianity in Northern Europe," in Johnson and Ross, *Atlas of Global Christianity*, 162.

sex scandals. They sincerely wait for the demise of Western Christianity. Although not perfect, non-Western Christianity is presented in a different light, with signs of vitality, authenticity and hope.[27]

This image points to a divergence between the statistical data and the interpretive essays of the atlas, raising questions about the essays. To what extent do the essays fulfill an interpretive role? Do they create a different image that the maps do not capture?

Migration as a factor in revitalization. A fourth, frequently repeated image in the atlas is that of migration as a factor in revitalizing European Christianity. The influence of Western Christianity is considered "waning but still powerful." However, due to migration of non-Western peoples, the influence of the South on the North has "greatly increased," leading to new vigor in the "often dwindling" churches of the North.[28] Migrants bring with them their Christian faith, "generally more dynamic and enthusiastic than their European hosts,"[29] creating some of the largest congregations in major centers of Western Europe. Some of them are part of growing movements of "reverse mission" from Protestant and independent churches, shocked by the decline of Christianity in countries from which they inherited the faith.[30] The future of Christianity in Europe is said to be "in the hands of immigrants, largely from the Global South."[31] The number of Muslims in Western Europe is said to have "skyrocketed" to eleven million, mainly due to the arrival of immigrants from Turkey and North Africa.[32]

Interestingly, this image displays immigration more or less as a success story, applauding the immigrants with their vibrant faith as a kind of solution to the problem of secularized Europe. However, the reality is much more complex. Many migrant churches serve their own ethnic communities while the historic European churches struggle to fit them into their national

---

[27]Daniel Jeyaraj, "The Re-Emergence of Global Christianity 1910–2010," in Johnson and Ross, *Atlas of Global Christianity*, 54.

[28]Sandra S. K. Lee, "Christianity by Major Tradition, 1910–2010," in Johnson and Ross, *Atlas of Global Christianity*, 66.

[29]Johnson and Ross, *Atlas of Global Christianity*, 172.

[30]Kirsteen Kim, "Missionaries Sent and Received, Europe 1910–2010," in Johnson and Ross, *Atlas of Global Christianity*, 273.

[31]Johnson and Ross, *Atlas of Global Christianity*, 156.

[32]Ibid., 172.

structures.[33] A great hindrance to the suggested cross-pollination is the issue of otherness and extreme right-wing tendencies in European society and the European "indigenous" churches. Immigrants often bring another form of Christian faith, derived from another cultural background, which does not fit the nation-building role that religion still plays in many European countries. The presence of migrant Christians in the indigenous European churches sometimes engenders attitudes of superiority toward migrants and their theological convictions.[34]

Growth of independent churches at the periphery. The growth of independent churches, at times referred to as the "Churches of the Spirit," is the fifth image that can be identified in the atlas. These independents are found to be not at the center of political power and economic wealth but at the periphery. All Christian traditions are said to have been affected by the renewalist movements, the majority being Pentecostal/charismatic, often leading to "a more vibrant faith."[35] According to the atlas, in Mediterranean Europe the independent churches are fast growing "on the margins of Europe, Portugal, southern Italy, Romania and Gypsy communities."[36] In Eastern Europe the charismatic renewal movement is "sweeping through all the Christian traditions," like the Lord's Army in Romania.[37] Pentecostal churches in Eastern Europe are said to be growing at a rate of 3.5 percent per year.[38]

It is striking that in the whole atlas this is the only instance where the Roma (Gypsy) communities are mentioned. In fact, the ten to twelve million Roma minority is considered one of the greatest challenges in Europe. Perhaps because of the massive exclusion of the Roma in Europe, because of widespread stereotypes,[39] they are hidden in the statistics, mostly as independents. Many Gypsy Pentecostal communities have their roots in the "Roma revival" that started in the 1950s in France and subsequently

---

[33]Cf. Bianca Dümling, "Migrationskirchen in Deutschland" (lecture, "Die Zukunft der Kirche in Europa," International Symposium sponsored by the Institut zur Erforschung von Evangelisation und Gemeindeentwicklung [IEEG] of the Universität Greifswald, Greifswald, Germany, May 28-30, 2015).

[34]See Kyriaki Avtzki et al. "Report WCC Consultation on Evangelism in Theological Education and Missional Formation in Europe," Bossey, Switzerland, October 28-31, 2012.

[35]Johnson and Ross, *Atlas of Global Christianity*, 172.

[36]Martin, "Christianity in Europe," 154.

[37]Johnson and Ross, *Atlas of Global Christianity*, 160.

[38]Ibid., 103.

[39]Bogdal, *Europa erfindet die Zigeuner*; Bogdal, "Europe Invents the Gypsies."

spread to Spain and beyond.[40] Currently more than two million believers
are considered to belong to this movement in forty-four countries.[41] In contrast to what is stated in the atlas, some nonmigrant types of new churches,
like the Pentecostal Church in Romania and the Faith Church (*Hit gyüle-
kezete*) in Hungary, are now very much at the center of political power and
wealth, especially in Central and Eastern Europe.

   A shift of European Christianity from center to margins. A sixth image
is related to what is perceived as a shift of European Christianity from center
to periphery in global Christianity. According to the atlas, what could be
considered a double marginalization is taking place: to be at the margins of
European society and to be relegated to the margins of global Christianity.[42]
Once the European continent was the primary base of Christianity; now
"the de-Christianization of the West [is making] the West a post-Christian
society."[43] Western Europe is presented as having changed from being the
Christian heartland to being the Christian wasteland, with recession in the
West and advance elsewhere.[44] The atlas affirms that one of the "ironies of
history" is that Western Europe at one time occupied a central position in
Christianity but is now "the secular champion of the world."[45] With the role
and existence of (overseas) missionaries and Western European churches
seeking new ways to reach out to an unchurched generation, "sea changes
in patterns of mission activity" in, from and to Europe have taken place.[46]

   The image of Christianity as a Western religion, which it acquired
through the missionary movement, persists and poses a problem for

---

[40]Anne-Marie Kool, "European Churches' Perspectives on Mission Work Among the Roma"
(Don McClure Mission Lecture, Pittsburgh Theological Seminary, Pittsburgh, PA, September
24-25, 2012).

[41]Anne-Marie Kool, "Eastern European Churches' Responses to the Roma People" (paper pre-
sented at Great Commission Center, International Roma Consultation: Roma for the Nations,
Budapest, Hungary, September 29 to October 3, 2014). See also my "Eastern European Churches
Engaging Roma People: Historical and Missiological Perspectives," in *Mission in Central and
Eastern Europe: Realities, Perspectives, Trends*, ed. Corneliu Constantineanu, Mihai Himcinschi,
Anne-Marie Kool and Marcel Macelaru, Regnum Edinburgh Centenary Series (Oxford: Reg-
num, 2016), forthcoming.

[42]Droogers, "Christianity in Western Europe."

[43]Moonjang Lee, "Future of Global Christianity," in Johnson and Ross, *Atlas of Global Christianity*, 104.

[44]Andrew F. Walls, "Christianity Across Twenty Centuries," in Johnson and Ross, *Atlas of Global
Christianity*, 48.

[45]Droogers, "Christianity in Western Europe."

[46]Kim, "Missionaries Sent and Received," 272.

non-Western Christianity. It is considered one of the stumbling blocks for evangelism in the non-West. Lee observes, "Though we talk about a post-Christian West and a post-Western Christianity, the prevailing forms of Christianity in most parts of the non-Western world are still dominated by Western influences."[47]

However, it is important to examine whether a shift has indeed taken place or whether this centralist image of European churches as the Christian heartland still persists. Has European Christianity accepted the historical reality of advance and recession, or does it still embrace the image of a "Christian continent" as a way to preserve its global influence? Although this question is outside the scope of this chapter, we probably should ask a similar question of North American Christianity.

CONCEPTUAL AND METHODOLOGICAL PROBLEMS

Having briefly outlined six major images of Europe and European Christianity in the *Atlas of Global Christianity*, let's now consider a second major issue: the matter of conceptual and methodological presuppositions underlying the atlas. With the focus on Europe, a number of conceptual and methodological problems can be identified in the emergence and formation of the images in the atlas. The methodological notes in the atlas are excerpted from the first edition of the *World Christian Encyclopedia* (1982), later updated for the companion volume, *World Christian Trends, AD 30–AD 2200*. These notes are intended to give the reader "some ideas"[48] of how the data behind the statistical images and maps were compiled and analyzed.[49] In fact, very little discussion of the underlying methodologies of the atlas has taken place.[50] Woodberry is right in emphasizing that "more transparency is needed."[51] Possibly the large quantity of detail and

---

[47]Lee, "Future of Global Christianity," 104.

[48]Johnson and Ross, *Atlas of Global Christianity*, 342.

[49]See also Todd M. Johnson and Kenneth R. Ross, "The Making of the *Atlas of Global Christianity*," *International Bulletin of Missionary Research* 34, no. 1 (2010): 12-16; Kenneth R. Ross, "Mapping Ecclesiology and Mission: Trends Revealed by the *Atlas of Global Christianity*," in *Walk Humbly with the Lord: Church and Mission Engaging Plurality*, ed. Viggo Mortenson and Andreas Osterlund Nielsen (Grand Rapids: Eerdmans, 2010), 27-35.

[50]Except for Becky Hsu et al., "Estimating the Religious Composition of All Nations: An Empirical Assessment of the World Christian Database," *Journal for the Scientific Study of Religion* 47, no. 4 (2008): 678-93.

[51]Woodberry, "World Religion Database," 22.

the breathtaking scope of the project silenced other critical voices. The data are simply taken as authoritative.

This chapter does not allow for more than a brief treatment of the conceptual and methodological problems of the atlas. These are fundamental issues that impact the statistical images presented of Europe. In the atlas, three principles are featured in presenting these images:

1. to establish broad parameters, giving a general order of magnitude

2. that "like must be compared with like, and like can only be compared with like"

3. that the numbers present, with a few exceptions, general-order estimates[52]

Concepts and definitions. The WCD and the World Religion Database (WRD) serve as sources for the data of the atlas. In 2001 a new methodology was introduced in the WCD to divide Christians into four different groups.[53] The first and broadest category is "Professing Christians": "those who profess publicly to be Christian when asked what their religion is, either in government censuses, or in public-opinion polls." The glossary defines them as "Followers of Jesus Christ of all kinds, all traditions and confessions, and all degrees of commitment."[54] The second category is "Affiliated Christians," those enrolled on the churches' books, the so-called church members. The third category is that of "Practicing Christians," those "affiliated Christians" or "active Christians," also referred to as "attending Christians" or "committed Christians," that attend a church service or public worship at least once a year.[55] A fourth category consists of "Great Commission Christians": "Believers in Jesus Christ [who] are aware of the implication of his Great Commission,"[56] measured by scoring at least five out of ten areas related to the Great Commission or by a simplified method of comparing "the number of cross-cultural missionaries sent or supported." This category is therefore considered to be "quite difficult" to measure.[57]

---

[52]Johnson and Ross, *Atlas of Global Christianity*, 342.
[53]Ibid.
[54]Ibid., 325.
[55]Ibid., 343.
[56]Ibid., 326.
[57]Ibid., 292.

It is significant that only the data of the first category of "professing Christians" are presented in the atlas when speaking about "Christians." These data are derived from government censuses or public-opinion polls, not from information provided by the churches, the (baptized) "church members" or "attending Christians." This key concept of "professing Christians" takes its starting point in the *Universal Declaration of Human Rights* (1948), emphasizing the right to freedom of religion, considered to be a synonym for professing to be a Christian. This legal concept then is justified from a biblical perspective drawing from Matthew 10:32 ("Everyone therefore who acknowledges me before others, I also will acknowledge before my Father in heaven.") and Romans 10:9 ("Because if you confess with your lips that Jesus is Lord and believe in your heart that God raised him from the dead, you will be saved."). Thus this category is considered a synonym for "confessing Christians." In other words, a legal concept, justified by a biblical text, is then linked to the concept of religious self-identification derived from the discipline of sociology of religion. The conceptually somewhat confusing conclusion is that a large religious sociological category of "professing Christians" is synonymous with "declared Christians," "confessing Christians" or "self-identifying Christians."[58]

This "self-identification" concept, rooted in sociology of religion, dominates the statistical images of the atlas. It takes precedence over the term "affiliated Christians," which means someone appears in somebody's church records. It is justified by legal and biblical arguments, leading to peculiar results when applied to Europe. In Europe, belonging to a Christian tradition is an identity marker. It identifies the person's religion, often closely linked to cultural and national identity. It tends to be an identity marker that has little or no bearing on the day-to-day lives of many people. In Europe, this category differs markedly from the concept of membership in a denomination or confessing Christ in North America. The idea of voluntary adherence to a denomination is rooted in North American history and culture and points to religious practice. But it is problematic to apply it to the European context, where one finds a completely different understanding of religious allegiance in the mainline churches.[59] We must

[58]Ibid., 343.

[59]Peter L. Berger, Grace Davie and Effie Fokas, *Religious America, Secular Europe? A Theme and Variation* (Burlington, VT: Ashgate, 2008); Emanuel L. Paparella, "Toward a Post-Secular Europe?: A Review Essay," *Metanexus*, December 4, 2009, www.metanexus.net/essay/toward-post-secular-europe-review-essay.

not confuse voluntary membership in a religious society, or church membership as understood in North America, with belonging to a mainline church in Europe, where such belonging is rather conceived of as an expression of cultural and national identity.

Another peculiar fact flowing from the "self-identification" principle as the central organizing principle is that the definition of Christians includes Mormons, Jehovah's Witnesses, Christian Science and others, referred to as "Marginal Christians," acceptable from a sociology of religion perspective. From a theological point of view this is problematic.[60]

It is important for us to ask why only this large religious category of "professing Christians" is presented in the atlas, eliminating categories that may offer a wider degree of diversification.[61] A more diversified understanding of religious belief is important if one is to understand the nature of European Christianity. The claim that the atlas offers a "nuanced picture" of global Christianity is not fulfilled with regard to Europe.

The statistical image of Europe that is presented reinforces the image of Europe as a kind of Christian continent by not taking into account the internal diversification and erosion of traditional forms of Christianity. Why is only this broad definition used? Is it for fear of losing power and becoming marginalized? Or is it intended to maintain the image of the numerically strong "World C" (see below) that provides the human and financial resources to "finish the task"? Are matters of Christian finance playing a role, with a worldwide annual budget for foreign mission of 32 billion USD?[62] Or does this image emerge out of a hidden resistance to accept that Europe is now also a mission field? Does it result from fear of ending up statistically weaker than the Muslims?[63] Or is this an attempt to implicitly perpetuate Western hegemony? The reality of European Christianity is less monolithic and more complex than has been hitherto recognized by those whose lenses are dominated by secularization theory. The situation involves blurred boundaries between Christians and atheists

---

[60]Brierley, "World Religion Database," 19.
[61]Johnson and Ross, *Atlas of Global Christianity*, 338-39. The fourth category of the Great Commission Christians is mentioned in the country-by-country overview.
[62]Johnson and Ross, *Atlas of Global Christianity*, 296.
[63]Marilynne Robinson, "Fear," *New York Review of Books*, September 24, 2015, www.nybooks.com /articles/2015/09/24/marilynne-robinson-fear/.

or agnostics, a factor better grasped by those who have written the interpretive essays in the atlas.

Underlying missiological theory and perceptions. Another major question has to do with the mission strategies and underlying missiological theories that are invoked. Eric Friede's analysis convincingly argues that the *Atlas of Global Christianitys* is ultimately written from the perspective of the so-called Great Commission Christians who engage in and support Christian missions.[64] Many essays address the issue of how to grow Christianity in a particular region.[65]

The mission strategy invoked is that of identifying the human resources needed for the task of world evangelization[66] and the finances needed to make that happen.[67] An assessment of major tools for finishing this task is offered in subsequent sections, followed by a section on evangelization, with a division of the world into A, B and C, according to the level of "being evangelized," as follows:

1. World A is 50 percent unevangelized.

2. World B is 50 percent evangelized but less than 60 percent Christian.

3. World C is at least 60 percent Christian.[68]

The aim of this division is to direct the focus to the unfinished task: the "unreached peoples" in World A, and to address the imbalance in missionary deployment. Over 85 percent of all Christian outreach is said to go to "professing Christians" in World C. This imbalance would then result in most Christian outreach never reaching the non-Christians in World A or B.[69] This involves a mission strategy that focuses on motivating individuals— Great Commission Christians from World C, the Christian world, that is, mainly from the West, the "Western world that remains predominantly

---

[64]Eric Friede, "Critical Review: *Atlas of Global Christianity*," *Theological Librarianship* 3, no. 1 (2010): 55.

[65]Ibid., 56.

[66]Cathy Ross, "Great Commission Christians, 1910–2010," in Johnson and Ross, *Atlas of Global Christianity*, 290-91.

[67]Jonathan J. Bonk, "Christian Finances," in Johnson and Ross, *Atlas of Global Christianity*, 294-95.

[68]Johnson and Ross, *Atlas of Global Christianity*, 312-13.

[69]Todd M. Johnson and Albert W. Hickman, "Interpreting Religion: Religious Demography and Mission Strategy," *International Journal for Frontier Missiology* 29, no. 1 (2012): 13-21.

Christian"[70]—to reach out to those still in World A or World B, many of whom are located in the so-called 10/40 Window (regions of the world between 10 and 40 degrees north of the equator), outside the West.[71] The statistical maps are used to stimulate funding for this missionary enterprise, pointing to where supposedly the greatest needs exist.

The atlas could thus be considered an example of statistics used to motivate missionaries and national workers to mission action. Christian mission is reduced to a manageable enterprise with a dominant quantitative approach and a well-defined pragmatic orientation "as a typical school of thought coming from modern United States."[72]

The question posed in this chapter is how this mission strategy can be applied to Europe. Since almost all of Europe (94 percent) falls in the category of World C, the message encourages European Christianity to focus attention on the unreached peoples in World A or on the partially or moderately evangelized non-Christian World B[73] and to provide funding for facilitating this missionary enterprise. But to classify as "reached" and "evangelized" a person who identifies as a Christian in a cultural sense and may never or only occasionally attend church can be misleading. Strictly speaking, this division of the world into A, B and C leaves mission in Europe in a vacuum.

The underlying missiological theory of this mission strategy is a subdiscipline of missiology called missiometrics, which seeks to assist churches in planning for mission by offering powerful tools to calculate the complexity of people groups and languages in today's world.[74] The importance of "counting" for mission strategy was elaborated by Donald McGavran, who pressed for a kind of strategizing that incorporated a sociological perspective. McGavran urged mission leaders to concentrate their resources on those initiatives with the greatest promise for numerical success over against

---

[70]Johnson and Ross, *Atlas of Global Christianity*, 313.

[71]Ibid., 314.

[72]J. Samuel Escobar, "Evangelical Missiology: Peering into the Future at the Turn of the Century," in *Global Missiology for the 21st Century: The Iguassu Dialogue*, ed. William D. Taylor, Globalization of Mission Series (Grand Rapids: Baker Academic, 2000), 109.

[73]David B. Barrett et al., *World Christian Trends, AD 30–AD 2200: Interpreting the Annual Christian Megacensus* (Pasadena, CA: William Carey Library, 2001), 80-81.

[74]David B. Barrett, "'Count the Worshipers!': The New Science of Missiometrics," *International Bulletin of Missionary Research* 19, no. 4 (1995): 154-60.

the strategy of someone like Roland Allen, who wanted missions to "stop over-planning, so that God's Spirit could do its work unfettered by human schemes."[75] Often the implicit goal of finishing the mission task by making it more manageable is to trigger the second coming of Christ.[76] This missiological theory uses such concepts as "unreached peoples" or "adopt a people" to convey a strong sense of urgency and to call for the use of all possible means to "get the job done."[77] This atlas could be considered one of those means.

The influence of missiometrics—with its measurable goals and focus on output that turn mission into a predictable, efficient, calculated and controlled mission strategy based on market principles—is gaining ground in church and mission circles in Europe. It offers an attempt to find a solution to the problem of European Christianity. Also for this reason, it is important to revisit the presuppositions of this missiology and to listen to the critical voices calling for a disclosure of its underlying assumptions.

Critical voices from Latin America. Samuel Escobar characterizes this school of thought coming out of Pasadena as managerial missiology.[78] Elsewhere referring to it as an "application of the Harvard Business School method,"[79] he considers this approach rather a "methodology for mission" than a missiology. Therefore he challenges it to "enter into dialogue with theology and other missiologies [to] make its valuable contribution to mission in the third millennium."[80] From an image-formation-theory perspective the essence of this dialogue with critical voices is to nurture missional integrity at all levels of our methodology of missiology: in our praxis, our mission theory and our worldview assumptions.[81]

---

[75]Stanley H. Skreslet, *Comprehending Mission: The Questions, Methods, Themes, Problems, and Prospects of Missiology*, American Society of Missiology Series (Maryknoll, NY: Orbis Books, 2012), 130.

[76]Robert T. Coote, "'AD 2000' and the '10/40 Window': A Preliminary Assessment," *International Bulletin of Missionary Research* 24, no. 4 (October 2000): 160.

[77]Escobar, "Evangelical Missiology," 109.

[78]Ibid., passim.

[79]As expressed in Paul Davies, "Managerial or Messy Mission," *Missional Musings: Scattered Ruminations from a Mission Theologian* (blog), August 25, 2015, http://pauljdavies.org/?p=656.

[80]Escobar, "Evangelical Missiology," 112.

[81]J. N. J. (Klippies) Kritzinger, "Nurturing Missional Integrity" (paper presented at the Károli Gáspár University of the Reformed Church in Hungary–Central and Eastern European Institute for Mission Studies [KRE-CIMS] Seminar, Budapest, Hungary, October 2011).

First, Escobar states that this missiology tends to reduce Christian mission to a manageable enterprise following marketing principles and operating within the frame of an "avowed quantifying intention."[82] Statistical analysis first serves the role of evaluating the effect of missionary action according to a narrowly defined concept of mission as numerical church growth and insistence on the unfinished task. For Donald McGavran, the dilemma was whether mission is "primarily evangelism, or . . . primarily all efforts to improve human existence."[83] For Escobar, McGavran's choice is clear: "Winning many to the Christian life must be the dominant concern of all Christians. . . . Once that is done . . . other steps toward the better life will become much more possible and more permanent."[84] Some extreme forms of managerial missiology like counting the number of printed pages distributed or the hours of broadcasting may not have been McGavran's intention. Yet such narrowing of the concept of mission has at times led to a managerial approach to mission that has been the object of severe criticism.

Second, Escobar notes the pragmatic approach, de-emphasizing theological problems in which tough questions are not asked because they cannot be reduced to a management-by-objectives process. It is geared "to provide methodologies for a guaranteed success."[85] This pragmatic bias results in a reductionist theological foundation for missiology, eliminating anything that hinders numerical growth. Suffering and persecution, holistic mission and participation in social transformation, and the slow process of developing a contextual theology are too easily replaced by prepackaged programs translated from English.[86]

The third point of Escobar's criticism involves the strong influence of American functionalist social sciences, with their structural-functional model of cultural anthropology based on a static view of the world that "undermines the hope of transformation which is central to the gospel."[87]

---

[82]Escobar, "Evangelical Missiology," 109.
[83]Donald McGavran, "Missiology Facing the Lion," *Missiology* 17, no. 3 (1989): 338, quoted in Escobar, "Evangelical Missiology," 110.
[84]Ibid., quoted in Escobar, "Evangelical Missiology," 110.
[85]Escobar, "Evangelical Missiology," 110.
[86]Ibid., 111.
[87]Charles Taber, quoted in Escobar, "Evangelical Missiology," 111.

Some proponents of managerial missiology have created suspicion about the underlying motivations. Such suspicion has been fueled by the great amount of data and technical resources used to promote their views and by their focus on the quantitative increase in the missionary force without much debate about the quality.[88] Some critics are suspicious of being used as objects of missionary action, as elements in a success story, ultimately directed toward enhancing the financial, informational and decision-making power of mission centers in the Global North. All of these three points of criticism by Escobar—the quantifiable and manageable frame of missiology, the pragmatic approach avoiding tough theological questions and the static view of the world derived from functionalism in cultural anthropology—call us to continue the conversation.

Critical voices from Central and Eastern Europe. This mission strategy with its quantitative emphasis has also given rise to critical voices in Eastern Europe. After the fall of the Berlin Wall and a period of euphoria (1989–1998), a period of disillusionment (1998–2008) followed with an ambiguous view of the role of Western missionaries. Although they were credited with positive contributions,[89] the models from the West they brought with them often did not address the many "shadows of the past." Disillusionment was strengthened by mission agencies and churches in the West that carried out short-term, output-oriented projects, many of which resulted in a clash of the Western paradigm of mission based on success with the Eastern European mindset that is more characterized by suffering. There has been a general discontentment with how Western missionary agencies handled their relationships with nationals.[90] Concerning cooperation with local churches, there was general consensus that many Western missions were building their own missionary empires as if no indigenous churches existed.[91]

Vladimir Ubeivolc has underlined the negative impact of the Western face of (evangelical) Christianity in Moldavia, Ukraine and Russia. He

---

[88]Escobar, "Evangelical Missiology," 112.

[89]Peter Penner, "Scripture, Community, and Context in God's Mission in the FSU," in *Mission in the Former Soviet Union*, ed. Walter Sawatsky and Peter Penner (Schwarzenfeld, Ger.: Neufeld Verlag, 2005), 31.

[90]Danut Manastireanu, "Western Assistance in Theological Training for Romanian Evangelicals to 1989," *East-West Church & Ministry Report* 14, no. 4 (2006): 7; and David Novak, "Czech Evangelicals and Evangelism," *East-West Church & Ministry Report* 13, no. 1 (2005): 8-10.

[91]Novak, "Czech Evangelicals and Evangelism," 7.

affirms that a strategy that aims to plant new churches in each settlement in Moldavia is an ineffective mission approach, demanding great spiritual, financial and emotional effort without the desired results.[92] He has proposed a holistic approach to mission in the Moldovan context, calling on evangelical Baptists to be "servants for the sake of victims of social injustice, prophets for social justice, witnesses of the Good News and peacemakers among all the groups that suffered from difficult conflicts."[93] Many strategies conceived by Western Christianity are considered a serious hindrance to the process of growing an indigenous church that can address the complex missiological challenges in its own context from a biblical perspective.[94]

When we take a closer look at the lenses that have shaped the statistical images of the atlas, we are challenged to focus more attention on the roots of the underlying missiological theory: its concepts, its methodologies and the worldview assumptions drawn from the social sciences that until recently have been dominated by secularization theory.

The question for a continuing dialogue on methodology is this: What would reconstructed images look like when seen through postsecular, post-Christendom lenses that redefine the concepts, take seriously the new attention for religion in sociology[95] and realign our mission strategy to be based on theological principles rather than on secular management principles based on power, control and predetermined outcomes?

CONCLUSION

Using contemporary image-formation theory, this chapter explored the construction and maintenance of images about Europe and European Christianity that have fueled and motivated specific types of missionary enterprises and strategies. We have examined some of the underlying missiological

---

[92]Vladimir Ubeivolc, "Rethinking *Missio Dei* Among Evangelical Churches in an Eastern European Orthodox Context" (PhD thesis, University of Wales and International Baptist Theological Academy, 2011), 230.

[93]Ibid., 272.

[94]Joshua T. Searle and Mykhailo N. Cherenkov, *A Future and a Hope: Mission, Theological Education, and the Transformation of Post-Soviet Society* (Eugene, OR: Wipf & Stock, 2014).

[95]Such as, for example, Christian Smith et al., "Roundtable on the Sociology of Religion: Twenty-Three Theses on the Status of Religion in American Sociology—A Mellon Working-Group Reflection," *Journal of the American Association of Religion* 81, no. 4 (2013): 903-38.

theories and perceptions found in one of the most remarkable sources of such images, the *Atlas of Global Christianity*.

We dealt with some of the conceptual and methodological problems, discovering that the statistical images of the atlas offer a distorted view of Europe and European Christianity. The lenses are blurred by secularization theory, unable to capture a resurgence of religion and spirituality on the ground. Such lenses are not able to inform a new mission engagement that can create an opportunity for a contextually appropriate strategy in Europe. The mission strategy underlying the atlas, based on missiometrics, perpetuates Western hegemony in mission and does not serve well the shift to global Christianity. It may also hinder the development of contextually relevant indigenous churches in many parts of (Eastern) Europe and the Global South. The mission strategy invoked by the statistical images of the atlas based on a division of the world into A, B and C leaves mission in Europe in a vacuum.

Furthermore, missiometrics turns Christian mission into a managerial enterprise based on secular values rather than on a movement flowing out of the *missio Dei*, based on theological principles.

Declaring the Wonders of God in Our Own Tongues

Africa, Mission and the Making of World Christianity

J. Kwabena Asamoah-Gyadu

INTRODUCTION

In the early 2000s Andrew F. Walls, clearly the doyen of studies in World Christianity in the twentieth century, drew attention to the wide recognition that Christianity had become a primarily non-Western religion in terms of both regional balance and ethnic composition. This observation is not necessarily original to Walls, but he has certainly been one of its main proponents. For our purposes here, it is the interpretation that Walls gave to the African continent in the changing phase of world Christianity that makes his observation more significant:

> This means that we have to regard African Christianity as potentially *representative* Christianity of the twenty-first century. . . . The Christianity typical of the twenty-first century will be shaped by the events and processes that take place in the southern continents, and above all by those that take place in Africa.[1]

The question then remains: what are the developments that have taken place within Christianity, as far as Africa is concerned? A number of these readily come to mind, including certain seismic changes generated by the activities of indigenous charismatic prophets and movements during the

---

[1] Andrew F. Walls, *The Cross-Cultural Process in Christian History* (Maryknoll, NY: Orbis Books, 2002), 85; emphasis added.

opening decade of the twentieth century. The salient factors in the movements we have in mind here are the experience, manifestations and power of the Holy Spirit as "lived experience" and the fact that they started "charismatizing" the African Christian landscape a few years before developments at Azusa Street came to attention.

AFRICAN REVIVALISM

In this discussion, I use the example of African initiatives in pneumatic Christianity as a focal point in reflecting on the relationship between Spirit-empowerment, religious transformation and mission as a non-Western endeavor. Every genuine revival of the Christian faith outside its former strongholds in the West demonstrates that, inspired by Spirit-empowered renewal, modern-day Gentiles are declaring the wonders of God in their own tongues. This is a process that in Africa has historically been facilitated by vernacular translations of the Bible and, for Pentecostals in particular, by active, conscious and even aggressive forms of evangelization. Walter J. Hollenweger in his book *The Pentecostals* also drew attention to how the oral cultures of African societies and the importance of expressive and experiential religions make it easier for Pentecostal/charismatic forms of the faith to blossom in such non-Western cultures.[2] It is thus not surprising that Pentecostal/charismatic Christianity is credited for the transformation of faith that has been underway in Africa since the middle of the twentieth century.

Paul Gifford was puzzled that "Africa is not reacting to globalization by revitalizing African traditional religion" but instead appeared to be opting into "exotic religions."[3] The "exotic" religions referred to here are the Spirit-empowered revivalist movements that started burgeoning in Africa from the beginning of the twentieth century. A number of them may have inveighed against aspects of African traditional religions, but these movements in their spirituality uniquely sustain African worldviews of the power of the supernatural and mystical causality. Throughout history, many of the leaders of African revivalist movements have rejected Western understandings of beliefs in witchcraft, for example, as a figment of the popular uneducated imagination or even a psychological delusion. African

---

[2]Walter J. Hollenweger, *The Pentecostals* (London: SCM, 1972).
[3]Paul Gifford, *African Christianity: Its Public Role* (London: Hurst and Co., 1998), 321.

pneumatic movements have operated on the basis that witchcraft is real and a major factor in African underdevelopment, accounting for poverty, squalor, disease and communal stagnation.

Ruth Marshall calls for an approach to the study of revival movements in Africa that "restores intelligibility to religion in its irreducibility, to make sense of the inherent rationality of its disciplines and practices, over and above its social, cultural, or political functions."[4] One may not appreciate the spiritual interpretations that the prophetic ministries of pneumatic movements recognize underlying the most mundane problems in African societies unless we take the faith of those in African pneumatic movements seriously. It is to the credit of Christian new religious movements in Africa that they create appropriate Christian ritual contexts for the restoration of disturbed persons and even restore physical spaces to proper functioning order in ways that take indigenous notions of causality seriously. In Ghana and Zambia, new governments have invited independent charismatic pastors with the requisite anointing or power to spiritually cleanse the seats of governments, and a Pentecostal archbishop in Ghana has prayed publicly for the Holy Spirit to "arrest" the declining fortunes of the local currency. These actions capture the inseparability of sacred and secular realities in the African religiocultural realm.

AFRICAN REVIVALISM AND THE PUBLIC SPHERE

The following reflections will illustrate how different Spirit-empowered communities in Africa are illustrative of the shift in Christian presence from the Northern to the Southern continents. The power of numbers comes with influence, and Spirit empowerment means, among others things, a call to impact the public sphere. In his book *In the Days of Caesar*, Amos Yong notes that the "apoliticism" that characterized the attitude of early Pentecostals in the public sphere has given way to a greater degree of political engagement because of the changing nature and demographic compositions of contemporary Pentecostal movements.[5] And even though Africa's older

---

[4]Ruth Marshall, *Political Spiritualities: The Pentecostal Revolution in Nigeria* (Chicago: University of Chicago Press, 2009), 3.

[5]Amos Yong, *In the Days of Caesar: Pentecostalism and Political Theology* (Grand Rapids: Eerdmans, 2010), 8.

independent churches, for example, may have appeared apolitical, as the first groups of religious mass movements in Africa, they demanded respect from political leaders, who were forced to heed them and even court their friendship. After Ghana's 1966 coup d'état, for example, the lot fell on Prophet C. K. Wovenu of the Apostles Revelation Society, a new independent church, to "exorcise" the seat of government. The deposed president Kwame Nkrumah was believed to have accumulated an array of non-Christian religious powers for his protection. The ability to deal with the supernatural was thought to be beyond the powers of the historic mission ministers, who possessed academic credentials but lacked charismatic power. Thus, when public officeholders seek persons who understand the language of spiritual power to deal with supernatural evil, the choice is always from the ranks of the pneumatic movements.

Co-option of the early independent churches into the political power struggles in Africa was one sign of the significance of those movements. As I point out below, the importance of the early independent churches was also recognized by academics interested in the study of Christianity in Africa; they were forced to take notice of them as important subjects of serious research. The newer Pentecostals are even more prominent in the public sphere given their better-educated leadership, the extensive uses they make of modern media and the youthful congregations they have attracted. Although the two sets of movements—the African independent/initiated/instituted churches (AICs) and the Pentecostal/charismatic movements—developed within different historical and sociocultural contexts, their spiritualities overlap in ways that indicate they offer something that touches a nerve within African religious sensibilities. Andrew F. Walls has this to say about their phenomenological differences and theological convergences:

> Until recently these prophet-healing churches could be held [sic] the most significant and the fastest-growing sector of the indigenous churches. This is no longer so certain. Nigeria and Ghana . . . are witnessing the rise of another type of independent church. Like many prophet-healing churches, they have often originated as prayer or revival groups outside older churches. Like the prophet-healing churches, they proclaim the divine power of deliverance from disease and demonic affliction, but the style of proclamation is more like that of the American adventist and pentecostal preaching. Gone are the

African drums of the aladuras; the visitor is more likely to hear electronic keyboards and amplified guitars, see a preacher in elegant agbada or smart business suit and a choir in bow ties. Yet these radical charismatic movements are African in origin, in leadership, and in finance. They are highly entrepreneurial and are active in radio, television and cassette ministries as well as in campaigns and conventions.[6]

The first group, the AICs or prophet-healing churches, started at the dawn of the twentieth century, and the second group, the charismatic churches or contemporary Pentecostals, at the end of the same century. What they have in common, as Walls suggests in the quotation above, is an emphasis on the power of the Holy Spirit for Christian life and public witness. In the words of Walls, "All the new movements share with the prophet-healing churches a quest for the demonstrable presence of the Holy Spirit and direct address to the problems and frustrations of modern African urban life."[7] There are both continuities and discontinuities between the two groups, but each in its own way reflects African options in the appropriation of Christianity. In both cases there are wide variations in the nature of these movements, so I use the expression pneumatic Christianity to refer to them in a bid to account for the diversity that they bring to the religious variety in Africa.

I take it for granted that both the old and new African initiatives in Christianity appeal primarily to the Bible for theological and ecclesiological legitimacy. People who begin attending these churches say that they do so because they offer a more vibrant, Spirit-filled and experiential worship than the historic mission denominations. They function within a theologically interventionist mindset that challenges the rational and cerebral nature of historic mission Christianity. The healing and prophetic ministries of the charismatic prophets of the AICs have proven very popular in Africa. This is why Harold W. Turner opted to call them "prophet-healing" churches.[8] The world has moved on, and young people in particular are attracted to the contemporary Pentecostals or "new paradigm churches" as Donald E. Miller

---

[6]Andrew F. Walls, *The Missionary Movement in Christian History: Studies in the Transmission of Faith* (Maryknoll, NY: Orbis Books, 1996), 92-93.
[7]Ibid., 93.
[8]Harold W. Turner, *Religious Innovation in Africa: Collected Essays on New Religious Movements* (Boston: G. K. Hall, 1979).

calls them in the North American context, partly because of their trendy Christianity, entertainment culture and media-driven worship services.[9]

Young graduates and business executives find career-advancing opportunities in the new charismatic churches, and these churches create a social context for young people to find future partners. These are important parts of the appeal of these churches to Africa's upwardly mobile young people. The churches' messages of motivation have also struck a chord among young people in search of new sources of inspiration away from the politics of corrupt African leaders. Beginning with the source of their appeal, which is the Bible, in the rest of this chapter I will discuss a number of ways in which African pneumatic movements have become important players on the world stage.

Spirit-empowerment and the biblical mandate. In Africa, most of the indigenous Christian movements take a pneumatic approach to church life even if some do not clearly and specifically identify with the Pentecostal/charismatic designation. The bottom line is the importance of the experience of the Holy Spirit in Christian mission. Jesus Christ set the tone for mission when in one of his post-resurrection appearances he made a connection between the sending of the disciples and the granting of the Holy Spirit:

> When it was evening on that day, the first day of the week, and the doors of the house where the disciples had met were locked for fear of the Jews, Jesus came and stood among them and said, "Peace be with you." After he said this, he showed them his hands and side. Then the disciples rejoiced when they saw the Lord. Jesus said to them again, "Peace be with you. As the Father has sent me, so I send you." When he said this, he breathed on them and said to them, "Receive the Holy Spirit. If you forgive the sins of any, they are forgiven them; if you retain the sins of any, they are retained." (Jn 20:19-23)

The sending and the granting of the Spirit occur in the same breath; in addition, there is a clear sense that the disciples have been given the authority to execute the task ahead. "The chief actor in the historic mission of the Christian church is the Holy Spirit," John V. Taylor wrote. "He is the

---

[9]Donald E. Miller, *Reinventing American Protestantism: Christianity in the New Millennium* (Berkeley: University of California Press, 1997).

director of the whole enterprise," he continued, and "the mission consists of the things he is doing in the world."[10] The questions are, what is God doing in the world, and how is he executing this mission? Quoting Taylor again:

> In Africa today it seems that the incalculable Spirit has chosen to use the Independent Church Movement for another spectacular advance. This does not prove that their teaching is necessarily true, but it shows they have the raw materials out of which a missionary church is made—spontaneity, total commitment, and the primitive responses that arise from the depths of life.[11]

The rise of pneumatic movements in Africa signified a popular rejection of a hypercritical approach to biblical interpretation. As with the early Pentecostal movements, indigenous expressions of the faith in Africa took a more "fundamentalist" approach to the Bible by first recognizing its place in Christian experience as the Word of God. Second, African Christians rejected scientific ways of explaining some of the miracles of the Christian Scriptures. This approach to the Bible, in which people have sought to experience the same signs and wonders and miracles that the Bible chronicles, has been an important element in African innovations in Christianity that distinguishes it from several expressions of the faith present in the Western context.

The impact on studies in world Christianity. It is impossible to talk about the academic study of Christianity as a non-Western religion without reference to what we have described as Christian religious innovation in Africa. We encountered Andrew F. Walls at the beginning of this chapter, and that for a reason. He has been an important figure in the study of Christianity in Africa much of the last half of the twentieth century. His experience of teaching as a missionary in Sierra Leone from 1957 to 1966 left Andrew Walls with no doubt that "the immediate future of Christianity lay in the southern hemisphere."[12] Walls's desire, then, was to do something about this "new and exciting chapter in Christian history" by providing the resources and context for the documentation and interpretation of "the rapid growth and

---

[10]John V. Taylor, *The Go-Between God: The Holy Spirit and the Christian Mission* (London: SCM, 1972), 3.

[11]Ibid., 54.

[12]Andrew Walls as quoted in Brian Stanley, "Founding the Center for the Study of Christianity in the Non-Western World," in *Understanding World Christianity: The Vision and Work of Andrew F. Walls*, ed. William R. Burrows, Mark R. Gornick and Janice A. McClean (Maryknoll, NY: Orbis Books, 2011), 51.

rich diversification of southern Christianity."[13] That Africans, like all others, must declare the wonders of God in their own tongues seemed to have been the underlying motivation. The result of this desire was the establishment in 1982 of the Center for the Study of Christianity in the Non-Western World in Aberdeen, later in Edinburgh and now at Liverpool Hope University.

The distinguished academics who joined Andrew Walls or were mentored by him included Harold W. Turner, Adrian Hastings, Lamin Sanneh, David Shank and Kwame Bediako. Andrew Walls also founded the still-active and important *Journal of Religion in Africa* in 1967 and was its editor until 1985. The scholars mentioned here are important leaders in the study of what became known as the African independent/initiated/instituted churches (AICs). Sanneh's *West African Christianity: The Religious Impact* has extensive chapters on the revivalist Aladura movement of Nigeria.[14] Hastings specialized in the history of the church in Africa; in virtually all his important works, he wrote about these AICs and their role in the transformation of Christianity in Africa.[15] David Shank's major work is on the prophetic ministry of William Wadé Harris, a powerful early-twentieth-century figure from Liberia who was nicknamed the "Black Elijah of West Africa" for his Holy Spirit–driven and charismatic ministry.[16] Today, centers for the study of world Christianity blossom around the northern continents, and in virtually every case the focus is on the study of non-Western forms of the faith, paying significant attention to developments in Africa. That a number of important studies continue to resurface on early African pneumatic movements is indicative of their importance in the history of such churches in world Christianity.[17]

Two things continue to bear testimony to the dominance of the African-initiated churches in the study of Christianity in Africa. First, these churches have provided research material for church historians, missiologists and

---

[13]Ibid., 51.

[14]Lamin Sanneh, *West African Christianity: The Religious Impact* (Maryknoll, NY: Orbis Books, 1983).

[15]Adrian Hastings, *A History of African Christianity 1950–1975* (Cambridge: Cambridge University Press, 1979).

[16]David A. Shank, *Prophet Harris: The Black Elijah of West Africa* (Leiden: Brill, 1994).

[17]Joel Cabrita, *Texts and Authority in the South African Nazaretha Church* (Cambridge: Cambridge University Press, 2014); and Chinonyerem Chijioke Ekebuisi, *The Life and Ministry of Prophet Garrick Sokari Braide: Elijah the Second of Niger Delta, Nigeria, (c. 1882–1918)* (Oxford: Lang, 2015).

theologians interested in religious innovation in Africa. The evidence for this is the massive bibliographical material available on indigenous Christian movements in Africa in libraries around the world. In the middle of the twentieth century, according to Hastings, the study of independent churches became something of a "cash crop" among scholars interested in religious innovation:

> The scholar looking . . . for an interesting research topic in the field of African religion at that time could hardly fail to be attracted by one of the almost innumerable new churches springing into vibrant existence in Zaire [now Democratic Republic of the Congo], Kenya, Zambia or Ghana in those years. . . . "African Christianity" was now, suddenly, a popular subject indeed but almost entirely in terms of independent churches.[18]

Second, the *Journal of Religion in Africa* (*JRA*) has emerged as and continues to be the single most important journal to report on the ministries of these revitalization movements across Africa. The *JRA* has in the last two decades become the periodical that has given the most extensive coverage to the study of contemporary Pentecostalism in Africa.

The impact on ecclesiology. The AICs changed the face of Christianity in Africa from the early years of the twentieth century. Prayer has always been a factor in African-initiated Christianity. The term *Aladura*, used to describe the Yoruba version of these movements, means "people of prayer." Pentecostalism understands fundamentally that prayer has the power of transformation and change. Prayer can overcome resistance to the message of the gospel, the work of evil powers and situations of misfortune. When prayer is delivered in tongues, it is considered even more effective because, being the tongue of angels, it "confuses" the devil. Out of vigorous and aggressive prayer sessions and demonstration of acts of power, prophecies emerged directing certain persons to start independent churches in sub-Saharan Africa. As one Nigerian member of an independent church noted,

> In our [previous historic-mission-founded] churches with their set services there was not sufficient time for us to develop spiritually. When you do a thing you must reap the benefits; what we were taught in church we do not experience

---

[18]Adrian Hastings, "Christianity in Africa," in *Turning Points in Religious Studies: Essays in Honour of Geoffrey Parrinder*, ed. Ursula King (Edinburgh: T&T Clark, 1990), 204.

in practice. We Africans are so low in everything, but by prayer we may win everlasting power in God's Kingdom. In a word, practical Christianity.[19]

There are reasons for this. First, the way to have an alternative to Western ecclesiology was to focus on the neglected dimensions of the faith by being fundamentally biblical. That meant opting for a form of Christianity that took seriously the promises of Scripture concerning the Holy Spirit. Christian G. Baëta, one of the first people to study these movements in their Ghanaian context, described them as groups "engaged in a prodigious struggle to prove the reality of spiritual things in general and the biblical promises in particular, taking these in a fully literal sense."[20] Second, focusing on the Holy Spirit and experiencing the Spirit's power of speaking in tongues, exorcism, healing, deliverance and the like helped African Christians to appreciate the resonances between Spirit-empowered Christianity and traditional religiocultural practices.

Indeed, it is precisely in this area of contextualizing church life within an African setting based on biblical understandings of the work of the Spirit that Lamin Sanneh suggests African churches made their unique contribution to the faith:

> A process of internal change was thus initiated in which African Christians sought a distinctive way of life through mediation of the Spirit, a process that enhanced the importance of traditional religions for the deepening of Christian spirituality. . . . Biblical material was submitted to the regenerative capacity of African perception, and the result would be Africa's unique contribution to the story of Christianity.[21]

On the importance of the Spirit in ecclesiological experiences in the AICs, consider the following observation from John D. Y. Peel's study of the Aladura movement in Nigeria. He notes that a belief in the significance of dreams was nothing new in the world of the Yorubas. What may have been new was the conscious search for supernatural visions through prayer and fasting. The members of the movement were instructed in their use by their

---

[19]John D. Y. Peel, *Aladura: A Religious Movement Among the Yoruba* (Oxford: Oxford University Press, 1968), 73.

[20]Christian G. Baëta, *Prophetism in Ghana: A Study of Some Spiritual Churches* (London: SCM, 1962), 135.

[21]Sanneh, *West African Christianity*, 180.

leader Orimolade. At meetings, Orimolade would keep silent for a long time in prayer while all present waited expectantly. Eventually he might say, "The Holy Spirit has descended." Then, following prayer, Orimolade would tell those present any visions he had seen. This was how the charisma of seeing visions developed among the Aladura.[22] An important dimension, to which Aladura spirituality was directed, was attention to the existential needs of members: marriage, employment, health, promotion, success in business and general well-being. In a sense, that which developed as an orientation toward practical salvation among the early independent churches comes full circle in modern prosperity preaching.

Gospel and prosperity. On more contemporary developments, Amos Yong makes an important observation when he notes that "prosperity is a central feature of the globalization of Pentecostalism and that the prosperity message, or message of dominion, is traveling in multiple directions—from the 'north' to the 'south,' and back again."[23] Most of those who write on the prosperity gospel from outside the Pentecostal/charismatic movement attack its materialistic orientation. Prosperity preaching is, however, about something more profound than just the flamboyant lifestyles and consumerist values of those who preach it. Prosperity is about a felt call to dominate the earth, and such dominance is seen as a God-given right to develop the earth for human well-being. There are several ways to understand the new dominion theology, and one of these is through the slogans of the prosperity-preaching churches. In London, Matthew Ashimolowo's Kingsway International Christian Center advertises itself as a church that is "Taking Territories and Raising Champions." Mensa Otabil's International Central Gospel Church in Ghana is "Raising Leaders, Shaping Vision and Influencing Society Through Christ."

These slogans have one thing in common: that God has called into being a new crop of churches and church leaders filled with his Spirit to transform society through the innovative hermeneutics of prosperity. Mensa Otabil has stated several times in his *Living Word* broadcasts that the cardinal test guiding his preaching is Genesis 1:28:

---

[22]Peel, *Aladura*, 72.
[23]Yong, *In the Days of Caesar*, 15.

God blessed them, and God said to them, "Be fruitful and multiply, and fill the earth and subdue it; and have dominion over the fish of the sea and over the birds of the air and over every living thing that moves upon the earth."

It is an important text that drives the motivational messages of contemporary Pentecostalism and also informs its theology of dominion. The result of exercising dominion is prosperity in both physical and spiritual dimensions. As Yong notes of the prosperity mindset of Ezekiel Guti of the Zimbabwe Assemblies of Africa, the church's success was established on its "exemplifying power of the prosperity gospel." As he explains, "upward social mobility, a growing middle class membership, and Guti's affluent lifestyle were convincing indicators that association with the church brought with it not only eternal salvation but also material blessings."[24] It is not uncommon for charismatic church pastors to demand that those who have prospered materially under their ministry "sow" some apostolic offerings in return. The wealth of these leaders is then cited as an indicator that the gospel of prosperity is viable not just for individuals but also for nations.

This prosperity message, especially in terms of physical and human development, is directed particularly at the black race, specifically Africans, because we have allowed ourselves to be mentally enslaved decades after the collapse of the colonialist project. I have explained elsewhere how dominion theology also informs the choice of symbols, the eagle being the preferred choice.[25] The eagle symbolizes dominion because not only is it the king of birds but its ability to soar higher than all birds, piercing vision, strength as a bird of prey and power of flight make it the ideal example of what God created human beings to be—that is, to dominate spaces. An incredibly high number of contemporary Pentecostal/charismatic churches frequently indulge in eagle hermeneutics, and some even go by names such as Eagle Charismatic Church or Eagle Christian Center.

Across Africa the word *dominion* also occurs in the names of many contemporary Pentecostal churches. The Action Chapel International has even named its new university Dominion University College, and the Kingsway International Christian Centre (KICC) temple in Accra is simply Dominion

---

[24]Yong, *In the Days of Caesar*, 16.
[25]J. Kwabena Asamoah-Gyadu, *Sighs and Signs of the Spirit: Ghanaian Perspectives on Pentecostalism and Renewal in Africa* (Oxford: Regnum, 2015), chap. 3.

Center. The churches in question have transformed the African urban skyline with their imposing "cathedroms," and there is a tacit competition to build the auditorium that accommodates the highest number of worshipers. This same spirit of dominion drives the desire to have megachurches appear on electronic media platforms, such as the Internet, and transcribe sermons and turn them into books for wider circulation beyond weekly Sunday audiences. The worldwide peregrinations of the new crop of Christian leaders, whether by invitation or self-sponsored trips, are an important positive index of the prosperity gospel they preach. The words *global*, *international* and *worldwide*, which appear in the name of every charismatic church, emphasize their dominion-theology mindset.

Spiritual warfare. There is an important connection between dominion theology and spiritual warfare. The ministry of spiritual warfare, which deals with the deployment of supernatural resources in the name/blood of Jesus and by the power of the Holy Spirit to free people from all kinds of bondage, releases victims into lives of prosperity. The dominion mindset accounts for the reinvention of spiritual warfare within contemporary Pentecostal spirituality. Whereas Western missionaries regarded the African belief in demons as superstitious paganism, African prophets "demonstrated the power of God to overcome them through the driving out of the spirits."[26] I refer to this ministry in its current forms as reinventions because it was an important part of the spirituality of the AICs. So the idea of taking territories and raising champions refers to something more than building businesses and increasing investments. It also means exercising dominion over the "principalities" and "powers" (Eph 6:12 KJV) that threaten the prosperity of God's people. An emerging strategy to handle these powers is by the positive declarations developed by charismatic pastors for their churches in lieu of the historic creeds recited by the older mission denominations.

One booklet, issued by Archbishop Nicholas Duncan-Williams of Action Chapel International, has documented the following declaration against demons working to sabotage a person's prosperity:

> I decree a divine cleansing upon my land, and my household. I declare that my land is flowing with milk and honey. I lift up counter petitions against

---

[26]Opoku Onyina, *Witchcraft and Demonology in Ghana* (Dorchester, UK: Deo, 2012), 111.

every strange voice that makes demands on my dividends and I command a permanent halt to such voices. In the name of Jesus Christ, I speak from the throne room perspective and command permanent closure to all forms of vain labor, financial desecration and setbacks. By the warrant of the blood of Jesus, I command the arrest of disembodied spirits assigned to rob me of my treasures and fortunes. In the name of the Jesus Christ, I confront and break the powers of any entity or entities mandated by ancestral curses to deny me of my financial liberty.[27]

This is a classic example of how Pentecostal/charismatic Christianity provides its followers with "spiritual tools" for dealing with the power of evil and thereby the ability to "access their God-given promises of prosperity."[28] For an African ministry, it is significant not only that the declaration makes reference to demonic powers associated with Satan but also that African ancestral practices are denounced as a "demonic doorway" of affliction. This is a mark of the heightened sense of opposition to traditional religion by Pentecostals from the years of historic mission Christianity. In the demonization of traditional beliefs, Pentecostal spirituality has been widened to accommodate various aspects of culture. Most important, though, in the public sphere, words have a certain performance effect, and one can send them forth on incapacitating missions against supernatural powers that work against Christian prosperity. This notion of spiritual warfare from the older AICs finds new expression in indigenous Christianity to denounce contemporary lifestyles like homosexuality and transgender surgeries as demonic or satanic.[29] All this is to reiterate Yong's point that in Africa "the prosperity gospel is alive and well" and involves "not only belief in material blessings but also deliverance from evil spirits, healing of the body, and expectations of a social uplift as a whole."[30] Therein lies the importance of prosperity for the public sphere.

Immigrant Christianity and African Pentecostal witness. My Pentecostal dominion-mandate theory is good for explaining the high percentage

---

[27]Nicholas Duncan-Williams, *Enforcing Prophet Decrees* (Accra, Ghana: Design Solutions, 2015), 37-39.

[28]Yong, *In the Days of Caesar*, 20.

[29]Ruth Marshall, *Political Spiritualities: Pentecostal Revolution in Nigeria* (Chicago: University of Chicago Press, 2009), 79.

[30]Yong, *In the Days of Caesar*, 17.

of African immigrant churches that belong to the Pentecostal/charismatic streams of the faith. In African thought generally, the colonial project ensured that the West became the best gateway to personal well-being. In contemporary Africa, the pursuit of visas for international travel comes next to healing in the search for God's intervention. The recent high casualties on the Mediterranean illustrate the desperation with which Africans seek refuge abroad. What is not often recognized, though, is the religious motivation that pushes young people to attempt such adventures. The most common reason for international travel is economic, but when Europe and North America are perceived to be locations of divine breakthrough, or key achievement and accomplishment, that increases the desire to migrate to a level that supersedes any practical considerations. In the charismatic hermeneutics of prosperity, international travel is key evidence of God's favor.

At some point the means by which people travel to the West ceases to matter. Documented and undocumented migrants consider their arrival in Europe and North America as a breakthrough from God. Much testimony in the African immigrant churches, most of which are either Pentecostal or possess a charismatic culture, focuses on opportunities for better living. At the same time, these churches struggle to mitigate jarring cultural disparities for these new immigrants, whose religious sensibilities are traumatized on seeing the transformation of cathedrals into restaurants and mosques throughout the North. Gerrie ter Haar writes about how Dutch communities, even the Christian ones, are reluctant to accept African immigrants as brothers and sisters in Christ despite their strong Christian faith. The Dutch place more emphasis on "the African" rather than the "Christian" identities of these immigrants. In contrast to this negative attitude, African Christians take the opposite view and aspire to use their Christian faith as a means of integration into Dutch society.[31]

According to Bediako, the observation by ter Haar "points to some specifically 'Christian' dimensions of the African participation in globalization that might escape secular-minded observers." For ter Haar stresses that "the development of these 'African initiated' churches

---

[31]Gerrie ter Haar, "Strangers in the Promised Land," *Exchange* 24 (February 1995): 29.

outside the African continent, propagating a 'self-confident Christianity' and 'claiming universal qualities for a religious worldview which, as it happens, has important roots in Africa' is a significant departure that should lead to a renewed appreciation of Africa's role in the world."[32] Timothy Tennent describes current developments in world Christianity as one of the most dramatic shifts in Christianity since the Reformation.[33] The churches we describe here look on themselves as "international churches" and express their aspirations to be part of the international world in which they believe they have a missionary task. Most of these churches, we have noted, have a Pentecostal/charismatic orientation. Their presence is so important that Jehu Hanciles concludes in *Beyond Christendom* that we would have been moving much more rapidly toward a post-Christian status were it not for the faith of non-Western immigrants in the West.[34]

CONCLUSION

Considering that just over a century ago Christianity was still synonymous with Western cultures and civilizations, the story of its recession in the Global North and its accession in the South may in some way reflect Paul's thoughts concerning the mind of God on the bearers of mission:

> But God chose what is foolish in the world to shame the wise; God chose what is weak in the world to shame the strong; God chose what is low and despised in the world, things that are not, to reduce to nothing things that are, so that no one might boast in the presence of God. (1 Cor 1:27-29)

The critical expression here is this: "that no one might boast in the presence of God." In other words, when it comes to the workings of God in mission, one needs to guard against interpreting things in a triumphal and hegemonic manner for, as Kwame Bediako of Africa notes,

---

[32]Kwame Bediako, "Christian Witness in the Public Sphere: Some Residual Challenges from the Recent Political History of Ghana," in *The Changing Face of Christianity: Africa, the West and the World*, ed. Lamin Sanneh and Joel Carpenter (Oxford: Oxford University Press, 2005), 120.

[33]Timothy C. Tennent, *Theology in the Context of World Christianity* (Grand Rapids: Zondervan, 2007), 2. See also Wesley Granberg-Michaelson, *From Time Square to Timbuktu: The Post-Christian West Meets the Non-Western Church* (Grand Rapids: Eerdmans, 2013).

[34]Jehu H. Hanciles, *Beyond Christendom: Globalization, African Migration and the Transformation of the West* (Maryknoll, NY: Orbis Books, 2008).

The significance of the modern shift in the center of gravity of Christianity is not that its former centers of dominance cease to matter, but rather that the faith now acquires new centers of its universality. Accordingly, the study of one manifestation of it must help toward understanding its character in general.[35]

If Christianity is under siege in university departments for the study of religion and in theologically liberal seminaries, it must find refuge in those institutions of higher learning that uphold conservative evangelical theological values. In Paul's writing to the Corinthians, this sort of intellectual resistance to falsehood was all too familiar:

> Indeed, we live as human beings, but we do not wage war according to human standards; for the weapons of our warfare are not merely human, but they have divine power to destroy strongholds. We destroy arguments and every proud obstacle raised up against the knowledge of God, and we take every thought captive to obey Christ. (2 Cor 10:3-5)

It is unlikely that Paul was simply talking here about marshaling intellectual theological arguments against falsehood and heresies, important as those may be. From my context in Africa a number of these forms of resistance are also considered spiritual in nature, and "the weapons of our warfare" have included prayer and those spiritual disciplines that make the Christian life something more than a mere mental accent to historic credos inherited from the Western Christian tradition. I should think that this experiential and simple approach to the faith would be part of Africa's contribution to the growing field of study in history, mission and theology in non-Western contexts, now known as world Christianity. The changes that we discern in Christianity in Africa and the contributions the churches are making to world Christianity in a sense amount to speaking of the wonders of God in indigenous tongues, suggesting that the presence of the Spirit has never been alien to the African Christian experience.

---

[35]Kwame Bediako, "Five Theses on the Significance of Modern African Christianity: A Manifesto," in *Landmark Essays in Mission and World Christianity*, ed. Robert L. Gallagher and Paul Hertig (Maryknoll, NY: Orbis Books, 2009), 110.

Eschatology and Mission

A Latin American Perspective

Pablo A. Deiros

INTRODUCTION

As we move further into the new millennium, we need a new hermeneutical key to understand our present history, the mission of the church and what the people of God in the world are experiencing today, particularly in Latin America. We must reflect on our theology and propose our missiology from a perspective (or context) that is situated in the future, not in the present. Thus the *locus theologicus* and the *locus missiologicus* of our reflection should be placed in the future, and the Sitz im Leben, our situation in life, that functions as our point of reference is a reality that has not happened yet. Examples of this, from a Latin American perspective, are the globalization of the Christian mission, the lure of the future, the pursuit of the unity of the church in mission, the theological and missiological homogenization process currently underway, the proclamation of an integral gospel and a polyhedral model of missiology, among other manifestations.

Before considering each of these elements, let us consider the contrast between the two hermeneutical loci for the completion of the Christian mission.

LOOKING AT THE FUTURE FROM THE PRESENT VERSUS LOOKING AT THE PRESENT FROM THE FUTURE

Let us try to understand these two perceptions, one at the end of the nineteenth century and the beginning of the twentieth century and the other as an expression of more recent developments.

At the end of the nineteenth century and in the beginning decades of the twentieth century, both in Europe and North America—the two places where scholars were reflecting both theologically and missiologically—the prevalent idea was one of unrestrained and infinite progress. This general perception of reality was based on the scientific and technological developments of those days. Humankind was *progressing* toward its own maturity and perfection. The ideas behind this kind of thinking had to do with Darwinism, historicism, positivism, Freudianism and, later, other variations of the understanding of reality. All these ideologies had in common a positive perception of human evolution that went hand in hand with science and technology and had the goal of furthering the progress of humankind.

As far as the Christian mission is concerned, that was a time when the superpowers of the North Atlantic were enjoying their most formidable expansion. Theirs was a colonial as well as an imperialist expansion as they took Christianity to the ends of the earth. To be sure, when one spoke of Christianity, one meant basically the Western Christian civilization, which assumed typical values of the North Atlantic cultures. Such was the positive mentality of ad infinitum progress, which was the essential motivation behind so-called modern missions.

But it was exactly in that optimistic North Atlantic world that the First World War took place. And soon a second World War ravaged the region as well. The United States was involved as a superpower in both conflicts, which enabled an impressive leap forward in both their science and their technology. All the nations perceived, however, that the very science and technology that pushed the progress of humankind could also destroy the human race in seconds and transform it into cave dwellers the day after. Much of the literature and the art of the 1950s illustrate this kind of anticipation and fear.

However, certain optimism in the idea of progress still prevailed despite all the frustrations of the twentieth century. This led many evangelicals in the twentieth century to adopt a kind of naive optimism. The idea was that as the gospel was preached to every creature, the world would continually improve. And thanks to this Christian witness, the kingdom of God would establish itself and, with it, the justice and peace that rightfully belong in it. As a consequence, at the end of the twentieth century, the ideas of postmillennialism still enjoyed a widespread acceptance among eschatological theories.

In the span of the last two centuries, humankind has gone from a dramatic sequence of naive optimism to skeptical pessimism. On the one hand, people believed that science and technology would solve all their problems, and on the other there was a firm belief that this same science and technology had the power to sweep the human race off the face of the earth.

In a sense, however, these were two sides of the same coin. We can summarize the dichotomy as follows: either the world progresses and we are capable of introducing the kingdom of God on earth, or the world will destroy itself by leaps and bounds and we can only hope for God himself to intervene and solve all our problems and inaugurate his millennial kingdom on earth. Either way, in both the postmillennialist as well as in the premillennialist understanding, the idea was that God himself would act miraculously in history. The idea of progress is present both in the excessive historical optimism of one understanding and in the excessive historical pessimism of the other. In both cases, the observer is looking at the future from the perspective of his or her present reality—a movement from the present to the future. The future, therefore, appears distant and remote.

However, one might also look at the present from the future. In order to understand the best missiological approach for reaching our goal, we ought first to ask, how do we look at the future?

In my view, the distance between the present and the future becomes shorter every day. Nowadays when we speak about the future, we ask ourselves, which future? This has to do, again, with the Sitz im Leben in which we find ourselves. It also has to do with the *locus theologicus* and *locus missiologicus* from which we seek to interpret our faith and our Christian commitment. One may say that there are various factors that explain this shrinking of the breach between the present and the future. We have the strange privilege of being actors at the beginnings of both a century and a millennium.

We know that every end of a century, and especially every end of a millennium, generates numerous millenarian, eschatological and apocalyptic expectations. In fact, we know this because Christian history has registered two such phenomena. The second millennium came to an end before our eyes only fifteen years ago. Nevertheless, we know that in times of transition, as we are experiencing now, there have been apocalyptic expectations because the Christian community has experienced the end of a century twenty times before.

In these times of transition, we have the impression that the future is closing in on us. We—evangelicals especially—are no longer looking at the future from the perspective of the present. On the contrary, it seems to me that we are looking at the whole process in the reverse. We are looking at the present from the perspective of the future.[1]

I believe we have here a hermeneutical key to understanding our present history, the mission of the church and what the people of God in the world are experiencing today, particularly in Latin America. I believe, however, that in such *eschatological* times as ours we need a different perspective. We must see reality from the *future* to the *present*, instead of the reverse. Therefore, any present phenomenon must be interpreted in light of the imminent future that we are expecting. If we adopt this perspective, we will need different hermeneutical keys in order to understand reality. If, for example, we are dealing with a revival in these last days, we will no longer use past experiences as our guide to interpret reality but rather the future events—precisely because we probably are in the last days.

This replacement (or redeployment) of our *locus theologicus* and *locus missiologicus*, not in the past but in the future, has profound consequences in terms of our reflection and our conclusions. Doing missiology from the perspective of the future will surely produce different understandings than if we take the perspective of the past, as we used to do.

THE GLOBALIZATION PHENOMENON

The most important consequence of such change in perspective, in my opinion, is not so much the change in the axis of our perspective but of the phenomenon of globalization. This phenomenon has its own identifiable roots in history.

I am referring to the globalization of the Christian faith with all its implications. There is a definite break with denominational barriers, not so

---

[1]David J. Bosch, *Misión en transformación: Cambios de paradigma en la teología de la misión* (Grand Rapids: Libros Desafío, 2000), 629.

much in terms of ecclesiastical structures but as a change in our under-standing of the experience of so many Christians around the world. Chris-tians everywhere are beginning to see the fulfillment of the Christian mission as a spinoff from their particular reality into the whole world and in all directions. We are becoming more and more citizens of the world, and we are engaging ourselves with human needs wherever they may be found.

This has a lot to do with our understanding of history—that is, our past. I am feeling increasingly uncomfortable with the traditional understanding we have had of Christian history since Augustine of Hippo. The idea of history as a linear movement that progresses infinitely toward its *telos*, its final fulfillment in Christ Jesus, may be adequate in our understanding of the future of humanity from a Christian perspective, but it has its limitations. I believe that it has been exactly this traditional understanding of Christian history—which was taken over by the Enlightenment and penetrated the Protestantism of the eighteenth, nineteenth and twentieth centuries—that has determined our philosophy of all history ever since.

This Augustinian understanding has controlled our thinking by forcing us to see all historical events from a bi-dimensional perspective (time and space). I am beginning to ask myself whether this bi-dimensional model is indeed the most appropriate in our understanding of the way in which God intervenes in history today.

Like the Greek cyclical (bi-dimensional) concept of history, the tradi-tional Christian (Augustinian) concept of infinite linear progress is also a bi-dimensional concept. Perhaps we need to incorporate a tri-dimensional model in our understanding of the history of Christian witness. In this new historical model, each event is linked to the other not so much as one of several links in succession but rather as several knots that are linked by the threads of a net (or network) or perhaps linked like the vertices of a polyhedron, which are interconnected by their intersecting lines.[2] I will come back to this later.

---

[2] A polyhedron is a geometric figure limited by plane polygons. It has a certain number of faces (or sides), themselves defined by a number of intersecting lines. The lines touch each other in vertices that define three or more intersections. I have in mind a figure similar to an icosahe-dron—a polygon with twenty faces—which is itself formed by equilateral triangles. (The geo-metric description is intended here only as a point of reference.) The important feature here is that the figure is *tri-dimensional* and makes for a good model in our understanding of historical facts and their multiple coordination.

What we need are fewer linear (bi-dimensional) models in favor of more organic (tri-dimensional) models to reflect our theology and our missiology. A new tri-dimensional model may well help us do a better job of creating more effective strategies to complete the mission that has been entrusted to us by the Lord.

A tri-dimensional understanding of the reality of mission better suits our understanding of a global reality. The bi-dimensional or linear understanding that differentiates between sending countries and receiving countries has been replaced by a more dynamic polyhedral network of multiple relationships in which all send and all receive at the same time under the lordship of Christ. This is the perception I discern about the world today regarding the Christian witness. This sending-and-receiving mutuality increases at a breathtaking speed when we understand it with a tri-dimensional perspective.

THE LURE OF THE FUTURE

If I situate myself in this eschatological future mentioned above, and if I am convinced that indeed Christ is coming soon, such assurance will affect my whole understanding of the present reality as well as my understanding of what is to come. My thinking, the way I make decisions, and my strategy and action are governed not by what I am experiencing now but by what lies ahead in the immediate future. It is on this conviction that I start to draw theological conclusions and to plan new strategies that are appropriate to the life of the church and its mission.

But someone will say, fine, but this future is imaginary; it exists only in your mind. Surely, no one knows exactly how the future will be in all of its details. Nevertheless, though I do not know *when* my future will come, I know for sure *what* my future will be. I know it by faith, by the witness of the Scriptures and by the witness of the Spirit in the heart of the believer. We read that the Spirit "will declare to you the things that are to come" (Jn 16:13).

The reality that governs me now as a theologian and a missiologist is my concept and conviction about what is going to happen tomorrow. All my understanding of the faith and mission of the church stems from the context from which I reflect. If this context is situated in the future and is linked to the immediate return of Christ, both my theology and my missiology will reflect that conviction. And I believe that the most appropriate perspective for the contemplation of our theological and missiological task is the future.

If we do not recognize that the author of 1 Corinthians was energized—at the moment in which he wrote the letter—by his assurance of the immediate return of Christ, we will not be able to understand his ethics, his ecclesiology and his theology as he discusses them in the letter. When, for instance, Paul says that women should not marry and men should remain single (see 1 Cor 7), we teach—as good exegetes—that we have to understand Paul's eschatological expectation in order to interpret what he says.[3]

If we are indeed living in a special *kairos*—special because it is final—and if God is acting today through his Holy Spirit in extraordinary ways all over the world and if we are closer to the end, then the future acquires a dominant role over the present. The future governs the present, and our understanding about anything in the present must take this future hope into account. In biblical terms, the direction of God's redeeming actions is located in the future—because he is the God of hope.[4] We may ask, what are the consequences of such a reflection?

Even the futurists in our days—people who occupy themselves with discovering the tendencies that govern reality—arrive at their conclusions starting from the present and working their way out into the future. Their basic question is, where are we going from this present situation? This is a fundamental question when we are dealing with tendencies. But since we are theologians and missiologists who are more concerned about the issue of contextualization from one millennium to another, we are not so much concerned about where we are going from the present. What concerns us is what may happen tomorrow, and what is it that we need to do now in view of that future. In other words, in what ways is the pressure of the future leading us to reflect on certain new questions? One might say, I am a product of my past, and from this I can surmise what is going to happen. Another very different perspective views life from an immediate and imminent future that should determine our present.

---

[3]William Barclay, *The Mind of St Paul* (London: Fontana, 1965), 156-73; D. E. H. Whiteley, *The Theology of St. Paul* (Philadelphia: Fortress, 1964), 233-73; and Archibald M. Hunter, *Interpreting Paul's Gospel* (Philadelphia: Westminster, 1954), 50-55.

[4]Arthur F. Glasser, *Announcing the Kingdom: The Story of God's Mission in the Bible* (Grand Rapids: Baker Academic, 2003), 27.

The Question of Unity

In view of the eschatological weight of this future, what are some of its theological and missiological consequences? The first consequence is that, in Christian terms, if the Lord is coming to take his bride, his church, we have to do something about this bride of his. Her state is deplorable. She is dismembered, divided, prostituted, filled with sin, confused, sterile, passive and defeated, to say the least. It is indeed a horrible picture. Above all, we must recognize that if the Lord comes soon, he will find not a beautiful bride but a shameful harem of selfish concubines, each one pretending to be the sole owner of the Bridegroom, of his truth and of the exclusive expressions of his kingdom.

This leads us to think especially about the question of Christian unity. It is a fundamental component of the context in which we perform our theological and missiological reflection from the perspective of the future. I believe that all our efforts to stimulate and promote the unity of the people of God have failed. This has happened because we have not understood the meaning of the church as the body of Christ and, especially, as the bride of Christ. Our theological conclusions have been wrong, or at least they have proven to be ineffective throughout the centuries in expressing the reality of the unity for which Jesus pleaded so earnestly with the Father (Jn 17).

In most of our ecumenical efforts—especially in the second half of the twentieth century—we have focused on achieving the unity of an *institutional* church. Every effort has been made with the aim of arriving at agreements (mainly political and formal) on issues of faith and order, life and work, liturgy and spirituality, and so on. We have tried to establish missionary strategies to avoid institutional competition, and we have signed mission declarations or agreements to improve our own statistics. But immediately following our *unity*, we discuss how best to *divide* the fruit, or we fight for prestige and power, if indeed there has been any fruit.

The truth is that we have invested more time and effort in *negotiating* our unity than in working together to the glory of Christ and the expansion of his kingdom. We have assumed that we have to agree on the Eucharist, baptism and ministry, among other things, in order to prepare ourselves to work together as the body of Christ. But this has nothing to do with the reality of the fact that we *are* the body of Christ.

First of all, the body of Christ is not an amoeba. It is not a single living cell. It has an amazing diversity. God willed it that way; therefore there is no room for dispute or envy among the members of the body. Diversity is an essential ingredient in the richness and unity of the body. A single human body, in comparison, is one because all members are connected in the same body, not because this member is the same as that. This is what Paul talks about in 1 Corinthians 12:12-27: "Now you are the body of Christ and individually members of it."

If it is true that Christ is coming, we need an urgent ecclesiological agenda. We have to work hard to dilute the barriers that still separate us. It is precisely because of this increasing awareness, which Christians are experiencing worldwide about Christ's immediate return, that the ideology of denominationalism—which has characterized our way of being Christians—is beginning to undergo a crisis of disintegration. I am not suggesting that we get rid of the traditional denominations. I do believe, however, that we are realizing that we are more than a *hand* of the body of Christ; we are *one* of the hands, and others are the *eyes, ears* or *feet* of the same body.

We are beginning to realize that the body is more than the individuality; the collective reality is more than the individual reality. The organic nature of the church is more than its institutional nature. Because of this, I believe that if we choose to look from the future to the present, then one of the main tendencies defined by our context is the unity of the body of Christ.

THEOLOGICAL AND MISSIOLOGICAL HOMOGENIZATION

Another tendency in our context—again looking from the future into the present—is the theological and missiological homogenization that is currently underway. If the Holy Spirit that lives in you is the same Holy Spirit that lives in me, it is a plain contradiction that you would understand God in a certain way whereas I would understand him in another way. If the Holy Spirit's task is to lead us into all truth and to reveal to us what the Father wants us to know and the things to come (Jn 16:13), how is it possible that our conclusions are disparate most of the time? It is understandable that your *weltanschauung*, your worldview, and your concept of reality would provide particular nuances to your understanding of God and that such nuances might be different from the ones I hold. But surely—in theological and missiological terms—your essential understanding of God has to be close to mine because we are both objects of the same pedagogical work of one and the same Spirit of God.

We know the scriptural truth that "we were all made to drink of one Spirit" (1 Cor 12:13). In these last days, as we grow in our understanding of the work of the Spirit, we feel that we are all going in the same direction. Beyond our local colors and nuances, and beyond the way we each express our understanding of the truth of God, I have the impression that the people of God all over the world are increasingly experiencing a spiritual consensus. I see, therefore, a growing homogenization among Christians as an essential part of this perception of the present from the perspective of the future.

The tendency today is to minimize all that divides us because what drives us is the mission and the imperative of accomplishing the task we have received—because the Lord is coming. He wants to find us, his servants, busy doing his mission, not discussing dogmatic minutiae. The imperative of the present hour is missiological, and the need to win this world for Christ has more value than all theological negotiation or utopian dreaming. Urgency rests in the fact that if indeed Christ is coming, we do not want him to find us idle or empty-handed. We know that he wills the salvation of the whole world (2 Pet 3:9). However, if he is to find *faith* on earth and not *unbelief* (Lk 18:8), his people must proclaim the gospel of the kingdom with power and authority.

THE WHOLE GOSPEL

As denominationalism, Constantinianism and institutionalism lose strength, the idea of the kingdom gains more ground. This is the kingdom of God, which has come and is yet to come. We discover a principle here: the more these ideas lose their strength, the more the idea of the kingdom grows. Conversely, the more Constantinian (Christendom-dependent) theology and missiology lose their strength, the more kingdom theology and missiology grow. As this understanding grows, we start discovering the meanings and implications of the kingdom.

First of all, we know that the gospel is not *married* to any culture in particular—that is, to any form that acts as a means of communication of this gospel of the kingdom to the world. Consequently, the proclamation of the redemptive acts of God in Christ Jesus is not attached to the culture through which we communicate the message. In other words, the gospel has nothing to do with the way in which one dresses, eats or sleeps or any other customs one may have. The gospel is above all this. The gospel does not deny these things, nor does it ignore them, but it is definitely above all of them.

Second, the theology and missiology that the praxis of this gospel produces are just as unfettered by the cultural features of the person reflecting and acting. The banner that the Christian lifts up is the banner of the kingdom, not the banner of Great Britain, the United States, Germany or Argentina. The idea of the kingdom has the necessary ingredients to overcome these divisions and bypass the limitations that such divisions may impose on the church and its agents.

Third, the new theology and missiology will be global or globalizing. This is because they deal with the kingdom of God, and this kingdom has no frontiers. It is beyond time and space, although it expresses itself in both time and space.

Fourth, this new theology and missiology will produce a new ecclesiology. My brothers and my sisters in Christ will be all those who are identified with this kingdom of God, and not necessarily all those who are members of my particular church or denomination. My fellow citizen in the kingdom is not the person who worships God in the same way I do but the person who acknowledges Jesus Christ as his or her King and obeys Christ as his or her Lord. For this reason I see myself as a member of a kingdom that confesses that Jesus Christ is Lord in every language and that acknowledges him as Lord (owner) of all *ethnē*, all social groups.

The identity of this kingdom and the right of citizenship in it do not depend on the color of one's skin or the language of the Bible one uses—not even on whether one has a Bible. Participation in this kingdom is for all those who confess Christ as Lord—though the crucial point is not so much what one says with the mouth as what one lives. In other words, only those men and women who allow him to govern their lives give evidence of participating in his kingdom.

Therefore, in these last days, we see a new globalized theology and missiology in gestation. These are profoundly identified with the expectation of

Christ's immediate return and express a holistic understanding of the gospel. We are talking about *all* the gospel to *all* people, of all nations, in all the earth. Until this is fully accomplished, we cannot be satisfied as Christians. We cannot be sure that we have expressed the kingdom of God as it is supposed to be expressed unless we see to it that this goal becomes a reality.

A POLYHEDRAL MISSIOLOGY

We no longer speak about mission in terms of those who send and those who receive missionaries. This is a thing of the past. Today we talk about a mission in which *all* send and *all* receive at the same time. The church evangelizes and is evangelized. The Christian mission in the world today should be multidimensional.[5]

It is not a linear process, such as an action that connects opposite points by way of a succession of intermediate dots that bridge between the extremes. We do not identify a country that sends and another that receives. This was typical of our bi-dimensional, one-directional model until recently. Nowadays, mission resembles more a tri-dimensional model, and for this very reason it is more organic. This recalls the polyhedron model I mentioned earlier (see figure 14.1).

In the polyhedral model, the Christian mission is multidirectional—it expands in all directions all the time. All vertices touch all others in the structure through their interconnection. So the model is hyperdynamic and plurifunctional. This illustrates a new variety of possible contacts and relationships in mission.

The polyhedral model has the added advantage of being an organic structure without a defined beginning or end. Today, a particular church might have the personnel, another agency has the financial resources and somebody else opens an opportunity; still another church has prayer or experience, and another organization has the necessary know-how or the sending structures. We can all work dynamically with everyone else in order to missionize wherever the gospel has not yet been communicated. In the Constantinian model, the mission consisted of taking Christ to the nations. The new, polyhedral model—as far as I can see—takes the nations to Christ.

---

[5]Bosch, *Misión en transformación*, 623.

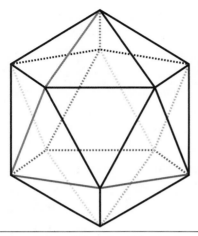

Figure 14.1. A polyhedral model of mission

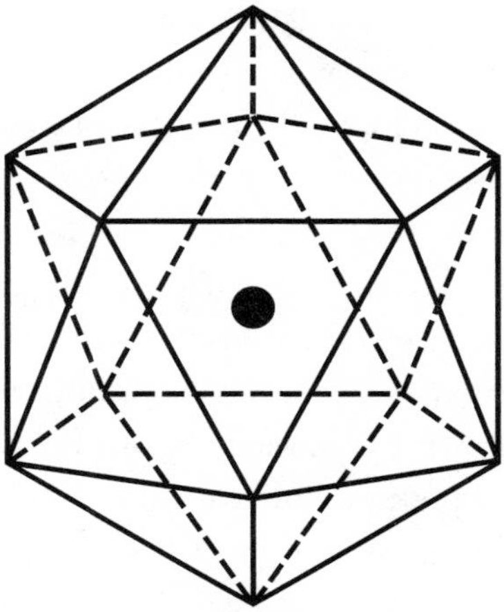

Figure 14.2. The polyhedral model with Christ at the center

A CHRISTOCENTRIC MODEL

Let us explore further the tri-dimensional polyhedral model. Let us now create an imaginary point at the center of the structure equally distant from all its vertices (see figure 14.2). In our missiological model let us imagine this central point to be Christ himself. He is in touch with all the nations, and all the nations are drawn to him. From this central stance, Christ maintains and gives meaning to the whole structure. Its geometric perfection, as well as the evenness of all its faces and the perfect spacing between the vertices, depends on the perfect centrality of this imaginary central point—Jesus Christ.

The *missio Dei* places Christ precisely at the center of all things. I believe that this is what Paul refers to when he skillfully speaks about the pre-eminence of Christ in Colossians 1:15-23. The goal of our participation in God's mission, under Christ's headship, is to build a network of relationships centered in Christ and united to him until Christ himself "is above all and through all and in all" (Eph 4:6). In other words, until "Christ is all and in all" (Col 3:11).

Missiologically speaking, one point or vertex advances along with all the others, which are closely connected to it. At the same time, all vertices are connected to the central point, which gives meaning and stability to the whole structure.

In tectonic terms, beyond the force that each vertex exerts on all its contacts, the structure finds its equilibrium in the strength (or force) of each radius linking the central point to each vertex. This central point, though invisible, keeps the whole polyhedral structure together. That this is so can be verified by the fact that if the distance between the vertices is changed—that is, if the intersections are unequal—the whole structure collapses. The same would happen if the radii were not equal: the structure would lose its tectonic equilibrium and would collapse because it would have lost its basic format. But in the ideal polyhedron, the symmetry is dynamically perfect and the structure maintains itself in place.

I believe this polyhedral model can help us to represent the theological-missiological network that is being developed all over the world today. As we continue into the twenty-first century, we need a new model to help us in our reflection and action. The centrality and force of the central point in this model may be an appropriate representation of the centrality and power of Christ in the whole process.

Futurology Versus Eschatological Missiology

The polyhedral model does not see the Christian mission as futurology sees it. Many Christians have adopted the futurology model of thinking. Futurology says, I look at how things are evolving, and, in accordance with their direction and intentionality, I try to devise how things might look in the foreseeable future. This exercise produces tendencies and identifies the forces that generate a movement in a predictable direction. It is similar to measuring the force and speed of the wind, registering its direction, and making calculations, estimates and prognoses. Futurology starts in the present and works toward the future.

From our own eschatological perspective—as we have posited above—the observation point is in the future, not in the present. Looking at things from the future—that is, with the assurance that the Lord is coming soon—what is going to be our vision of the church and its mission? How can we reflect missiologically in these new terms?

An important element in this new perspective is a sense of urgency in relation to the fulfillment of the mission. The person who is convinced that these are the last days and that the Lord is near knows that our world has no other chance. The consciousness of an imminent parousia does not allow us to say, well, if not now, maybe later; if not in this generation, maybe others will evangelize the world; if we are not successful in uniting the church, perhaps our successors will be able to do it.

If we perceive the future as immediate and as closing in on the present, then we do not have much time left. If, for example, you know that the roof of your house is about to collapse at any moment, though you are not sure when, you are going to do something about it. It does not matter whether this was your grandparent's house, or whether this is the house where you were born, or whether this roof has withstood other hurricanes before. You will do something. Your behavior will be determined by your unshakable assurance that the roof is about to collapse at any moment. Your thinking will be determined by your conviction at that moment. Our faith models our theology and missiology. Our faith in the glorious return of Christ and the end of history has a deep impact on our missionary theology and practice.[6]

LISTENING TO THE SPIRIT

If we take this new approach, and if indeed the end is near, the logical consequence is that we need to listen to what the Spirit is saying as he calls the churches into a renewed commitment to the mission of God (Rev 2–3). Equally important, we must listen to what the Lamb of God is saying to the churches in these days, through the Spirit: "See, I am coming soon! . . . See, I am coming soon. . . . Surely I am coming soon" (Rev 22:7, 12, 20). Also, we have to heed what the bride is saying as the Spirit moves her: "Come. . . . Amen. Come, Lord Jesus!" (Rev 22:17, 20). We have no grounds to postpone our eschatological expectation for yet another millennium!

Neither do we uphold the optimistic idea of progress that was developed at the end of the nineteenth century. Nor do we naively sustain that, with a little effort on our part, we will be able to make the new century into the Christian century. I am *not* waiting for a Christian century. What I am waiting for is the coming of the King! And if the King is coming, there is not much time left to accomplish our mission. The nations have to know

[6]A. Scott Moreau, Gary R. Corwin and Gary B. McGee, *Introducing World Missions: A Biblical, Historical, and Practical Survey* (Grand Rapids: Baker Academic, 2006), 85.

that the King is coming. The largest possible number of peoples must have the opportunity to confess Jesus Christ as Lord so that "everyone who calls on the name of the Lord" will "be saved" (Joel 2:32). On the other hand, I believe that we are beginning to see the fulfillment of the prophecy of Joel. The elderly are dreaming and the young are beginning to see visions, while the servants are filled with the Holy Spirit and are working in the kingdom through fantastic manifestations of the power and authority that they have found in Christ.

Let us hear what the Spirit is saying to the churches at this time. Christ is coming soon, and there is little time left for us to accomplish the mission that he has entrusted to us. This is what I feel personally. And I do not apologize for this feeling, because another Christian, a respectable man of God, had the same expectation, the same eschatology and the same sense of urgency some two thousand years ago. Surely the Lord did not come during the days of the apostle Paul, as Paul himself expected. But the work that he did, motivated by this expectation, continues to draw admiration and respect. Thank God for the apostle Paul and his eschatological missiology.[7]

Someone may say, Paul was mistaken about his eschatology. It may have been so, but his missiology was correct. Thanks to his eschatological missiology, Paul won thousands of people for the kingdom, helped in the transformation of families, moved whole cities with his preaching, filled the places he visited with the gospel of Christ and had the courage to live and die for Christ.[8]

Maybe my own eschatological expectation is mistaken. But I desire with all my heart, if the Lord does not come soon, that twenty centuries from today someone may say that my missiology was correct. We need to understand missions as an eschatological reality.[9]

The Future as an Appropriate Context

Definitely, each Christian has to decide from which context he or she is going to reflect theologically and missiologically so as to determine his or her mission in the present. In my judgment, the future is a more appropriate context for that reflection than the present.

---

[7]Juan Luis Segundo, *The Humanist Christology of Paul* (Maryknoll, NY: Orbis Books, 1986), 179.
[8]Bosch, *Misión en transformación*, 196-97.
[9]Harry R. Boer, *Pentecost and Missions* (Grand Rapids: Eerdmans, 1964), 139, 148-60.

Certainly, this future is not yet designed in all its details. The most important thing is this punctual event in the future, which is the glorious return of Christ. But that is not merely a millenarian expectation with a program *for* the future. It is an event, a definitive and redemptive irruption of God into history, which puts an end to history itself. When Jesus came the first time to establish his kingdom, he did not do it with a millennial kingdom in mind—so we read in the Gospels. On the contrary, this was the idea that the *disciples* had in mind. Even before Christ's death on the cross, they were disputing among themselves who would sit on the right hand and on the left hand of the King. But Jesus said clearly, "My kingdom is not from this world" (Jn 18:36), not even in the form of a millennial kingdom.

The Christian hope, then, does not consist in a determined program for the future or an agenda for what is to come. The Christian hope is grounded on the fact that the King is coming. And if the King is coming, as Jesus explained in dramatic yet simple terms in the eschatological parables, we his servants better be watching and waiting for him. This means that our action in the present will not be defined by what happened in the past or even by the specific moment when we may be living. As Christians who are committed to the kingdom, our actions in the present toward the future are defined by this fundamental event that we await: the glorious return of Christ. We do not have any salvific event of greater importance ahead of us. Our mission today can only be understood in the light of this glorious future event.[10]

The death and resurrection of Jesus have already happened. As redemptive acts, they define our present. However, the span that goes from our present to the future is not defined by Christ's death and resurrection; it is rather defined by Christ's immediate return. If our definition of the mission of the church and our missionary strategies have to do with what is happening today, as we move into the future, then the return of Christ becomes the appropriate context for our missiology.

---

[10]Jürgen Moltmann, *Theology of Hope* (New York: Harper & Row, 1967), 83.

Conclusion
....

A Historian's Hunches

Eight Future Trends in Mission

Scott W. Sunquist

It is not wise for a historian, or any Christian for that matter, to make predictions about the future. Prophecy is a dangerous occupation: false prophets were killed, and even true prophets were often persecuted. Recently I have been amazed at what terrible prophets the greatest of Christian leaders were at the beginning of the twentieth century. The best and brightest Christian leaders in the early 1900s had no idea of what was happening all around them concerning global Christianity. No one predicted that Christianity would be so populated by the poor, by Asians, Africans and Latin Americans as it became in the twentieth century.[1] And of course, no one in the West (caught up in the optimistic and progressive thinking of the early twentieth century) guessed that the West would tear itself apart in two "great wars" and embrace the purely secular as it did.[2] Those who attempted to look at the future were blinded by their own cultural hubris. Europeans and North Americans looked at the dominance of (Christian) Western empires ruling the world and called it a "Christian century." The present moment is not that different, so we proceed with caution.

Prophecy is an inexact science and a dangerous calling. And yet, missiologists must read the "signs of the times." This is our dilemma. Looking around and then looking ahead are important pursuits for missiologists. Christians are to be attentive to the world in order to interpret the times. For

---

[1]Scott W. Sunquist, *The Unexpected Christian Century: The Reversal and Transformation of Global Christianity, 1900–2000* (Grand Rapids: Baker Academic, 2015).
[2]Ian Kershaw, *To Hell and Back: Europe 1914–1949* (New York: Viking, 2015).

example, changes in laws regarding religions, changes in governments and growth in violence (or the abating of the same) mean something and should be signs for the church. These are social changes of which we need to be aware. There are also signs that come from Christian movements: the rise of new mission societies and movements, people movements to Christ (McGavran's "Christward movements"), newer Christian institutions and others. In light of these changes, missiologists need to adjust their teaching and planning. Missiologists, by definition, are constantly focusing on changes and adaptations that are needed to effectively engage in the *missio Dei*. Missiologists are driven to find better ways to incarnate the life of Christ— "constants in context" to quote one of our writers (chapter six).[3]

Another way of looking at this is that missionary leaders of the church have always been more innovative (and sometimes more heretical) than the bishops and priests. Until the past generation, worship has tended to be conservative and mission innovative. This is to be expected. Mission involves contact with the ever-changing world of humanity, a world in constant change and turmoil. Worship is rooted in the great tradition and must re-center the Christian and the Christian community every week. Missionaries have had to adapt to new slang, new technology, new travel routes and new cultures they encounter. When they do not adapt or innovate, they become irrelevant at best, irritating and obnoxious at worst. One wonders how much persecution of Christian missionaries has been caused by their irritating and uncompromising approach to cultures.

Worship, which tends to be concerned with conserving orthodoxy and orthopraxis, needs mission and vice versa. Worship grounds mission in the foundational message and practice of the followers of Christ. Mission breathes back into the liturgy the reality of the power of the message to save, transform and heal. When mission refuses to innovate, it turns into something like a mission station, a static place of community living, worship and institutional development. It was this approach that Donald McGavran was reacting against when he wrote *The Bridges of God: A Study in the Strategy of Missions*.[4]

---

[3]Stephen Bevans, who, with Roger Schroeder, wrote, *Constants in Context: A Theology of Mission for Today* (Maryknoll, NY: Orbis Books, 2004).
[4]Donald A. McGavran, *The Bridges of God: A Study in the Strategy of Missions* (1955; repr., Eugene, OR: Wipf & Stock, 2005).

What McGavran described in looking for and responding to "bridges of God" that connect with people groups is similar to the type of adaptation that mission leaders have undertaken from the earliest times. The idea of monastic centers for copying Bibles, for translation and for church planting was a type of innovation. The development of Christian "sutras" along the Silk Road and then in China was a type of innovation as Syrian monks tried to connect the eternal message with ancient kingdoms.

The major innovations of the early modern period came from the Society of Jesus (Jesuits). Their attention to cultures (including art, history and philosophy) was an innovation that was followed by the early Protestants in the eighteenth and nineteenth centuries. Their preparation for missionary engagement included the best of modern learning from Renaissance Europe. This approach to culture and history was applied to the study of Japanese culture, Indian religions and Confucianism in China. Jesuit innovation was not appreciated by many fellow Christians, missionary and ecclesiastical leaders alike.

Classic conflicts occurred in China, centering on the rites and terms controversies; in India conflicts centered on caste. The Jesuits' innovations emphasized careful study of the translation and adaptation of the message for other cultures. What was appropriate and what was misleading? Protestants later encountered similar conflicts when they innovated in approaches to missionary work among slaves in the Caribbean, in methods of translating the Bible into so many languages and dialects, and in their bold outreach to indigenous peoples in the mountains of the Pacific, South America and Southeast Asia.

This volume has in part reviewed some of the innovations that came out of the early founders of the School of World Mission and Institute of Church Growth at Fuller Theological Seminary. Key to most of the innovations was the concern to make the gospel more accessible to more people. Thus, McGavran's call to find and support "bridges of God" and Ralph Winter's extensive application of theological education by extension were both concerned with supporting local leaders and initiatives as the most efficient method to reach the most people. Winter's focus on "unreached" and "hidden" peoples was a development of McGavran's call to reach "peoples." Innovations of the last fifty years proved to be important in the development of missiological

thinking and practice. Innovations in the future will be of a different order.
Here we mention a few that require further research and discussion.

EIGHT MISSION TRENDS TO GUIDE US

Rather than try to describe *innovations* in mission that might develop in the
coming decades, I think it is more sensible to identify recent *trends* in mission
that will continue to guide us toward newer innovations. Some of these
trends are obvious, others less so. Each trend will require further attention
and analysis from scholars, mission agencies and global church leaders.

   1. Technology. The past two centuries have been dominated by the use
of new discoveries and inventions for the sake of mission. The discovery of
germs and their relationship to disease in the 1860s increased the value
of medical missions. Clinics, nurses' training, surgery and vaccinations
all were added to "normal" missionary practices in the later part of the
nineteenth century and continue today. About the same time, more rapid
forms of transportation (and spread of European empires) opened up new
areas for Christian mission. In the twentieth century newer technologies of
radio began to be used by evangelists like Charles E. Fuller (first broadcast
in 1929) and for overseas missionary outreach (e.g., HCJB ["Voice of the
Andes"], founded in 1931, and Far East Broadcasting Company [FEBC],
founded in 1945). Many of these were criticized by the Christian West until
we began to hear stories of villages and cities that were reached by the gospel
where no missionary had visited. Radio has connected the heart of God,
through the heart language of local peoples, to the heart of the unreached.

   Today and in the future, computer and satellite technologies will prove
to be more and more significant. Technological communications will not
be stopped by governments or armies. Satellite and Internet connectivity,
like urban rats or raccoons, will continue to adapt and continue offering
both the most excellent and most evil of human life. In terms of mission,
Iranian pastors, for example, receive a thorough theological education
through satellite courses taught from most anywhere in the world. The
same is true for Arab and Indian classes delivered electronically. When
countries and local religious rulers are oppressive, denying basic freedoms,
local people will search for more. Many are receiving new ideas through
the Internet (often a smartphone is all they need) and through satellite

programs. Training courses and Bibles (along with multiple translations) are all found on cellular phones.

Technology can and should facilitate more global community classes so students from Muslim West Africa, Egypt, Turkey and Malaysia can study Christian witness together in Islamic contexts. Ministry to migrants from Syria can be provided by a community class or ministry class with pastors and missionaries from Germany, Greece, Boston and Orange County, California. This is not just an interesting possibility; it is important to pursue this since mission is from everywhere to everywhere, provided by ubiquitous technological connectivity.

2. Insider movements. Since the death of Muhammad in 632, Christianity has decreased where Islam has increased (usually through empires, but also through trade and jihad). Some conversions from Islam to Christianity have occurred, but usually these conversions were related to the spread of empires and military conquest. Only in the last decades of the twentieth century, for the first time in 1,350 years, have we seen movements of Muslims toward Jesus *within* Islam. These are not typical movements to Jesus that are initiated through missionary contact or even migration. Many of these movements start from a dream or a vision, sometimes from contact with the written or spoken Gospels. From Southeast Asia to West Africa these "insider movements" have been observed for three or more decades. What does this mean? Much has been written about this, but only recently has more systematic study been done.[5]

Insider movements as a current Christian trend are controversial in the global church. Still, it is an observable and even measurable trend, not only in Islam, but also among Hindus, Buddhists and even Communists, who follow the Jesus of Scripture within their religious communities of origin. This trend needs more study and reflection in the coming decades. How can such movements be supported and encouraged by the global church? Are there ways that the Western church has discouraged such movements in the

---

[5]Harley Talman and John Jay Travis, *Understanding Insider Movements: Disciples of Jesus Within Diverse Religious Communities* (Pasadena, CA: William Carey Library, 2015). See also Dudley Woodberry's earlier volume, *From Seed to Fruit: Global Trends, Fruitful Practices and Emerging Issues Among Muslims* (Pasadena, CA: William Carey Library, 2008); and David Garrison, *A Wind in the House of Islam: How God Is Drawing Muslims from Around the World to Faith in Jesus Christ* (Monument, CO: WIGTake Resources, 2014).

past? What resources need to be developed for these movements, as well as for the global church, to better connect these movements with the global church? History makes it very clear that any isolated or parochial church—such as a "church" of Muslims following Jesus in a specific village—tends toward heterodoxy through an overly contextualized theology. Future innovations in mission will require attention to various insider movements.

3. Preemptive peacemakers. Many Western Christians now ask, "Is there a place for the Western Christian missionary anymore? We don't seem to be wanted or needed." Affirming that the Great Commission is a call to all Christians to the end of time and to the ends of the earth, we must say, "Yes, but . . ." There is a place for the Western missionary. But now it is much more in the roll of team player and specialized servant. Western missionaries will no longer have the protection of their governments or empires, or even financial support. Places where Western missionaries travel now will be difficult places with less security and comfort than in the past. Few are the places in the world where governments support, protect or even tolerate missionaries.

Specifically, one missiological area that needs to be explored in such a violent and hostile world where there is so little trust in the Western missionary is that of "preemptive peacemaking." Christians need to place themselves in difficult areas where ministries of mercy, compassion and peacemaking are needed. Places of potential violence are where many of the unreached and unloved people of the world live. Because of the great sacrifice required and the higher level of risk, preemptive peacemakers may need to develop non-Catholic religious orders taking vows of poverty and celibacy. Most of these regions of high risk require single persons without the responsibility of spouse and children. It may be time for such Protestant religious orders.

Displaced people are in need of the love of Christ and the creative and loving presence of Christians. Whether the place of tension, violence and displacement involves Muslims, Hindus or secularists, it should not be avoided by Christians; it should be embraced as a place needing the Prince of Peace. In years to come, as we have seen many times in the past, local people will come to notice that their own people or their own neighbors persecuted them, but Christians did not abandon them. We hope this will be the future claim about Christians. Such intentional missionary presence we can call preemptive peacemaking.

4. Scripture. One of the strongest lessons of the past half century in mission is that missionaries are part of the larger *missio Dei*, but God's mission is carried out in a myriad of ways with or without apostolic figures. One of the ways his kingdom is spread is simply through the availability of the Bible translated into local languages and linked with literacy efforts. Movements have been started by people hearing the Word read over radio, but this happens more effectively when they read the Bible for themselves in small groups or families. Families and even villages have come to faith through the reading and study of the Bible. Small groups reading the Bible in Mao's China sustained the faith during a period of thirty years when there were no missionaries serving in China and then inspired a surprising revival of Christianity. Small groups studying the Bible in Latin America connected the liberating work of Jesus Christ with local contexts. Pentecostalism and liberation theology alike have developed indigenous Christian movements throughout Latin America.

The formula that has emerged is a simple one: Christian growth and development ("evangelization") simply require access to the Bible in a local language with increasing cross-cultural Christian contacts. When either of these (Bible and ecumenical contacts) is missing, Christianity does not develop, or it will develop into a cultic expression. Ecumenical, or cross-cultural, Christian social interaction is a necessary element for healthy Christian development. This contact may be missionary contact (receiving or sending), migration, periodic conferences or any other regular contact.

In the past we assumed much more was required in the form of specific missionary teaching or preaching. We have now learned that the Bible, when understood by local indigenous peoples, has power to transform and convert. Linked with some of the concepts above, it is clear that we must continue to emphasize biblical translation and availability in the future.

5. Migration and displacement. In recent decades the importance of migration (and diaspora) in mission has been a growing field of scholarship. Migration has always been important in mission (including all the history of Christianity and Judaism), but it is just now getting the attention

and study it needs.[6] From Adam and Eve's expulsion from the Garden, to
Israel's exile in Egypt and later in Babylon, to the displacement of the
Messiah in his first years of life, to the persecution and exile of Christians
in the Roman and then Persian Empires, movement, migration and displacement have been central to Christian life and theology. Today we are
recognizing the complexity of migration and displacement. Immigration
to Europe has meant a decline in the percentage of Christians and an increase in the number of people to be reached with the gospel. Immigration
to the United States has meant an increase in the Christian population
along with greater diversity of cultures and languages in American Christianity. In urban areas of North America, Christianity has become more
Asian, more African and more Latin American.

In our globalized world poor immigrants are being received by nations
far away, and wealthy immigrants are choosing to bring their gifts and
talents mostly to the West. The poor displaced populations today include
about thirty million children.[7] Never has there been such a multitude of
needy children separated from their homes, their local villages and their
extended families. There is no sign that this massive number of children at
risk will abate in the near future. Christian mission must make such suffering and hopelessness a top priority for missiology. Many communions
today are working on this problem, but most notable is the work of the
Lausanne Committee.[8] Migration is complex and comes to us today as a
major crisis for the exposed and defenseless, as well as opportunity for those
who have resources.

6. Holy Spirit. In October of 2015, at the fiftieth anniversary celebration
of the School of Intercultural Studies, we heard again and again how the

[6]See Jehu Hanciles, *Beyond Christendom: Globalization, African Migration and the Transformation of the West* (Maryknoll, NY: Orbis Books, 2008); Charles Van Engen, "Biblical Perspectives
on the Role of Immigrants in God's Mission," *Evangelical Review of Theology* 34, no. 1 (2010):
29-43; J. D. Payne, *Strangers Next Door: Immigration, Migration and Mission* (Downers Grove,
IL: InterVarsity Press, 2012); Enoch Wan, *Diaspora Missiology: Theory, Methodology, and Practice* (self-published, CreateSpace, 2012); Chandler H. Im and Amos Yong, eds., *Global Diasporas
and Mission* (Eugene, OR: Cascade, 2014); and Michael Pocock, *Diaspora Missiology: Reflections
on Reaching the Scattered Peoples of the World* (Pasadena, CA: William Carey Library, 2015).
[7]Jake Silverstein, "The Displaced," *New York Times Magazine*, November 8, 2015, 44-86.
[8]See Lausanne Consultation on Children at Risk, *Quito Call to Action on Children at Risk*,
Quito, Ecuador, Lausanne Movement, 2015, www.lausanne.org/content/statement/quito-call-
to-action-on-children-at-risk.

work, concept and reality of the Holy Spirit came up repeatedly in the first half-century of this particular school. Some of the innovations or major topics that came out of the School of World Mission included Paul Hiebert's famous article "The Flaw of the Excluded Middle," the concept of "power evangelism" from John Wimber, and "signs and wonders" and "Third Wave" as missional perspectives of Charles Kraft and Peter Wagner.[9] All these discussions related to the work of the Holy Spirit. Discussions of the work of the Holy Spirit took place beyond Fuller Theological Seminary, but this one seminary reflected what was going on in the world, specifically in global mission. The explosion of pneumatic forms of Christianity began with the opening of the twentieth century, and there is no sign that this will change. Future Christian mission will be guided and empowered more by unmediated means (the direct influence of the Holy Spirit) and less by what is mediated by human efforts (Enlightenment reasoning and programs).

This does not mean that we are driving a wedge between human reason and divine intervention. It means that we should reaffirm the direct work of the Holy Spirit in mission and be more attentive to these themes. In Africa this has meant not that missionary work was wasted in the past but that God's intervention has breathed new life and even correction into that work. Ogbu Kalu has a nuanced view of missionary work and the miraculous work of the Holy Spirit in Africa. He has expressed it in the following way:

> One may need a foreign missionary to hear the gospel for the first time, but not necessarily for experiencing the baptism of the Spirit. . . . The Pentecostal experience broke out without missionaries or any foreigners and often to the consternation of missionaries who deployed the colonial government's clout to contain the flares. In many cases, the indigenes invited the foreigners. . . . African Pentecostalism did not originate from Azusa Street and is not an extension of the American electronic church. We should analyze the relationship with external change agents carefully to show that the movement emanated from the missionary churches and evangelical spirituality.[10]

---

[9]Paul Hiebert, "The Flaw of the Excluded Middle," *Missiology* 10, no. 1 (1982): 35-47. See John Wimber, *Power Evangelism* (New York: Harper & Row, 1986); Charles Kraft, *Christianity with Power: Your Worldview and Your Experience of the Supernatural* (Ann Arbor, MI: Vine Books, 1989); and many books by C. Peter Wagner, e.g., *The Third Wave of the Holy Spirit: Encountering the Power of Signs and Wonders Today* (Ann Arbor, MI: Vine Books, 1988).

[10]Ogbu Kalu, *African Pentecostalism: An Introduction* (Oxford: Oxford University Press, 2008), viii.

The missionary has always been part of the development of Christianity in Africa, but two other agents are central: the appropriation of that message by indigenous peoples and the surprising outpouring of the Holy Spirit. Pentecostal experiences make perfect sense in the flow of religious life and expressions in Africa—less so in the Enlightenment West. Thus, a recovery of pneumatic Christianity has occurred and continues to develop, not only in Africa but also in most of Asia and Latin America. Christian mission must shed many of the Enlightenment assumptions that prevent the fullness of the development of Christianity in each context.

7. Poverty and promise. Jesus said that it was harder for a wealthy person to enter the kingdom of heaven than for a camel to go through the eye of a needle (Mk 10:25). This is becoming more evident in the twenty-first century as the Christian movement grows more and more among the displaced and the poor. Christianity has developed most rapidly among Africans (living on the poorest continent); in Chinese villagers; recently, in countries like Cambodia, Nepal and Mongolia; and among migrants. In contrast, Christianity continues to decline in wealthy Western nations. There is a strong and growing missionary movement on the Indian subcontinent in which Indians migrate to unevangelized regions for the purpose of sharing their Christian faith. Closely related is the growing missionary movement among Chinese from China, moving out across Asia and even to Africa.

But the place of poverty in mission is not just that the poor are being reached and are reaching out. Poverty has now become the place of missiological reflection and missionary integrity. Christian development work requires partnership, prayer, reflection and long-term commitment to communities. The history of Protestant missions has been a history of the powerful and the wealthy reaching out to the weak (often oppressed) and poor. Now the poor are once again the subjects but also the leaders of mission and of the church in ways that have not been true for over a millennium. Poverty has become a place of blessedness. "Blessed are the poor" (see Mt 5:3; Lk 6:20) has taken on new meaning for the church in mission.[11] It is a promise being fulfilled. This theme for the future must be studied closely with the previous theme of pneumatic Christianity, for the poor are much more

---

[11]See chapter 8 by Jayakumar Christian.

aware of the Holy Spirit, and more aware of other spirits. Poverty, blessedness and power are three strands of a single cord for mission in the future.

8. *Mission from the South and the East.* Finally, it hardly needs to be mentioned that missionary work continues to grow outside of the Western world. The missionary movement is growing from Asia (especially from East and Southeast Asia), from Africa and from Latin America. We can expect the number of African churches in Europe and North America to continue to grow, but we should also expect the number of Chinese evangelizing Asia, Europe and Africa to continue to grow. Latin Americans will continue their outreach to the Americas, as well as to Europe and the Muslim world. Most of these missionaries are less formed by Enlightenment assumptions and thus more willing to be guided by faith, and dependent on the Holy Spirit.

This does not mean that missionaries will no longer be going from North America and from Europe. But when they do, they need to work closely with non-Western missionaries. On the other hand, non-Western missionaries would do well to learn from Western missionaries. We in the West have made many errors in the past three hundred years; it would be irresponsible not to pass on what we have learned. There have also been some remarkable missionaries and movements from whom Asians, Africans and Latin Americans can learn.[12]

Historically, we can observe missionaries from the early church moving out from Jerusalem in all directions. One of the strongest and most extensive movements in the first seven hundred years was from the West (Syria) to the East (China). Then we have a long period of Christianity that is mostly hemmed in by Islam until the sixteenth century. During this long period, from the mid-seventh century through the fifteenth century, European Christian mission atrophied. From the sixteenth century through the twentieth century the movement was from the West to the rest, moving out from the center (Europe/North America). Today the missionary movement is mostly from the Global South to the North and from the East to the West. Any innovations in terms of strategy and investment must recognize that this is not a temporary shift. Mission will be from many centers and from the margins.

---

[12]In fact, it would be very helpful if Western missionaries also learned from their own heritage. Far too many Western missionaries go out in mission today with little or no understanding of the Western mission tradition.

HOPE AND FUTURE

When we look at these eight trends, it is easy to turn melancholy. The ubiquity of technology can be seen as a rising idolatry; in fact, for some it is. As we try to connect with other people "in person," say, talking to a person on an airplane or in a bus station, we often find that they are already connected to YouTube, Vimeo or movies or listening to music. Personal encounters are blocked by technological fixations. Technology is our ever-present reality. People need to be connected, tuned in to their devices. This is part of our missional context.

Similar discouragement may strike us if we see insider movements as moving the church away from orthodox understandings of the church, or we might question what it means to give our absolute and undying loyalty to Jesus Christ. Has such a thing ever happened before? Are insider movements an ecclesial and christological compromise? And what about calling people to be preemptive peacemakers? Aren't we really asking people to risk their lives by living in places with the most conflict and potential violence? In addition, so many of these themes make it difficult for Western Christians to find their places in the future of God's mission. Is there a place for the highly motivated American or European? These and other themes seem so dark, dangerous and depressing. Many of us (not wanting to admit it) may long for the days of colonial or semicolonial missions when there were clearer lines regarding safety and orthodoxy—times when a friendship really meant sitting down and sipping tea and talking to each other (in the same country and even the same room).

But mission has always been full of such ambiguities and dangers. The double meaning of *marturia* as both witness and martyr is our guide now as it has been from the beginning. Pneumatic developments in Christianity around the world should be one of the guiding themes for Christian mission. Moving from technique and strategy to spirituality and power is, I propose, a recovery of earlier forms of Christianity that were neutralized by Enlightenment assumptions and forgotten because of Christendom realities. Something must die in our Western mission assumptions in order for a resurrection of Christian mission to ensue. Christianity will flourish in the future almost solely in nations and cultures that are opposed to Jesus or are pluralistic. No longer will it flourish in Christendom cultures and contexts.

And yet, with all the exciting developments in Christianity in recent history, and all the developments we look forward to, we must remember that the percentage of Christians in the twentieth century declined slightly (34.8 percent to 33.2 percent). God was doing great new things, but for the future we might surmise that deeper prayer, reflection and commitment are called for, keeping in mind the eight themes mentioned above.

Worship and mission are the two great purposes of the church. Worship must flow out into mission, and mission should always lead to thanksgiving and worship. All the nations are to be included, and all the tears are to be wiped away. Innovation in mission must always be pulled forward by the future vision. Another way of saying this is that missiology that tracks the current trends must be grounded in eschatology (Rev 7:9-17). To God be the glory.

Contributors

J. Kwabena Asamoah-Gyadu is Baëta-Grau Professor of Contemporary African Christianity and Pentecostal/Charismatic Theology at Trinity Theological Seminary, Accra, Ghana.

John A. Azumah is professor of world Christianity and Islam and director of International Programs at Columbia Theological Seminary, Decatur, Georgia.

Pascal D. Bazzell is Swiss National Science Postdoc Fellow in the Department of Religious Studies, Missiology and Ecumenism at Humboldt University of Berlin, Germany.

Stephen Bevans, SVD, is Louis J. Luzbetak Professor Emeritus of Mission and Culture at Catholic Theological Union, Chicago, Illinois.

Jayakumar Christian provides leadership for World Vision International's Faith & Development efforts from his base in Chennai, India.

Pablo A. Deiros is the vice president of the International Baptist Theological Seminary, Buenos Aires, Argentina.

Sarita D. Gallagher is associate professor of religion at George Fox University, Newberg, Oregon.

Anne-Marie Kool is professor of missiology at Evangelical Theological Seminary, Osijek, Croatia; associate professor of missiology at Baptist Theological Academy, Budapest, Hungary; and vice president of the Central and Eastern European Association for Mission Studies.

Moonjang Lee currently serves a local church in Korea as a full-time pastor, having lectured in North America, the United Kingdom and Singapore.

Wonsuk Ma is Distinguished Professor of Global Christianity at Oral Roberts University, Tulsa, Oklahoma.

Gary L. McIntosh is professor of Christian ministry and leadership in Talbot School of Theology at Biola University, La Mirada, California.

Mary Motte is a sister of the Franciscan Missionary of Mary and director of the Mission Resource Center, North Providence, Rhode Island.

Terry C. Muck is a scholar of religion, with special research interests in Theravada Buddhism and relationships among Buddhists and Christians, and most recently executive director of the Louisville Institute, Louisville, Kentucky.

Shawn B. Redford is an adjunct professor in the School of Intercultural Studies at Fuller Theological Seminary and faculty member of the Missions Department at Africa International University–Nairobi Evangelical Graduate School of Theology (AIU-NEGST), Nairobi, Kenya.

Scott W. Sunquist is dean of the School of Intercultural Studies and professor of world Christianity at Fuller Theological Seminary, Pasadena, California.

Charles Van Engen is the Arthur F. Glasser Senior Professor of Biblical Theology of Mission in the School of Intercultural Studies at Fuller Theological Seminary, Pasadena, California.

Index

MISSIOLOGICAL ENGAGEMENTS

Series Editors: Scott W. Sunquist,
Amos Yong and John R. Franke

Missiological Engagements: Church, Theology and Culture in Global Contexts charts interdisciplinary and innovative trajectories in the history, theology and practice of Christian mission at the beginning of the third millennium.

Among its guiding questions are the following: What are the major opportunities and challenges for Christian mission in the twenty-first century? How does the missionary impulse of the gospel reframe theology and hermeneutics within a global and intercultural context? What kind of missiological thinking ought to be retrieved and reappropriated for a dynamic global Christianity? What innovations in the theology and practice of mission are needed for a renewed and revitalized Christian witness in a postmodern, postcolonial, postsecular and post-Christian world?

Books in the series, both monographs and edited collections, will feature contributions by leading thinkers representing evangelical, Protestant, Roman Catholic and Orthodox traditions, who work within or across the range of biblical, historical, theological and social scientific disciplines. Authors and editors will include the full spectrum from younger and emerging researchers to established and renowned scholars, from the Euro-American West and the majority world, whose missiological scholarship will bridge church, academy and society.

Missiological Engagements reflects cutting-edge trends, research and innovations in the field that will be of relevance to theorists and practitioners in churches, academic domains, mission organizations and NGOs, among other arenas.

Finding the Textbook You Need

The IVP Academic Textbook Selector
is an online tool for instantly finding the IVP books
suitable for over 250 courses across 24 disciplines.

www.ivpress.com/academic/